HTML

Complete Course

Donna L. Baker

Hot Beaches - Hot Times

We started Sizzle Resorts to meet our own
needs, and those of other like-minded young
vacationers.

WILEY

Wiley Publishing, Inc.

HTML Complete Course

Published by:

Wiley Publishing, Inc.
111 River Street
Hoboken, NJ 07030
www.wiley.com/compbooks

Published simultaneously in Canada

For general information on our other products and services or to obtain technical support please contact our Customer Care Department within the U.S. at 800-762-2974, outside the U.S. at 317-572-3993 or fax 317-572-4002.

Library of Congress Cataloging-in-Publication Number: 2003111889

ISBN: 0-7645-4092-0

Manufactured in the United States of America

10 9 8 7 6 5 4 3 2 1

1K/SU/QZ/QT/IN

»Credits

Publisher: Barry Pruett
Project Editor: Cricket Krengel
Acquisitions Editor: Tom Heine
Editorial Manager: Rev Mengle
Technical Editor: Kyle Bowen
Copy Editor: Gwenette Gaddis Goshert
Production Coordinator: Nancee Reeves
Layout and Graphics: Beth Brooks
Joyce Haughey
Lynsey Osborn
Heather Pope
Quality Control: Laura Albert
Indexer: Tom Dinse
Proofreader: Joanne Keaton

»Dedication

For my friend Margaret Werdermann.

»Acknowledgements

Years ago when I was first introduced to JavaScript I had a very good friend who also happened to be a programmer. She helped me wade through the confusion and patiently read my frenetic e-mails about things like concatenating strings (never knew the word before that time!). Thank you my dear friend—look how much you helped me learn.

Thanks to my husband Terry and daughter Erin for the support and encouragement; I do believe this book is going to be on shelves long before the renovations are finished. Thanks to Deena for the chats as usual.

Thanks to my agent Matt Wagner for keeping me busy and Tom Heine at Wiley for the opportunity to write this book. A special thank you to my friend and editor Cricket Krengel. Tough and amusing—quite a combination. Thanks to Kyle Bowen for the skillful tech editing and to all at Wiley.

As usual, thanks to Tom Waits for keeping me company during the long and quiet nights of work.

»About the Author

Donna L. Baker has worked as a graphics designer, information developer, and instructor for many years. Donna is the author of *CourseBuilder for Dreamweaver f/x and Design* (The Coriolis Group, 2001), *Acrobat 5: The Professional User's Guide* (Apress, 2002), *How to Use After Effects 5.5* (Que, 2003), and *Premiere 6.5 Complete Course* (Wiley, 2003). She writes monthly articles on graphics applications for the online magazine *WindoWatch*. Donna can be found on any given day in her office building something visually interesting. She lives on the Canadian prairies with her husband, daughter, and dogs.

» Table of Contents

Part IV Adding Graphics and Images to Pages

113

Part V Organizing the Site

159

Part VI Visually Enhancing Your Site

193

Part VII Using Advanced Features in Your Site 233

Session 11 Adding More Pages and Objects to Your Site 234

Session 12 Using JavaScript 254

Session 13 Adding a Form to Your Site 274

Part VIII Showing Your Site to the World 295

Session 14 Constructing an Accessible Site 296

Session 15 Evaluating and Testing Your Site 320

Bonus Session Posting Your Site 338

Introduction

When I started online, browsers didn't have fancy graphics or motion. In fact, the browser didn't even display color—unless you count violent yellow letters against a greenish-black-background as color. Not only was the screen difficult to view, but the content was very difficult to understand because each line of text was accompanied by long strings of Unix code.

The first browsers capable of showing text and graphics were available in 1992-93. Browsers and Web development software continue to evolve, and the uses and applications of the World Wide Web and Internet technologies expand on a seemingly daily basis.

In this book, you learn how to join the millions of people using, working with, and working on the Web.

Is This Book for You?

This book is for you if you are interested in designing your own Web site but don't want to purchase expensive specialized software. This book is for you if you are interested in "what's under the hood"—understanding how a Web page is built and what goes into creating a Web site. The sessions offered in this course were designed with you in mind.

What's in This Book?

To introduce you to Web site building and show you what you can create using no software other than the utilities included with your computer's operating system and some freeware (a terrific image-editing program by Serif Software named PhotoPlus 5.5), the book begins with a quick-start tutorial called the Confidence Builder; this is followed by eight sections.

» "Confidence Builder" is a hands-on introduction. At the end of it, you'll have a three-page Web site, complete with links and your own artwork!

» **Part I: Course Setup**—This introductory section of the book contains information about how the Web works and about this course:

» "HTML Basics" includes an overview of the markup languages and scripting you use to write Web pages and how content and appearance of Web pages have become separate coding processes.

» "Project Overview" includes an explanation of the project that you create as you work through this course.

» "General Work Tips and Source File Instructions" explains how the tutorial files for this book can best be used and how to work with the files, different browsers, and different operating systems.

» **Part II: Getting Started**—The tutorials that get you started in your Web site building adventure begin in this section.

» Session 1, "Constructing the Basic Site," includes tutorials to show you how to start a new Web site; organize folders for your files, the layout of the site, and the structure of your site; and, how to build your first page.

» Session 2, "Using Tables for Layouts," includes tutorials to show you how to use tables. You also learn to construct a table template.

» **Part III: Working with Graphics**—This section shows you how to work with Serif Software's PhotoPlus 5.5.

» Session 3, "Drawing Graphic Elements," shows you how to create some simple graphic objects that add impact to your site.

» Session 4, "Building the Web Site's Logos," shows you how to work with layered drawings and construct a logo.

» **Part IV: Adding Graphics and Images to Pages**—This part combines customizing and styling tables and working with pictures.

» Session 5, "Customizing Tables Using Styles," shows you how to change tables to accommodate images and graphics. You learn how to combine parts of tables into larger segments and how to create and apply styles.

» Session 6, "Working with Pictures," teaches you how to use images in your Web site.

» **Part V: Organizing the Site**—In this part, you learn about ways to structure your Web site, including controlling what you see on different parts of the page and navigating between pages.

» Session 7, "Constructing Frames and Links," shows you how frames control the content of different parts of the page, how to build a frameset and assign pages to different frames, and how to customize the frames' characteristics.

» Session 8, "Adding More Navigation Options to the Site," explores different ways to link pages.

» **Part VI: Visually Enhancing Your Site**—In this section, you create and apply styles for the text, navigation table, and other elements on the Web site.

» Session 9, "Using Styles for Text and Positioning," shows you how to create and apply styles and how to position content on a page using styles.

» Session 10, "Attaching Navigation Styles and Elements," teaches you how to write and apply a series of styles to the links on your site. You also add styles to the navigation page to color and position the table.

» **Part VII: Using Advanced Features in Your Site**—In this section, you learn how to use an assortment of features and processes to add impact to your site, including a form, an imagemap, and some JavaScript elements.

» Session 11, "Adding More Pages and Objects to Your Site," shows you how to work with a Flash movie, how to build an imagemap for navigation, and write your first scripts.

» Session 12, "Using JavaScript," covers more JavaScript for your site. You write and apply scripts for navigation buttons. You add some styles and make final adjustments to the project's layout.

» Session 13, "Adding a Form to Your Site," covers the process of building a form and adding form elements as well as writing some more scripts.

» **Part VII: Showing Your Site to the World**—This final section discusses making your site accessible and how to post your site to a server.

» Session 14, "Constructing an Accessible Site," teaches you how to make your site usable by people using screen reader devices and special types of browsers.

» Session 15, "Evaluating and Testing Your Site," is a look at the processes required to test your site.

Introduction to the Web

You have decided to learn how to build your own Web site. You are joining millions of people worldwide who have created their own Web sites.

The number of people building Web pages can only be roughly estimated. Statistics released by the Cyberatlas division of internet.com in March 2003 reported the world's internet population in 2002 at between 580 and 655 million (based on different studies). Projected numbers of users for 2004 is estimated at between 709 and 945 million (again, based on different studies). That is a lot of people potentially viewing your site! If you want more information on the studies and statistics, you can access the full reports from http://cyberatlas.internet.com.

Table IN-1 shows estimated users for several countries.

Where to Start

Now you have an idea of the world you are about to enter. Ready to get your feet wet? Try your hand at building a small site. The Confidence Builder is designed for that express purpose—to give you a chance to see what's involved in the Web site building process.

Table IN-1: Estimated Numbers of Internet Users

Country	Population	Internet Users
Australia	19.5 million	10.5 million
Brazil	176 million	19.7 million
Canada	31.9 million	16.84 million
China	1.3 billion	45.8 million
Germany	83 million	41.8 million
Hong Kong	7.3 million	4 million
India	1 billion	5.0 million
Japan	127 million	56 million
United Kingdom	59.8 million	30.4 million
United States	280.5 million	168.6 million

Confidence Builder

Introduction

As you work through this book, you learn to use markup language and style sheet processes to create a finished Web site. Not sure you can do it? This introductory chapter, called the Confidence Builder, is designed to show you that you can indeed build a Web site using very simple tools. You use Notepad, a text editor that is part of Windows' accessories. The supplied logo image that you use was created in a freeware image-editing program from Serif Software called PhotoPlus 5.5. You work with PhotoPlus starting in Session 3.

In the Confidence Builder, you work through several short tutorials that not only give you a taste of what is to come, but also guide you through building a basic site from scratch!

TOOLS YOU'LL USE
Notepad, Internet Explorer (version 5 or higher)

CD-ROM FILES NEEDED
```
logo.gif, dark_stripes.gif, guitar.jpg,
keyboard.jpg, stripes.gif
```

TIME REQUIRED
60 minutes

Tutorial
» Building the Basic Page for Your Site

Regardless of how big or small, complex or simple a Web page is, a set of tags exists that is always required for a browser to display a Web page. In this first tutorial, you create a folder for your site, add the image files you need, and then build a page using the basic tags.

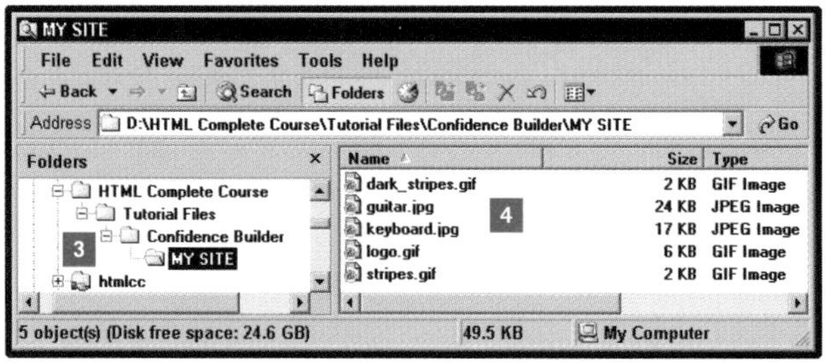

1. **Create a new folder on your hard drive, and name it** MY SITE.

2. **Open the HTML Complete Course CD.**
   You use several images from the CD in the Confidence Builder site.

3. **Open the Tutorial Files folder, open the Confidence Builder folder, and then open the MY SITE folder.**
   The folder contents display.

4. **Select these images:**
   ```
   dark_stripes.gif
   guitar.jpg
   keyboard.jpg
   logo.gif
   stripes.gif
   ```
   You use the images in the Confidence Builder project.

5. **Paste the images into the new folder, MY SITE, created on your hard drive in Step 1.**
   You add the images for the project.

6. **Open Notepad. Choose Start→Programs→Accessories→Notepad.**
   A blank window opens, but it isn't as intimidating as it looks!

Typing the Code

Your site is developed in Notepad, a text utility that is part of the Windows Operating System. The tutorials contain figures of code on a page, as well as figures of how your pages look in a browser. The instructions include references to line numbers as well as locations within a line. Notepad tracks the line numbers, although you do not see them on the page. You can choose Edit→Go to to identify the line the cursor is sitting on. If you prefer to arrange the content of your Notepad file exactly as described in the tutorial and shown in the figures, choose Format→Word Wrap. Then drag the resize handle at the bottom right of the Notepad window until the page holds the same number of characters as those shown in the tutorial. You can either use the Go to command or the Word Wrap command; you can't use both at the same time.

7. Type the HTML code for the page:

```
<html>
<head>
<title>Untitled Document</title>
</head>
<body>
</body>
</html>
```

Start each entry on a new line; you can add blank lines between the entries for clarity.

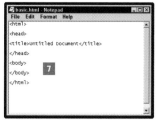

<TIP>

In the figure, blank lines are added between the entries. This allows you to see the content more clearly, but it has no effect on how the page works. HTML isn't fussy about spaces or capitalization. However, in the book's main project you use XHTML, which is case sensitive.

8. Choose File→Save.

The Save As dialog box opens.

9. Browse to the new folder that you created in Step 1.

Select the folder; it opens in the Save As dialog box.

<TIP>

You can choose File→Save or File→Save As. Notepad doesn't distinguish between the two commands.

10. Name the file basic.html.

The file is named basic; you must add the file extension manually. Notepad does not have options listed for saving a file in any format other than plain text.

<NOTE>

You can use one of two file extensions, either .htm or .html. The three-letter extension was required for older computer systems that couldn't process four-letter file extensions, but all computer operating systems built in the last several years can understand either.

11. Click Save.

The dialog box closes, and the name of the file appears at the top of the Notepad window. You have saved your first Web page file. Leave Notepad open to continue in the next tutorial.

Tutorial
» Creating a Site Page

You built a basic (very basic!) page. In this tutorial, you add some content to the basic page file, make copies for the site, and start customizing the pages. The Notepad view in the Confidence Builder is different from what you are using. I use a text editor that is very similar to Notepad, but it allows color coding of the different elements on the page and line numbers for you to use as reference.

1. **If you closed the** basic.html **file, reopen it in Notepad. Choose File→Save As, and save the page as** page1.html**.**
   This creates a copy of the basic.html file for you to work with.

<TIP>
Notepad doesn't automatically display .html files; its default format is .txt (text). When you open Notepad and choose File→Open, browse to the location of your site files. You won't see a list of files shown, but they aren't gone! At the bottom of the dialog box, click the drop-down menu for Files of Type and choose All Files. Now your .html files are visible.

2. **In line 2, select** "Untitled Document" **and delete the words. Type:** Welcome to Diamond Dog Productions! **in its place.**
   The page is titled.

3. **In line 5, add a background to the <body> tag. After** <body **type:** background="stripes.gif"
   Make sure that the text is added inside the right bracket. A striped background is added to the page. The line now reads <body background="stripes.gif">

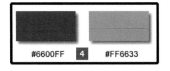

#6600FF   4   #FF6633

4. **In line 5, add link color tags following the <background> tag. Type:** link="#6600FF" vlink="#FF6633" **before the right bracket of the tag.**
   These numbers assign color to the page links. The line now reads <body background="stripes.gif" link="#6600FF" vlink="#FF6633">

5. **Save the file, and leave Notepad open.**
   You check your page in a Web browser.

6. **Open Internet Explorer. Choose File→Open.**
   The Open dialog box displays.

<NOTE>
The colors used are defined in the hexadecimal color system, discussed in Session 3. You can see the link color in the color swatch figure. When you add links to the pages later in the Confidence Builder, the text is blue and changes to orange after you have clicked the link.

7. Click Browse, locate the `page1.html` **file, and click Open.**
Your page is listed in the Open dialog box.

8. Click OK.
The dialog box closes, and your page is loaded into the browser.

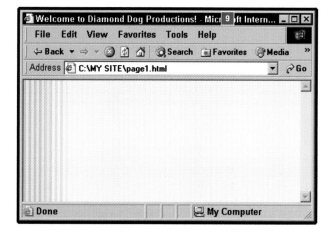

9. View your page.
You see the background image applied to the page. Look at the top of the browser window to see the title that you added.

10. Minimize your browser window.
When you want to preview the page again, expand the browser window.

11. Back in Notepad, press Enter after the `<body>` **tag in line 9 to add a blank line.**
You add a heading in the blank line.

12. On line 10, type: `<h1><font color="#330099">`
`Welcome! </font></h1>`
The Web page starts with a heading at the top, identified by the <h1> tag. A dark blue color is chosen for the text. The welcome message, `Welcome!` uses the heading size and color that you specified. You must tell the browser that the one-word message is the only text that uses the special font settings, which is done by closing the tags after `Welcome!`.

13. Press Enter to start another new line. Type: `<p>This is the`
`first content page. Add some general`
`info.</p>`
You add some general text. The <p></p> tags define a paragraph.

14. In Notepad, choose File→Save to save the `page1.html` **file.**
You built the first page for your sample Web site.

15. Maximize the Internet Explorer window. Click Refresh to reload the page.
A browser stores the content, and unless it is refreshed, you won't see the changes. Note the color of the heading text (a deep blue). The paragraph of text is placed below the heading. Minimize the browser. Leave Notepad and the `page1.html` page open for the next tutorial.

Tutorial

» Creating the Second Site Page

In the previous tutorial, you built the first page for your site. You added a background and some customized text to the page. In this tutorial, you create the second page for the site.

```
5  <title> Diamond Dog Details</title>   2
6
7  </head>
8
9  <body background="dark_stripes.gif" link="#6600FF" vlink="#FF6633">   3
10 <h1><font color="#330099">Here are the Diamond Dogs </font></h1>   4
```

1. **If you closed the** page1.html **file, reopen it in Notepad. Choose File→Save As, and save the page as** page2.html.
   You create the second page for the site.

< C A U T I O N >
Don't use the File→Save command, because that merely resaves the file as page1.html.

2. **On line 5, change the page's title to** Diamond Dog Details.
   The line now reads: <title> Diamond Dog Details</title>

3. **On line 9, change the background image in the** <body> **tag. Replace** background="stripes.gif" **with** background="dark_stripes.gif"
   The page2.html page uses a different background image.

4. **On line 10, replace the welcome message text. Type:** Here are the Diamond Dogs.
   Use the same heading size and font color. The line now reads: <h1><font color="#330099">Here are the Diamond Dogs </font></h1>

```
8
9  <body background="dark_stripes.gif" link="#6600FF" vlink="#FF6633">
10 <h1><font color="#330099">Here are the Diamond Dogs </font></h1>   5
11 <h1><font color="#330099">Here are the Diamond Dogs </font></h1>   7
12
```

5. **Select the <h1> text in line 10.**
   Choose Edit→Copy to copy the text.

6. **Click the start of line 11, and press Enter to add a blank line.**
   You add a second heading to the page.

7. **Choose Edit→Paste to paste the text into the blank line that you added in Step 6.**
   The text is added to line 11. You modify the text for the second heading.

8. **Modify the text in line 11 to read:**
   `<h2><font color="#330099" In All Their Glory!</font></h2>`
   You add a second heading level with the <h2> tags. The font color is the same as the <h1> tag options. Like you did with the <h1> titles, after adding the title's text, you must close both the <font> and <h2> tags.

9. **Go to line 13. Modify the text within the <p> tags to read:**
   `<p>This is the linked page.</p>`
   The text on the page changes.

10. **Choose File➔Save to save the** `page2.html` **file.**

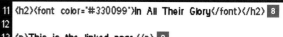

11. **Open Internet Explorer, and choose File➔Open. Browse to the location of the** page2.html **file, and click Open.**
    Your page is listed in the Open dialog box.

12. **Click OK.**
    The dialog box closes, and the page is loaded into the browser window.

13. **View the Web page.**
    You see the darker striped background on the page. The new title displays at the top of the browser window. The added text displays according to the headings that you assigned. Note that the color and font for the two heading levels are the same, but the size of the text is quite different.

14. **Close your browser.**
    You finished the second page for the site, adding background images, headings, and text.

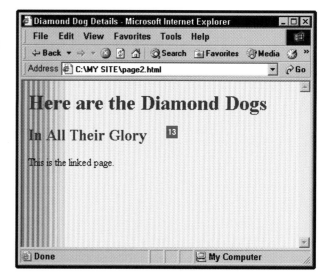

Tutorial
» Adding More Text and Images to the Site's Pages

In the previous tutorial, you built the second page for the site. Now you have two pages, each containing headings, background color information, and link color information. In this tutorial, you add more text and images to complete the content for the first site page, and then you add the text and images to the second site page.

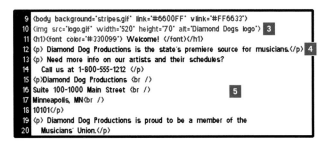

<TIP>

Remember that Notepad doesn't display any file formats except .txt files. To find your HTML file, click the Files of Type drop-down list and choose All Files. Now your html files are listed.

<NOTE>

The content of a page is added in sequence from top to bottom. You added the logo image, which displays at the top of the page. The heading is next, and you add text in the next steps that displays below the heading.

<NOTE>

When you view the page in your browser later in the tutorial, you see that the image displays the logo elements over a transparent background, a feature of the .gif file format.

<NOTE>

Tags generally have an opening and a closing segment that surround the content defined by the tag, such as the heading or paragraph tags with which you have worked. Some tags, such as the
 (break) tag, have no content, so they are opened and closed in the same tag. The "/" signifies closing of the tag.

1. **In Notepad, choose File→Open. Browse to your folder's location, and choose** `page1.html`**.**
   The page opens in Notepad.

2. **Go to line 10. Press Enter to add a blank line after the <body> tag.**
   You add an image to the page, and type the tag in line 10.

3. **On line 10, type:** `<img src="logo.gif" width="520" height="70" alt="Diamond Dogs logo">`
   You add an image to the page. The <img> tag refers to an image; the `src` attribute is the file's name; the `width` and `height` attributes are the dimensions of the image in pixels; the `alt` attribute is a text caption for the image.

4. **On line 12, replace the placeholder text that you added in the earlier tutorial. Between the <p> and </p> tags, type:** `Diamond Dog Productions is the state's premiere source for musicians.`
   The first line of text forms its own paragraph.

5. **From lines 13 to 20, type the rest of the text for the first page. Type:**
   ```
   <p> Need more info on our artists and their
   schedules?
   Call us at 1-800-555-1212. </p>
   <p>Diamond Dog Productions <br />
   Suite 100-1000 Main Street <br />
   Minneapolis, MN<br />
   10101</p>
   <p> Diamond Dog Productions is proud to be a
   member of the Musicians' Union.</p>
   ```
   You add the rest of the text in three additional paragraphs, each identified by the <p> and </p> tags at the start and end of the paragraphs. You also break the line as it appears in the browser using the <br /> tag.

6. **Save the** `page1.html` **file.**
You added text and an image to the page.

7. **Open your browser. Choose File→Open, and browse to the storage folder location. Choose the** `page1.html` **file, and click Open.**
Your page is listed in the Open dialog box.

8. **Click OK to view the page.**
You see the logo at the top of the page with the striped background of the page showing through the transparent background of the page. Look at the text—note how the text is spaced differently when the <br /> tags are used.

9. **Close the browser.**
You previewed the contents for the first page of your site.

10. **In Notepad, choose File→Open. Your site's folder contents display. Choose** `page2.html`**, and click Open.**
The `page1.html` file closes, and `page2.html` opens.

11. **Go to the placeholder paragraph in line 13; press Enter twice to move the text down two lines on the page to line 15.**
You add an image to the page before the text.

12. **On line 13, type:** `<img src="keyboard.jpg" width="200" height="144" alt="Joe Smith at the keyboard" >`
An image is added to the page, along with its dimensions and alternate text. In the figure, the text wraps from line 13 to 14.

```
12
13  <img src="keyboard.jpg" width="200" height="145" [12]
14    alt="Joe Smith at the keyboard">
15  <p>This is the linked page.</p> [11]
16
```

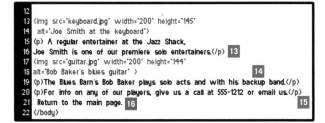

```
12
13  <img src="keyboard.jpg" width="200" height="145"
14    alt="Joe Smith at the keyboard">
15  <p> A regular entertainer at the Jazz Shack,
16  Joe Smith is one of our premiere solo entertainers.</p>  13
17  <img src="guitar.jpg" width="200" height="144"
18  alt="Bob Baker's blues guitar" >                          14
19  <p>The Blues Barn's Bob Baker plays solo acts and with his backup band.</p>
20  <p>For info on any of our players, give us a call at 555-1212 or email us.</p>
21  Return to the main page.  16                               15
22  </body>
```

13. **On line 15, within the <p> tags, type:** `<p> A regular entertainer at the Jazz Shack, Joe Smith is one of our premiere solo entertainers.</p>` A caption is added for the first image. In the figure, the text wraps from line 15 to 16.

14. **On lines 17 to 19, type:**
    ```
    <img src="guitar.jpg" width="200"
    height="144"
    alt="Bob Baker's blues guitar">
    <p>The Blues Barn's Bob Baker plays solo acts
    and with his backup band.</p>
    ```
    You add another image and a caption.

15. **On line 20, type:** `<p>For info on any of our play-ers, give us a call at 800-555-1212 or e-mail us.</p>` You add text used for links in the next tutorial.

16. **On line 21, type:** `Return to the main page.` The text is used for a link in the next tutorial.

17. **Choose File→Save to save the** `page2.html` **file.** You added text and images to the second page of the site.

18. **Open your browser. Choose File→Open. Browse to the location of your site folder, select the** `page2.html` **file, and click Open. When the page's name displays in the Open dialog box, click OK.** The page loads in your browser.

19. **Resize the window using the handle at the bottom right of the browser window.** Notice how the text on the page wraps according to the width of the window.

<N O T E>
The text resizes, but the images do not. When you added the images to the page, you defined their sizes, meaning that the images display at the defined size at all times.

20. **Move your cursor over the images.** The alternate text messages display.

21. **Close your browser.** You added text and images to both your site's pages. You used different tags to organize the text on the page. You specified size and alternate text attributes for the images. You tested the pages in your browser. Leave `page2.html` open in Notepad to continue with the next tutorial.

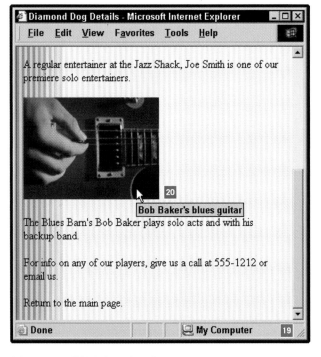

Tutorial
» Finishing the Site

You have reached the last tutorial in the Confidence Builder! All that remains is to add some links to both pages. On page 2, you add an e-mail link and a link to return to the first page. On page 1, you add a link to an external Web site and another tag. At the end of the previous tutorial, page2.html is open in Notepad; you start the tutorial by adding tags to the second page.

1. **In Notepad, go to line 20. Press Enter to add a blank line.**
   You add a tag to the empty line.

2. **On line 20, type:** ⟨hr /⟩
   You add a horizontal dividing line to the page.

3. **In the paragraph following the <hr /> tag,**
   find the phrase "email us." Before the phrase, type:
   ⟨ahref="mailto:bigdave@diamonddogs.com"⟩;
   after the phrase, type:⟨/a⟩
   Add the code before the closing </p> tag. The anchor tag is used for e-mail. You see the text highlighted when you view the page in your browser later in the tutorial, but you do not see the mailto portion because it is only used by the browser. Clicking the e-mail address on the page instructs the browser to open your default e-mail program.

4. **Go to line 23. Before the text on the line, type:** ⟨a
   href="page1.html"⟩; **after the text, type:** ⟨/a⟩
   You add a link to the last sentence on the page. When the link is clicked in the browser, the first page of the site displays.

5. **Choose File→Save to save the** page2.html **file.**

6. **Open your browser. Open the** page2.html **file.**
   You preview the links that you added to the page.

7. **Move your cursor over the e-mail link at the bottom of the page.**
   You see the mailto tag displayed in the status bar at the bottom of the page.

8. **Click the "Return to the main page" link to test it.**
   The page1.html file loads into your browser window. You tested the second page of the site.

10. **In Notepad, choose File→Open, browse to the site's storage folder, and select the** page1.html **file.**
   You add some tags to the first page.

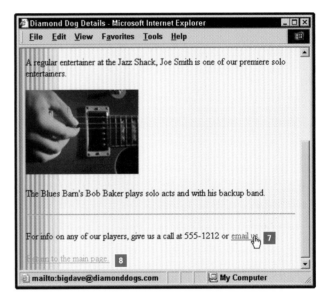

```
18   alt="Bob Baker's blues guitar")
19   (p)The Blues Barn's Bob Baker plays solo acts and with his backup band.(/p)
20   (hr /) [2]
21   (p)For info on any of our players, give us a call at 555-1212 or
22   (a href="mailto:bigdave@diamonddogs.com")email us.(/a)(/p) [3]
23   (a href="page1.html")Return to the main page.(/a) [4]
24   (/body)
```

<NOTE>
In the figure, the text wraps over lines 21 and 22 when the tag is added.

<NOTE>
If your links don't work for some reason, go back to the Notepad files. Check the structure of the links and make sure you haven't made any spelling errors.

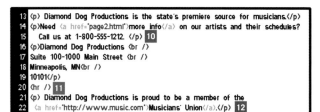

11. **On line 14, after "Need" type:** `<a href="page2.html">` **After the phrase "more info," type:** `</a>`
    You add a link to the phrase "more info" that opens page 2 of your site in the browser when clicked.

12. **Insert a blank line before the last <p> (in line 20).**
    Type: `<hr />`
    The <hr /> tag inserts a horizontal line used to visually separate content in different parts of a page.

13. **On line 21, before the phrase "Musicians' Union," type:**
    `<a href= "http://www.musicians.com">`**; type:** `</a>`
    after the phrase. Make sure that the closing </a> tag is within the closing </p> tag.
    The hypertext reference is a link to an external Web site. The words `Musicians' Union` become the link and use the colors set for tags in an earlier tutorial. On the figure, the text wraps over lines 21 and 22.

< N O T E >
The link used in the tutorial is for an actual Web site, but it is unrelated to this tutorial.

14. **Choose File→Save to save the** `page1.html` **file. Close Notepad.**
    Your pages' content is complete.

15. **In your browser, choose File→Open. Browse to your site folder, select** `page1.html`**, and click Open.**
    The first page of the site loads in the browser.

16. **Click the "more info" link.**
    The second page of your site loads in the browser window.

17. **Click the Back button on the browser.**
    Page 1 of your site reloads in the browser window.

18. **Click the Musician's Union link to test it.**
    As you move your cursor over the Musicians' Union link at the bottom of the page, note the address displayed in the status bar at the bottom left of the browser window. The musicians.com site loads in your browser.

19. **Close the browser.**
    You tested the pages in your site.

20. **Give yourself a round of applause—you built your first Web site!**
    You constructed a two-page Web site. You added images and text to both pages. You used different tags to format the text on the pages. You added links between the pages and to an external Web site. You also added an e-mail link.

Part I
Course Setup

HTML Basics

You could start the Sessions right now and finish with a very attractive and usable Web site using (X)HTML, Cascading Style Sheets, and JavaScript. Before you start into the book's project, you should understand what these terms mean and how your browser actually interprets what you write.

HTML

HTML stands for Hypertext Markup Language. And the fascinating thing about HTML is that it is based on a simple text file. It isn't magic—it's hypertext markup. The markup tags tell your browser how to display the page.

It seems that the Internet world changes completely every few years. We are on the brink of change now. Since the early 1990s, HTML has evolved through several language specifications. The last HTML specification, HTML 4.01, allowed you to use both uppercase and lowercase tags. The next generation of HTML is XHTML, which stands for Extensible Hypertext Markup Language. The first XHTML spec, XHTML 1.0, was recommended as a standard by the W3C World Wide Web Consortium in 2000.

<NOTE>
The W3C is a worldwide consortium of computer manufacturers, countries, agencies, and professional bodies that work on developing different standards for Web use and languages. A W3C Recommendation means that the specification has been reviewed by the W3C membership and approved as a Web standard. In this book, you deal with XHTML, CSS, and WAI (accessibility) standards.

When you worked on the Confidence Builder project, you saw how tags could have attributes, or custom characteristics. You attached font colors and faces, border color to your table, and so on. You don't arbitrarily attach an attribute to a tag, however. There are standard attributes for different tags. Attributes are written in the same way. For example:

```
name="value"
```

In the example <body bgcolor="330099", the name of the attribute is bgcolor (background color) and the value is a shade of orange for the tag <body.

After the attributes are completed, the tag must be closed. In this example, if there were no other attributes for the <body> tag, it would be typed as <body bgcolor="330099">.

How HTML got complicated

HTML, as it was originally written, was never intended to allow formatting. HTML was intended to define the content of a document. When HTML 3.2 was approved, attributes and formatting tags suddenly became usable. No longer were you forced to use plain default text in a default black color. However, developing sites using fonts and color information for every single piece of text that appeared on a page is a long and tedious process. Think back to the Confidence Builder project that you just completed. Each time you added text to the page, you also added attributes for the fonts and colors. Granted, you could copy and paste this information from line to line (and I hope you did!), but it is still a time-consuming process subject to lots of simple errors.

The repetitious description of attributes changed with HTML 4.0. All the formatting information required for a document could be moved out of the HTML document and into a separate style sheet. The document content stays in the HTML page; the styling information moves to a Cascading Style Sheet (CSS) file. Think again of your Confidence Builder project. Wouldn't it be much simpler to write the information about a text's color once and then assign the information, as a style, to your page's content? Sure it would.

XHTML—The next generation

The differences between HTML 4.01 and XHTML are actually very slight. I mentioned that you could use either uppercase or lowercase tags in HTML 4.01; XHTML requires lowercase tags only. The differences are small, but they result in a much more consistent code.

XML (Extensible Markup Language) is a markup language used to define the structure of a document. XML doesn't do anything—it is designed solely as a means to describe the data contained in a document. HTML is designed to display data. Put them together, and you get XHTML.

The goal of XHTML is to create properly constructed documents. Consider the range of devices that currently can or will be able to use browsers in the near future. Everything from telephones to PDAs to televisions can now use browser technology and read Web pages. XHTML is intended to work with any device or system; it works in all browsers, and it is backward browser compatible (that is, the language works in current browser versions but also in previous browser versions as well).

The XHTML specification requires lowercase text for tags, among other things. Other requirements for XHTML are covered in the sessions as you build your site.

You can test Web pages against the specification. A page that complies with the specs may display the image shown here to indicate compliance.

Separating Content from Appearance

Each HTML tag is defined using a similar tag format, like this:

```
<b>Complete Course</b>
```

The HTML tag itself is made up of two parts—the <b> and </b> elements. The tag instructs the browser to display the text written between the start tag <b> and the end tag </b> as bold. HTML tags are not case sensitive; you can use either uppercase or lowercase tags—for now. And this is where your experience with HTML gets interesting.

HTML 4.0 allowed for the creation of separate style sheets that contain style information for different elements on your page. CSS define how a browser displays HTML elements. You generally create and store styles in an external file using the css extension. The "style sheet" portion of the name is straightforward. "Cascading" refers to a sequence of style definitions that flow into one another. Both Netscape Navigator and Internet Explorer have supported the use of CSS since the version 4 release of their browsers.

In many ways, styles parallel HTML tags. Just as you can use standard HTML tags, such as paragraph, list, and table, you also can use standard CSS for color and size for example. The CSS language rule (or syntax) is made up of three parts: a selector, a property, and a value (together referred to as the declaration) and is written in this form:

```
selector {property: value}
```

The selector is usually the HTML tag that you want to define, the property is the attribute that you want to target, and the value is how you want the property defined. Separate the property and value with a colon, and surround the pair with curly braces like this:

```
body {color:ffff33}
```

This style means that the body of the page, which you see as the page's background, is colored the lovely yellow shown in the illustration.

When the value features multiple words, use quotes around the value, just as you did when you used the font-family attribute in your Confidence Builder project.

```
p {font-family: "Arial, Helvetica, sans-serif"}
```

As you learn throughout the book, you can specify more than one property for a style.

Working with a Style Sheet

Style sheets can save lots of work. You used font tags and color attributes in your Confidence Builder project. Since the time of the HTML 4.0 specs, these tags could be removed and defined as styles in another document. Suppose that your Confidence Builder site were 50 pages instead of 2. Now suppose that you decided to change all the h3 (heading level 3) text in your site from dark blue to dark green. What a lot of work! Now suppose that you moved all the style information to its own document and then referenced the style sheet from your pages. You change the color value in the CSS document, and instantly all h3 tags change their text from blue to green when viewed in a browser.

Style sheets are used in several ways. You can specify a style inside a single HTML element, inside the <head> element of a Web page, or in an external CSS file. You can even refer to multiple style sheets from the same HTML document. The styles are applied in a specific order, which is how the "Cascading" part of the term came to be.

Browsers use a default style. In the Confidence Builder tutorial, your default page still had some style—the heading was a larger font and centered; the regular text was smaller and left aligned. The heading and text are examples of default styles.

The most common way to use a CSS is through external style sheet files. The styles for elements in your page are defined using the CSS syntax, and the file is referenced at the start of the page's HTML. You can also create an internal style sheet, which is contained within the <head> tag of your page. Finally, you can also create an in-line style, which is added to an individual HTML element.

The application of a style follows in order from default to in-line. In other words, the browser style is used unless an external style sheet exists, which is used unless an internal style sheet exists, which is used unless an in-line style exists. This sequence of rules applies except for one case—a reader may use a personal style sheet to adjust for visual or physical impairments. In that case, the user's personal style sheet overrides any styles attached to the page.

The CSS1 spec was approved in December 1996; CSS2 in 1998. CSS3 has been a working draft since mid-2001. You can test Web site pages against the CSS specification. A page that is in compliance with the specs can display the image shown here.

Adding Action and Interaction

So far, creating content and creating appearance has been touched on. The last item to consider is creating interactivity. Millions of Web pages are enhanced through the use of JavaScript. JavaScript was developed by Netscape and is the most popular scripting language on the Internet. Netscape Navigator and Internet Explorer browsers version 3.0 and newer may use JavaScript.

JavaScript is a scripting language, not a full-blown computer program. The difference primarily lies in how the code is processed. True languages require compiling or processing before they run. JavaScript is an interpreted language, which means that it is processed as the browser and/or user interacts with the page. JavaScript is not the same thing as Java. Java is a programming language developed by Sun Microsystems.

You can use JavaScript in a Web page in literally hundreds of ways. Anything you can imagine a page doing or a user doing to interact with a page can use JavaScript. You don't have to be a computer programmer to use JavaScript, because it uses quite simple language rules. Nor do you have to write complex scripts to get effects in your pages. Small scripts, called "snippets" can be added to HTML pages. JavaScript reacts to events, such as when a user clicks a link or page element, when a user completes a form and submits it, or when a page loads or unloads in a browser.

The action that triggers the JavaScript is called an event handler. JavaScript has more rules than HTML and CSS. JavaScript components are case sensitive. For example, `variablea` is not the same thing as `VariableA`. Like HTML and CSS, you close symbols with brackets. JavaScript doesn't care about blank spaces added to a line, but breaking up a line of JavaScript must be done in a particular way. You work with JavaScript and its rules in Sessions 11 through 13.

Using JavaScript in Your Web Pages

Like other HTML elements, JavaScripts are identified by tags. You use <script></script> tags to enclose JavaScript. Scripts execute when the page loads into a browser. Sometimes, that is what you want to happen; other times, you want the user to interact with the page in some way to make the script run. You know from the Confidence Builder project that a page requires <head></head> tags. If you want to control when a JavaScript runs, the script is added inside the <head></head> tags, and its triggering event is included in the body portion of the page.

You also know from the Confidence Builder project that a page requires <body></body> tags. If you want a JavaScript to run when the page has loaded, add it to the body section of the page.

You can add multiple scripts to the same page, in both locations. You can also use an external file in a similar way to using an external style sheet. An external JavaScript file is saved with a `.js` file extension and attached to a page using a `src` (source) attribute.

Now, armed with this new background information, it's time to carry on with the course. In the next chapters, you learn about the book's project and how to work with the project files.

Project Overview

The Complete Course Project

This book is a tutorial-based course in Web site building designed for students and educators. People with two different types of experience will benefit from working through the book. You don't need any experience with either graphics or (X)HTML to use this book. Those who have no experience in Web page building can use the book as a systematic way to learn to build Web pages and Web graphics. If you have used Web page development software, you will also find this book useful. Rather than approaching the development of a Web page visually by using a program that offers menus and buttons, you learn how the pages are structured, how to create the pages manually, and how to add and configure page elements.

You can use this book in sequence—Session 2 builds on the knowledge and work completed in Session 1, and so on. You can also use the book starting with any session and using the supplied material. A complete set of files for each session can be found on the CD.

The Book's Web Site

In this book, you build a Web site for Sizzle, a trio of fictitious Caribbean resorts. The completed site contains a three-frame interface (that is, the page you view in a browser is composed of content from three pages). There are several types of pages that you build in this site. The top of the browser window shows a logo page and an imagemap used to navigate to different parts of the site. The lower-left portion of the window holds navigation links. The content of the large central frame displays the site's content. You create most of the graphic artwork, such as the main logo, page logos, and buttons.

The site contains information on each of the three resorts. It also includes a slideshow and a Flash video. You build a form and links pages. You also add some custom JavaScript elements to display dates, add messages, control windows, and so on.

Developing the Project

Does it sound scary? Well, it can be unless you approach site design and construction in a methodical way. Through the process of building this project, you pass through several stages. The site's development is presented in two ways. In general, you work from the basic to more complex. This way, you have an understanding of certain concepts applied across the pages in your site. Not only does this approach reinforce your newfound knowledge, but it simulates how a "real" Web site is developed. Some exceptions exist. For example, you complete the form for your site in one session starting from table creation and ending with JavaScript. This process takes you step-by-step through the construction of a single complex page—and a "real-life" approach.

The book is divided into several stages that correspond with the sections in this book:

» **Basic site creation:** Construct the basic pages for your site, and add tables for content placement.

» **Graphic development:** Build the site's graphic elements including logos, backgrounds, and buttons.

» **Adding visual content:** Customize the tables added earlier to accommodate the sizes and shapes of images and graphics.

» **Organizing your site's information:** Work with framesets to control page visibility and links to navigate through the site. Organize your site's appearance using style sheets.

» **Adding other elements:** Work with a range of advanced features including forms and JavaScript.

» **Distributing your site:** Make your site accessible to those with disabilities. Post your site to a Web server.

I suggest an experiment: Build the introductory project in Confidence Builder now (if you haven't already), and then work through the book. When you are finished, come back to the introductory project and modify and enhance it. You'll be surprised by how much you have learned.

General Work Tips and Source File Instructions

Working with the Tutorial Files

The CD contains a folder called Tutorial Files. This folder houses all the material you need for finishing the Complete Course project, samples of the project contents as they exist at the end of each session, and the book's Confidence Builder project. Depending on your computer's resources, you can copy the entire folder to your hard drive, or add the content from the CD as you work through the book. If you copy the files to your hard drive, create a folder in the root of your hard drive (usually C: drive) and name it Tutorial Files.

You'll find several categories of files on the CD, all contained within the Tutorial Files folder:

» **Artwork**—These are the source files and intermediate step examples for the images that you draw or compose for the site.

» **Confidence Builder**—This folder contains the image and HTML files needed to complete the book's introductory project.

» **Image Sources**—These images are used for the book's project; some are in their final form, others need modification.

» **Images**—These are the final images used in the book's project site.

» **Storage**—Here you'll find copies of text and HTML files that you use as template or source material for the book's project.

» **Session 01 through Session 15**—Folders for each session contain the HTML and CSS pages complete to the end of the numbered session. The iteration folder for Session 3 contains only one HTML page that you use for experimentation; the Session 4 folder contains no HTML or CSS files, because the session uses images only.

» **Sizzle**—This folder contains all the finished images, artwork, HTML pages, and CSS pages for the final Sizzle Web site. The Sizzle folder on the CD contains subfolders named Artwork, Image Sources, Images, and Storage.

Each session has its own folder. **Do not use the files directly from the CD.** Each file (as it appears in the sessions) has a corresponding set of files in subsequent sessions. For example, `sizzle_east.html` is created in Session 1. The CD has a total of 16 copies of this file, one for each session, and one for the finished site. On a session-by-session basis, the file name is prefaced by the session number—`01sizzle_east.html` to `15sizzle_east.html`. The finished site uses the file named `sizzle_east.html`.

The beginning of each tutorial picks up where the last one leaves off. For example, to start on Session 5, you can open the files that you created as you worked through the sessions and start working if you have completed each tutorial up to the end of Session 4.

If you do not have the project complete to the end of Session 4, you can update the tutorial content using files from the corresponding folder on the CD. Refer to the file list included at the start of each session.

Updating tutorial files

Because each session contains links and references to other files used to build your Web site, using the files directly from the CD or a storage location results in errors. To update tutorial files, follow these steps:

1. Open the session folder located on the CD in the Tutorial Files folder for the session prior to the one on which you want to work. For example, if you are ready to work on Session 9, open the Tutorial Files folder and then the Session08 folder.

2. To start work in a session, for example Session 9, read the opening of Session 8 in the book for the list of pages modified or created. Locate the first file to update from the CD or your hard drive storage folder, such as `08contacts.html`.

3. Copy the file to your Sizzle site folder.

4. Delete the last version of the file from your Sizzle site folder; for example, delete `contacts.html`.

5. Rename the copied file, and delete the numbered prefix; in this case, rename the file from `08contacts.html` to `contacts.html`.

Working with image files

Working with image files is not as complex as working with text files. For the most part, you use the photographs in the Images file just as they are; copy the files from the CD to your Sizzle site folder into one of the three graphics folders. You are instructed where to store or save a file in the tutorials. There are several pictures that you modify in PhotoPlus 5.5. These are indicated by "x" prefacing the file's name. For example, your site's slideshow uses many images. An image named `xss2b.jpg` means that this is the second image for the second page of the slideshow, and it requires modification before using it in the site (the "x" designation). The images are referenced in the sessions, and you are instructed to save the modified file using a final name, such as `ss2b.jpg` for use in your project.

More instructions for copying files and folders to your computer are in Appendix A.

Understanding the Tutorial Instructions

Your site is developed in Notepad, a text utility that is part of the Windows Operating System. The tutorials contain figures of code on a page, as well as figures of how your pages look in a browser. Take care when reading the instructions. You'll find references to line numbers, as well as locations within a line. Working with Notepad, you do not see any line numbers, although Notepad tracks the line number and you can use a Go To command to find a particular line on a page.

All the material in the course was developed in Notepad and then displayed in an editing program to show both line numbers and color-coded code elements. Both of these devices are intended to make finding specific locations on a page simpler for you.

Your line numbering may differ slightly from that shown in the tutorials. HTML isn't governed by line wrapping or leaving blank lines, so your pages are correct in your browser. In the tutorials, the lines are often wrapped (carried over to the next line) to show you the content in the figures. Use the line numbers as references to different areas of a page, but read the content of the line carefully as you follow the steps to ensure you are modifying or adding code to the correct line. When you are instructed to type text into a page, it is generally prefaced with a location and then the instruction, such as:

1. **On line 2, after the <body tag, type:** `color="663300">`
   Make sure the color attribute is followed by the closing bracket.

To complete this step, go to line 2 on your Notepad file. Partway through the line, following the opening segment of the tag starting with <body, type the text that follows the type: instruction, which is `color="663300">` in this example. Text for you to type is never placed in quotation marks, because they are used for the code itself. Code for you to type is in regular text within a line of bold text.

Please make notes in the margins of the book as you are working through the project. A good tutorial book always includes plenty of highlighting, dog-eared pages, and cryptic (sometimes even to you!) notes. And please, above all, experiment as you learn.

System Requirements

Any Windows-based computer is sufficient to complete the tutorials with the exception of the graphics sessions. To use the supplied image manipulation program, PhotoPlus 5.5 from Serif Software, Inc. your computer must meet these requirements:

» IBM compatible Pentium PC with CD-ROM.

» Windows 95/98/98 SE,2000,ME or Windows NT 4.0. XP compatible.

» 16MB (Win 95/98), 24MB (Win 98SE), 32MB (Win NT), or 64MB (Win 2000) RAM.

» 20MB free hard disk space for recommended installation.

» SVGA (16-bit color) display or higher.

» Additional disk resources and memory are required when editing large or complex documents.

In addition, you must have an Internet connection in order to validate files and access online resources.

Part II
Getting Started

Constructing the Basic Site

```
basic.html - Notepad                                              _ □ ×
File   Edit   Format   Help
<!DOCTYPE html PUBLIC "-//W3C//DTD XHTML 1.0 Transitional//EN"
"DTD/xhtml1-transitional.dtd">
<html xmlns="http://www.w3.org/1999/xhtml">

<head>
<title>Page Title</title>
<meta http-equiv="Content-Type" content="text/html; charset=utf-8" />
</head>

<body>
Add the page content here.
</body>
</html>
```

Discussion: **Organize Your Thoughts to Organize Your Site**

Tutorial: **Creating the Site Folders on Your Hard Drive**

Tutorial: **Building Your First Page**

Tutorial: **Previewing and Testing the Basic Page**

Tutorial: **Creating the Main Interface Pages**

Tutorial: **Constructing a Set of Similar Pages**

Tutorial: **Starting a Slideshow**

Session Introduction

Building a Web site isn't a casual undertaking. You must learn to do and use many things. You have to code the pages, pick colors and fonts, write the text that the reader sees, find or create images for your pages—the list seems almost endless. No, it isn't simple, but Web site building is a fascinating process. This is a chance for you to exercise both sides of your brain—the artistic side to develop color and draw images and the analytical side to build and organize the pages and their code.

You will find this a challenging process. I think you will be pleased with the final Web site that you create in the Sessions.

First things first. In this session, you start at the beginning. You organize the folders for your site's files and learn how to use Notepad to write the code. You build a number of the basic pages for the site. Before you start, read the Discussion on how the Sizzle site is organized.

TOOLS YOU'LL USE
Notepad, Internet Explorer, W3C Validator

CD-ROM FILES NEEDED
dk_bkgd.gif, east1.jpg, south1.jpg, west1.jpg

FILES CREATED
basic.html, main.html, nav_left.html, sizzle_east.html,
sizzle_south.html, sizzle_west.html, ss1.html

TIME REQUIRED
90 minutes

Discussion

Organize Your Thoughts to Organize Your Site

Several approaches to Web site design exist. What appears to be the simplest approach is to dive right in—you build some pages, add some links, drop in a few pictures, and the site is finished. Or is it?

To continue the example, imagine that the hastily constructed site is posted to a Web server and available for the world to see. Someone happens along and takes a look. After following the first couple of links, the reader can't seem to go any further and can't find a way to get back. Not only that, but the pages don't have titles, and the pages use different color schemes and text, so it's difficult to determine if it is really all part of the same site at all. Annoyed, the reader clicks the Back button on the browser a few times and returns to the rest of the Web. He can view millions of other sites, so a return visit to your site isn't likely.

On the other hand, if you take the time to plan how and why a reader uses your site, you can prevent such a scenario from occurring. Before you jump into Web page construction, consider how a site is designed. There are three key elements to successful site design—a logical structure, consistent appearance, and usable navigation.

Pages in a site should be organized into logical groupings. The Sizzle site features groups of pages that provide the same type of information in a similar way. You construct a set of six slideshow pages, each showing the same type of information. The site also has a set of three information pages, one for each Sizzle resort. Not only is the information presented in a logical way, but the reader has many visual cues that he is in the Sizzle site. The layouts, color schemes, and backgrounds are repeated and use a consistent color palette. This gives the reader visual cues that the information on the sets of pages belongs together. All pages have titles that display at the top of the browser window.

An effective way to organize a site is by using frames. A master file (a frameset) defines how much of the page is used by different pages. When you add links, you define which area of the window displays the linked page. The Sizzle site uses a total of three frames.

The illustration shows how your project site is broken up and what each segment displays. The primary purpose of structuring a site using frames is to make the information as readily available as possible while maintaining the site's integrity. That is, the reader can click many links from the main page of the Sizzle site, but aside from some external links to airlines and so on, all the information is loaded into the same location on your page.

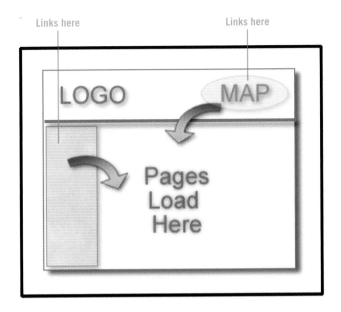

Site navigation can take numerous forms. Your project site gives the reader several ways to move through the site. The left side of the page contains a frame displaying navigation links. Links available from a picture of the Caribbean islands at the top of the page, called an imagemap, go to the main resort pages. Internally, links are available through the slideshow sequence. The user starts at the beginning of the slideshow and can either continue to the end or exit to the site's introductory page at any time. Other pages have links to site pages as well.

Basing site design on the user's needs rather than the needs of the designer or programmer, also known as user-centric design, is the key to making a site work for your readers. Your goal is to design the page features to accommodate their needs and plan their route through your site. You want to give them information; you also want them to come back again.

Folder Structures

Folder structure is an important consideration in Web site design. Folders can contain files, images, programs, and even other folders. The outermost folder is referred to as the root folder. Within the root folder are any number of other folders. The folders within the root folder are considered subfolders. If you open a subfolder, and add more folders, you create subfolders within the subfolder, and so on. The key to staying organized (and avoiding gnashing of teeth) is to use only the folder levels necessary. Not only can you remember where the content is more readily, but it is much simpler to type a path to a file that isn't buried six sets of subfolders deep! (The path is a file's location on your hard drive or remote server.) For example, folders for the site could be structured as C:\Sizzle\main\booking\airlines\images\tdair.jpg. Your Sizzle site has a root folder, named Sizzle, and several subfolders. You can reference all the content for the site from the root folder and from within the Images folder. On your hard drive, the path to a file looks like C:\Sizzle\filename; to an image file, the path is C:\Sizzle\images\imagename.

Tutorial
» Creating the Site Folders on Your Hard Drive

It is important that your files be assigned to appropriate storage locations. As you work with the site, adding pages and images, you quickly learn that what you type is important. A misplaced letter can mean the difference between viewing a page in a browser and seeing only an error message. In this tutorial, you build a root folder and then several subfolders to hold different elements of your site.

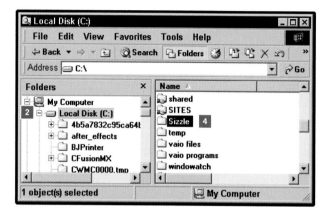

1. **Right-click Start on your desktop menu bar, and choose Explore.**
   The Explorer window opens.

2. **In the Explorer window, select the root of your main drive, usually C.**
   It is simpler to identify the locations of your pages and their content if the main site folder is at a drive's root level.

3. **Right-click in the right pane, and choose New→Folder.**
   The folder icon appears in the list and is selected.

4. **Name the folder Sizzle, and click outside the folder.**
   The file is named and deselected.

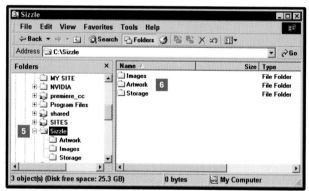

5. **Open your new folder.**
   If you don't see your new folder, scroll through the main drive listings in the left pane until you find it. Double-click the folder to open it in the right pane of the Explorer.

6. **Repeat steps 3 and 4 three times to create three additional folders.**
   Name the three folders Images, Artwork, and Storage.

7. **Close the Explorer window.**
   You built the folder sequence for your site. Your Web pages and style sheets are saved to the Sizzle folder; completed images are stored in the Images folder; parts and layers of images are stored in the Artwork folder; and the Storage folder can be used to store copies of files, files from the CD, and so on.

Working In Notepad

The tutorials include references to line numbers. Notepad doesn't show line numbers, although they are tracked and you can use the Edit→Go To command to find a particular line on a page. Your line numbering may differ slightly from that shown in the tutorials.

However, HTML isn't governed by line wrapping or leaving blank lines, so your pages are correct in your browser. In the tutorials, the lines are often wrapped (carried over to the next line) to show you all the content. Use the line numbers as references to different areas of a page, but read the content of the line carefully as you follow the steps to ensure you are modifying or adding code to the correct line.

You can make Notepad display the content the same, or very nearly the same as that shown in the figures. Begin by making sure that Word Wrap is active. Click Format on the menu bar and look for a checkmark to the left of Word Wrap. If there is no checkmark, click on Word Wrap to activate it. Then, type some code as outlined in the tutorial. Drag the bottom right corner of the Notepad page left, reducing the width of the window, until the length of the line displayed on the Notepad page is the same as that described in the tutorials.

Both the Go To command and the Word Wrap features in Notepad are very useful. However, if you have Word Wrap turned on, you must turn it off in order to use the Go To command.

Tutorial
» Building Your First Page

Now that your folder structure is built, it's time to make your first Web page. You already have some page-building experience if you completed the Confidence Builder tutorial. The Confidence Builder site was designed to give you an overview of the process and create viewable pages. In this tutorial, you start from scratch again. This time, along with making viewable pages, you make the pages well formed and compliant to the standards. Please note that the figures of the code look slightly different than you see in Notepad. To make it easier for you to follow along, I display the code in an editor to show the line numbers and color-code the different code elements. You may find some minor discrepancies between the lengths of the lines in the figures and your version in Notepad.

1. **From the desktop, choose Start→Programs→ Accessories→Notepad.**

2. **On line 1 and 2, type:** `<!DOCTYPE html PUBLIC "- //W3C//DTD XHTML 1.0 Transitional//EN" "DTD/xhtml1-transitional.dtd">`
   The first tag in a pair is the start tag, the second tag is the end tag, and text between the tags is the element content. A correctly coded (X)HTML Web page must define a Doctype (document type definition or DTD) to state what version of (X)HTML the Web page uses.

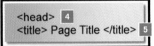

3. **On line 3, type:** `<html xmlns="http://www.w3.org/ 1999/xhtml">`
   This line includes the opening tag for the page's HTML code. It also identifies what type of elements and attributes are used on your page. In this case, xmlns refers to the XML name space.

4. **Leave a blank line; on line 5, type:** `<head>`
   The first portion of the Web page proper, the head defines content that is applied to the page, but isn't usually visible in a browser, such as scripts and metatags. (The tag applied in Step 5 is an exception.)

```
<head>  4
<title> Page Title </title>  5
```

5. **In line 6, type:** `<title>Page Title</title>`
   The title is a visible `<head>` tag; it displays on the title bar at the top of the browser window. When a reader adds a book-mark to a page, the title is the default name of the bookmark.

< N O T E >
Whenever you are introduced to a new HTML tag, it is shown as a tag image— the tag is shown on a blue background and numbered according to the tutorial step where it is first used. The tag images are used in addition to the figures of the code editor, which identi-fies the tags as they appear in your page.

< N O T E >
HTML tags are not case sensitive, but XHTML-compliant code requires lowercase letters in tags.

< N O T E >
The W3C, identified in the code added in Step 3, is the body responsible for identifying and maintaining Web standards; this organization also provides the page validation process that you use throughout this book.

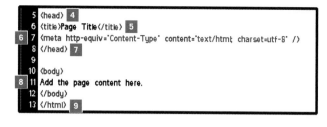

<TIP>
HTML tags are surrounded by the two characters < and >, called angle brackets.

<NOTE>
HTML isn't affected by blank lines in the code. You can separate the code in the Notepad page with blank lines to make it easier to read. If you press Enter on the keyboard to move text to another line or to break a line of text, it has no effect on HTML. If you break the line in a line of text, the break is equivalent to a space when the text is seen in a browser. However, you cannot break lines arbitrarily when writing JavaScript as you learn starting in Session 11.

6. **In line 7, type:** `<meta http-equiv="Content-Type" content="text/html; charset=utf-8" />`
   This string of words and characters defines the type of content used in the page and the format to be applied to characters. <meta> tags provide information about your page to browsers and search engines. The attributes refer to languages and character sets used on the Internet.

<TIP>
The content of line 7 is commonly used on Web pages. You may see different attributes for the content. Although most tags use `content="text/html;` the `charset` values vary. You are using an international character set named `utf=8`.

7. **Close the <head> tag in line 8; Type:** `</head>`
   Each element (tag) added to the page must be closed. A closed tag is written the same as the opening tag with a "/" preceding the element name.

8. **Leave line 9 blank. In line 10, type:** `<body>` **In line 11, type:** `Add the page content here.` **In line 12, type:** `</body>`
   The opening and closing <body> tags enclose placeholder text that displays when you preview the page.

9. **In line 13, type:** `</html>`
   You added the opening <html> tag in Step 3; each open tag must be closed in sequence.

10. **Choose File→Save. Browse to the location of your Sizzle folder on your hard drive, and open the Storage folder.**

11. **Save the file as** `basic.html`.
    Notepad offers only the text (`.txt`) file format; you must type the extension `.html` as well as the filename. You have now created the basic page for your Web site. You use this page as a template for creating other pages in your site later in this session.

Basic Rules for Using XHTML

The difference between a page containing valid code and one with errors may be slight. Here is a checklist to use when writing your page's code:

>> All elements (tags) must be properly nested within each other.

>> Each element that can use attributes must be part of a pair; both opening and closing tags are required.

>> Tag names must be in lowercase as XHTML is an XML application; all XML applications are case sensitive.

>> Empty elements are elements that don't have attributes, such as horizontal lines and line breaks. Empty elements must be closed. This can be written in one of two ways; for example, <br/> is read the same way as
</br>.

Tutorial

» Previewing and Testing the Basic Page

You use the basic page that you constructed in the previous tutorial as a source for several other templates and then for the pages in your site. Before you make multiple copies of the page, you want to preview and test the page. In this tutorial, you load the page into your browser and test the site using the W3C's Validator. The pages in the book's site are viewed and tested using Internet Explorer.

1. **Open Internet Explorer.**
You use the browser to view your page and test the code.

2. **From the browser menu, choose File→Open. In the Open dialog box, click Browse. Locate the** basic.html **file, and double-click the filename to display it in the Open dialog box.**

<TIP>
You can also select the page in the dialog box and click Open.

3. **Click OK to load the page into the browser.**
Note the page title at the top of the browser window and the placeholder text on the body of the page.

4. **Type this URL into the address bar of the browser:**
http://validator.w3.org/
A URL is a Uniform Resource Locator. It is also named a URI (Uniform Resource Indicator). The URL is the address of the Web page. When you type the address, the W3C Validator page displays in the browser.

5. **Click Browse to open an Explorer window. Locate your** basic.html **file and double-click.**
The file loads into the W3C Validator page.

6. **Click Validate File.**
The site processes the content and structure of your file according to the specification that you added in line 1 of the page.

7. **Read the results.**
Your basic.html file is determined to be valid XHTML code.

8. **Close the browser.**
You built and saved a template file. You tested the file visually in your browser and also validated the code.

More on Document Types

There are three XHTML document types: Strict, Transitional, and Frameset. These formats are used for different purposes. The Strict format is used for machine-readable content with little presentation markup, used together with Cascading Style Sheets. The Transitional XHTML document type is more generic and allows HTML presentation features. It also works with browsers that can't understand Cascading Style Sheets. Much of your site is constructed using the Transitional type. Finally, XHTML 1.0 Frameset is used when you want HTML frames to partition browser windows into frames, which is covered in Session 7.

Tutorial

» Creating the Main Interface Pages

The discussion at the start of this session described the interface for the Sizzle site and explained that the main interface of your site is made up of three pages. In this tutorial, you modify the basic HTML page to create some of the interface pages. The process for duplicating pages uses the `basic.html` file created as a template; if you prefer, you can also save copies of the files in sequence as you work with them. Just make sure to check the names and content carefully. Before you begin, locate the `dk_bkgd.gif` image file from the CD or your storage folder location; move or copy the file into the Images folder within the Sizzle site folder.

1. **In Notepad, choose File→Open and browse to the location of your site's Storage folder.**

2. **In the Open dialog box, click the drop-down list and choose All Files.**
   Your `.html` file now displays in the dialog box.

3. **Choose the `basic.html` file, and click Open.**

4. **Choose File→Save As, and name the copy `main.html`.**
   Save the file in the root folder of your site, not inside the Storage folder where the original `basic.html` file is stored.

<NOTE>
When you open your Sizzle site folder, you see `main.html` listed with the three folders that you created in an earlier tutorial.

5. **Choose Edit→Go To...**
   The Goto line dialog box opens.

6. **Type 6 in the line field.**

7. **Click OK.**
   The dialog box closes, and the cursor jumps to the start of line 6 in your Notepad page.

8. **In line 6, replace the default title text. Between the <title> tags, type:** `Welcome to Sizzle!`
   The title appears at the top of the browser window when you preview the file.

9. **Delete the placeholder text in line 11.**
   You replace the text in the next steps.

```
6  <title>Welcome to Sizzle!</title>
7  <meta http-equiv="Content-Type" content="text/html; charset=utf-8" />
8  </head>
9
```

10. **In line 11, wrapping to line 12, type:** `<h1><font color="#003366" face="Arial, Helvetica, sans-serif"><strong>Hot Beaches - Hot Times </strong></font></h1>`

    You add a visual title to the page. The title has a number of attributes, or characteristics. It uses the largest default heading size, `<h1>`. You define a blue color for the font and assign font faces. The `<strong>` tag gives the text more weight, similar to using a bold font.

< N O T E >

Elements must be properly nested. Each tag pair, like the layers of an onion, has a position within a string of tags. This means the sequence of opening tags is reversed for the sequence of closing tags. In Step 10, the opening tags are `<h1><font><strong>` and the closing tags are written as `</strong></font></h1>`.

11. **In line 13, wrapping to line 18, type:** `We started Sizzle Resorts to meet our own needs, and those of other like-minded young vacationers. In 2000 we realized that we had finished college — but we hadn't finished Spring Break, or at least the concept of Spring Break. With that philosophy in mind, the first Sizzle opened on an experimental basis. There are now three Sizzle locations in the Caribbean, with more in the planning stage. The experiment is a success. Join us.`

    The text is organized into a table in Session 2.

< T I P >

You can add as many lines as necessary in the code page. HTML reads any number of spaces as one space. A new line also counts as one space so when wrapping text to the next line, it isn't necessary to add a space after the final word before the wrap.

12. **Save the file.**

    You return to the `main.html` file in the next session.

13. **Preview the `main.html` file in your browser.**

    Note the page title, the blue heading, and the text. Minimize your browser.

14. **Save the file again now that you know everything looks as it should.**

15. **Choose File→Open, and reopen the `basic.html` page.**

16. **Choose File→Save As, and name the page `nav_left.html`.**

    Store the file in the root of your Sizzle site folder.

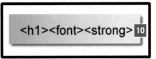

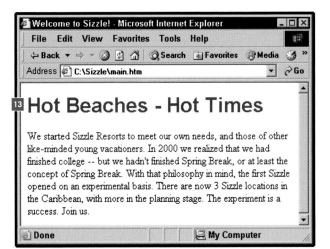

```
 5  <head>
 6  <title>Left Navigation Frame</title>
 7  <meta http-equiv="Content-Type" content="text/html; charset=utf-8" />
 8  </head>
 9
10  <body background="Images/dk_bkgd.gif">
11
```

17. **In line 6, replace the default title text. Type:** Left Navigation Frame **within the <title> tags.**
This page displays links at the left side of your site's interface.

18. **In line 10, expand the <body> tag. Type:** `<body background="Images/dk_bkdg.gif">`
You add a background attribute to the <body> tag. The value is an image stored in the Images folder within the Sizzle site folder. A blue/green striped image is added to the page.

< C A U T I O N >
The `nav_left.html` file is stored inside the Sizzle folder; the image is stored in a subfolder. In order for your browser to find the correct image and load it as the background, you must preface the file's name with the folder's name. If the image was stored in a folder within the Images folder, the value for the attribute would be prefaced by **./** meaning another folder level in addition to the Images folder level.

19. **Preview** nav_left.html **in your browser.**
Note the background image added to the page. Minimize the browser. You created the introductory page to your site, main.html and the first of two navigation pages.

Address 🔲 C:\Sizzle\left_nav.html   ▼   🔗 Go

📄 Done   🖳 My Computer

Working with Background Images

Background images are treated differently than inserted images on a Web page. In this tutorial, you add a background to the left_nav.html page. The background, dk_bkgd.gif, is a long narrow strip displaying the green/blue gradient you see in the preview. Your browser applies the image using a tiling method. This means that the image is copied as many times as required to fill the page background horizontally and vertically. A background image is not a standalone image. Rather, it is an attribute of the <body> tag. You work with inserted images starting in a later tutorial and continuing in several sessions throughout the book. The images are added using HTML elements and require a number of attributes to define them correctly.

Tutorial
» Constructing a Set of Similar Pages

The Sizzle empire is comprised of three resorts. Each resort has a main page that describes the focus, shows an image of the facility, and links to other parts of the site. In this tutorial, you construct the pages for the three locations. You add one image, a description, and text that is used for linking to each page. Complete the first page, and then duplicate it for the others to minimize typing. Remember that you can validate the code in the files whenever you want using the W3C Validator page.

1. **Copy or move these three images from your CD or your hard drive storage location to the Sizzle site's Images folder:**
   east1.jpg
   west1.jpg
   south1.jpg
   Each page has one of these images added during this tutorial.

2. **Open Notepad if you are not continuing from the last tutorial, and open the** basic.html **file.**

3. **Save the file as** sizzle_east.html **to become the first resort's page.**
   Each location's page is named in a similar way for consistency.

4. **In line 6, replace the default title text. Between the <title> tags, type:** Sizzle East - Where It's Spring Break All Year!
   The title appears at the top of the browser window when you preview the file.

5. **Replace the placeholder text in line 11, wrapping to line 12. Type:**
   <img src="Images/east1.jpg" width="240" height="180" alt="Sizzle East Resort - hotel and pool" />
   The <img> tag adds an image to your page and uses several attributes. The image source is defined the same way that you defined the background image in the previous tutorial. State the width and height of the image to define the image's location on the page. Width and height are optional attributes, but help to load pages faster. The width and height are understood to be in pixels; you don't have to specify the value. The alt attribute is a text label for the image. Readers with browser images turned off or using special devices and screen readers read about the image rather than view it. The tag is closed with />.

6. **Add an empty line below the image information.**
   Adding a blank line makes it easier to view the content on the page.

< N O T E >
The <img> tag can be closed in one of two ways. I use the shortened version, which uses a blank space and a slash before the closing bracket. You can also close the tag after the alt attribute and use </img>. Either version is correct, but don't use both—a tag needs to be closed only once!

```
14  <p>Sizzle East is located on the Berry Islands, a chain of 30 cays and islets.
15  Our resort sits on the northeastern edge of the Great Bahama Bank on Great
16  Harbour Cay. Sport fishing is famous in the area, and diving is becoming
17  popular. You can dive along the many reefs in the area. Or you can lie on
18  the beach. Have a few cold ones, watch the scenery, celebrate not being
19  at work -- the choice is yours.</p>
20
21  Watch our Sizzle slideshow
22  <hr />
23  Ready to visit? Book HERE. 10
24  </body>
25  </html>
```

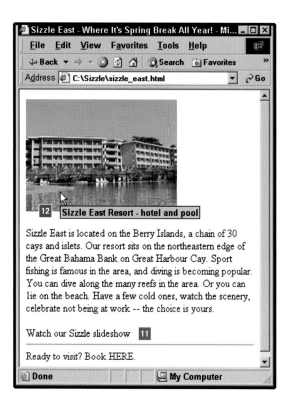

7. **In line 14, wrapping to line 19, type:** `<p>Sizzle East is located on the Berry Islands, a chain of 30 cays and islets. Our resort sits on the northeastern edge of the Great Bahama Bank on Great Harbour Cay. Sport fishing is famous in the area, and diving is becoming popular. You can dive along the many reefs in the area. Or you can lie on the beach. Have a few cold ones, watch the scenery, celebrate not being at work -- the choice is yours.</p>`
In Session 2 you separate the text into paragraphs and add the paragraphs to a table. You must encase the text with <p></p> tags, defining the start and end of a paragraph.

< N O T E >
Up to this point, the pages that you created didn't need to have the text in paragraph tags because the content of the <body> tag was only text. Now you have defined an image, and you must define the text with its own tags. When you start working with text styles, you identify all text on the pages with <p> tags or heading tags.

8. **Leave line 20 blank. In line 21, type:** `Watch our Sizzle slideshow`
The text is used for a link to the site's slideshow.

9. **In line 22, type:** `<hr />`
The <hr /> tag adds a horizontal rule across the page. The tag is structured as both the opening and closing tag for the element.

10. **In line 23, type:** `Ready to visit? Book HERE.`
The text is used to link to a booking page in the site.

11. **Save the file. Preview it in your browser.**
Note the elements you added to the page.

12. **Move the mouse cursor over the image, and read the alternative text that you added in the <img> tag. Minimize the browser.**

13. **In Notepad, choose File→Save As. Rename the page** `sizzle_west.html`.
The Sizzle West resort provides a similar range of information as the Sizzle East resort's page, so you can reuse the page as a starting point.

14. **In line 6, replace the title text. Between the <title> tags, type:**

    `Sizzle West - A Place For Couples`

    The title appears at the top of the browser window when you preview the file.

15. **Replace the placeholder text in line 11, wrapping to line 12. Type:**

    `<img src="Images/west1.jpg" width="240" height="180" alt="Sizzle West Resort - A Romantic Paradise" />`

    The image tag identifies the `west1.jpg` image. Replace the alternative text for the image as well.

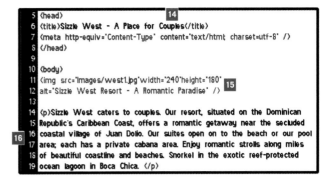

16. **Replace the text starting in line 14 and wrapping to line 19. Type:**

    `<p>Sizzle West caters to couples. Our resort, situated on the Dominican Republic's Caribbean Coast, offers a romantic getaway near the secluded coastal village of Juan Dolio. Our suites open onto the beach or our pool area; each has a private cabana area. Enjoy romantic strolls along miles of beautiful coastline and beaches. Snorkel in the exotic reef-protected ocean lagoon in Boca Chica. </p>`

17. **Save the file. Preview it in your browser. Move the mouse cursor over the image, and read the alternative text that you added in the <img> tag. Minimize the browser.**

18. **In Notepad, choose File➔Save As. Rename the page** `sizzle_south.html`.

    The Sizzle South resort uses the same type of information as the other two resorts' pages.

```
19  6  <title>Sizzle South - It's Hot Down Here!</title>
    7  <meta http-equiv="Content-Type" content="text/html; charset=utf-8" />
    8  </head>
    9
    10 <body>
20  11 <img src="Images/south1.jpg" width="240" height="180"
    12 alt="Sizzle South Resort - Grounds and Beach" />
    13
    14 <p>Sizzle South is for everyone. Young, not-so-young, couples, and singles.
    15 What brings everyone together? Sizzle South is a sports-oriented resort.
21  16 Spend your days on the water, in the water, under the water. Most
    17 activities are included with your vacation price. Not a water lover? Our
    18 grounds back a spectacular 18-hole golf course. Come to Barbados and
    19 hang out with us for a while. It's very hot down here! </p>
```

19. **In line 6, replace the title text. Type:** `Sizzle South - It's Hot Down Here!`
    The title appears at the top of the browser window when you preview the file.

20. **Modify the image text. On line 11, wrapping to line 12, type:**
    ```
    <img src="Images/south1.jpg" width="240"
    height="180"
    alt="Sizzle South Resort - Grounds and Beach"
    />
    ```
    The image tag identifies the `south1.jpg` image. Because the `south1.jpg` image is the same size as `west1.jpg`, use the same size attributes as you used in Step 14.

21. **Replace the text on lines 14 to 19. Type:** `<p>Sizzle South is for everyone. Young, not-so-young, couples, and singles. What brings everyone together? Sizzle South is a sports-oriented resort. Spend your days on the water, in the water, under the water. Most activities are included with your vacation price. Not a water lover? Our grounds back a spectacular 18-hole golf course. Come to Barbados and hang out with us for a while. It's very hot down here! </p>`

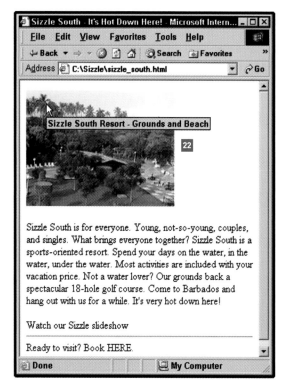

22. **Preview the** `sizzle_south.html` **page in your browser. Move the mouse cursor over the image, and read the alternative text that you added in the <img> tag. Minimize the browser.**

23. **Save the file. Leave Notepad open for the next tutorial.**
    You built a set of three pages, one for each of the Sizzle resorts. You added similar elements to the pages, including an image, text, and a horizontal rule.

Tutorial
» Starting a Slideshow

The Sizzle site uses a slideshow to present some images and provide bits of information about the resorts. A slideshow doesn't require any special code, but is instead based on layouts. The slideshow is a sequence of pages (six in total) that use the same types of images and text, and it has a navigation system for the reader to sequentially view the pages. In Sessions 2 and 5, you add and configure tables for the page; you build the rest of the slideshow pages in subsequent sessions. In the final tutorial for this session, you build the first of the slideshow pages.

1. **In Notepad, open the** `basic.html` **file.**
   You start configuring the slideshow page from the basic file.

2. **Choose File➔Save As. Browse to your site folder. Name the file** `ss1.html`**, and click Save.**
   Save the file in the root of the site folder.

3. **In line 6, replace the default title. Between the <title> tags, type:**
   `Slideshow 1`
   Each page of the slideshow is numbered.

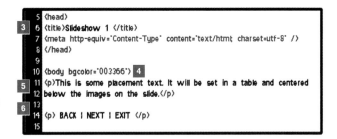

4. **In line 10, add a background color to the opening body tag. Type:**
   `<body bgcolor="003366">`
   Your original file included the <body> tag; add the color attribute after the element name and before the closing bracket.
   The page has a dark blue background.

5. **Delete the placeholder text beginning in line 11 and wrapping to line 12. Type:** `<p> This is some placement text. It will be set in a table and centered below the images on the slide. </p>`
   The slideshow uses text and images placed in a table. Both the text and the images are placed on the page in a table. You work with the slideshow pages in several sessions.

6. **Leave line 13 blank. In line 14, type:** `<p> BACK | NEXT | EXIT </p>`
   These words are used for text navigation.

7. **Save the file. Preview the page in your browser.**
   Note the background color, which is the same as the title that you added in an earlier tutorial to the `main.html` page. Close the browser.

8. **Save the** `ss1.html` **file. Close Notepad.**
   You added the first page of a slideshow sequence of pages to your site. You assigned a background color to the page and added some text to use for placement in a later session.

» Session Review

This session covered the initial site-building processes. You learned how to organize a folder structure for storing your site that is convenient and easy to work with. You created a basic Web page, shown in its written form in the first image in this session. You learned how to preview it in your browser and validate its code. You modified the basic page several times to create different pages and groups of pages for the site.

You built the main informational pages for the site, that is, the general information page that displays when your final site is loaded into a Web browser, as well as the information pages for each resort. One of the resort pages that you created is shown in the final image in this session. You created single files for some types of pages. The slideshow page is modified numerous times during several sessions. You create the rest of the pages when most of the content is complete. This saves copy and paste time and errors.

Here are some questions to help you review the information in this session. You'll find the answer to each question in the tutorial noted in parentheses.

1. What are the three key elements to successful Web site design? (See Discussion: Organize Your Thoughts to Organize Your Site.)

2. What are visual cues? Why are they important to Web site design? (See Discussion: Organize Your Thoughts to Organize Your Site.)

3. What is an appropriate storage location for a Web site's contents on a hard drive? Why? (See Tutorial: Building Your First Page.)

4. What is a document type? (See Tutorial: Building Your First Page.)

5. Why is it important to title Web pages? (See Tutorial: Building Your First Page.)

6. Why are tags (elements) in pairs? What does it mean to open and close a tag? (See Tutorial: Building Your First Page.)

7. Are XHTML tags case sensitive? What does that mean? (See Tutorial: Building Your First Page.)

8. Where does a page's title display in a Web browser? (See Tutorial: Previewing and Testing the Basic Page.)

9. What is a URL? What is a URI? (See Tutorial: Previewing and Testing the Basic Page.)

10. How do you nest elements? Why is it important? (See Tutorial: Creating the Main Interface Pages.)

11. Can you add extra spaces and extra lines when writing XHTML? (See Tutorial: Creating the Main Interface Pages.)

12. What is an attribute? (See Tutorial: Creating the Main Interface Pages.)

13. What attributes should you always use when inserting images on a Web page? (See Tutorial: Constructing a Set of Similar Pages.)

14. What are the two ways to close a tag? (See Tutorial: Constructing a Set of Similar Pages.)

15. What tag is used to define paragraphs of text on a page? (See Tutorial: Constructing a Set of Similar Pages.)

» Other Projects

You learned how to use the W3C Validator page to test your pages. In addition to testing your local files, you can test any Web page. Open the page that you would like to test. Click in the address bar at the top of the browser window, and drag to select the text. In the Validator, paste the text into the Address field. Can you find sites with compliant pages? Are you surprised at the results? Are the pages that you test primarily using HTML 4.01, or are they using XHTML 1.0 (as in this book)?

Sizzle West caters to couples. Our resort, situated on the Dominican Republic's Caribbean Coast offers a romantic getaway near the secluded coastal village of Juan Dolio. Our suites open on to the beach or our pool area; each has a private cabana area. Enjoy romantic strolls along miles of beautiful coastline and beaches. Snorkel in the exotic reef-protected ocean lagoon in Boca Chica.

Watch our Sizzle slideshow

Ready to visit? Book HERE.

Using Tables for Layouts

Address 🗐 C:\Sizzle\main.htm ▾ 🔗 Go

Hot Beaches - Hot Times

We started Sizzle Resorts to meet our own needs, and those of other like-minded young vacationers. In 2000 we realized that we had finished college -- but we hadn't finished Spring Break, or at least the concept of Spring Break. With that philosophy in mind, the first Sizzle opened on an experimental basis. There are now 3 Sizzle locations in the Caribbean, with more in the planning stage. The experiment is a success. Join us.

Cell A	Cell B
Cell C	Cell D
Cell C	Cell D

🗐 Done   🖳 My Computer

Session Introduction

One of the most important things to learn about Web page design is that you cannot expect to produce a page that looks the same to every reader. Some people use a high screen resolution, others a low resolution. Some use the latest browser versions, while others use older versions. More and more, people are using browsers that run on handheld devices or televisions, and many people use browsers in conjunction with screen reading or other assistive devices.

Designing a perfect layout is achievable in a publishing program as the page is static; but the relationships between letters and lines mean nothing in Web design as layouts are constantly changing. In addition to the options I listed, every time a reader resizes the window, the text is reformatted. The goal instead is to design a page that looks good and maintains appropriate relationships between the elements, regardless of how a reader views it.

Since the times of the early browser versions, tables have been used to organize content on a page. You use tables to organize your content in several sessions throughout the book. In this session, you build basic tables and add them to various pages in your site.

TOOLS YOU'LL USE
Notepad, Internet Explorer

WEB PAGES USED
main.html, sizzle_east.html, sizzle_west.html,
sizzle_south.html, nav_left.html, ss1.html

CD-ROM FILES NEEDED
main1.jpg, main2.jpg, main3.jpg, east2.jpg,
east3.jpg, south2.jpg, south3.jpg, west2.jpg,
west3.jpg

TIME REQUIRED
90 minutes

Discussion
Looking at Tables

A table is a straightforward structure. You write code for tables in layers. A number of basic tags and attributes are used with tables, rows, and cells. A table needs three sets of tags. The table is enclosed within <table> tags, each row is enclosed within <tr> tags, and each cell, defined by columns, is enclosed within <td> tags. Inside a <table> tag, you can also put table headers, other elements, and even other tables. The figure shows the basic layout of a table.

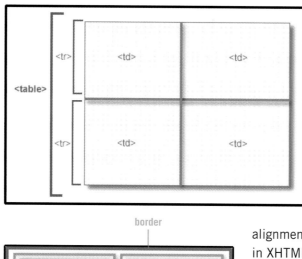

A table can use any of several attributes. The alignment of the table on a page (left, center, or right) and the background color of a table are two characteristics you use in your project. Rather than attaching the attributes to the <table> tags in the code, the alignment and color attributes are written as styles. The alignment and color are deprecated tags in XHTML which means that the tag still works in XHTML but its official use is not supported, and the tag is replaced by a style. Older browsers and versions of HTML recognize the tag.

The tables in this book use the following three attributes, shown in the illustration:

» **Border:** Value in pixels; specifies border width

» **Cellpadding:** Value in pixels or percentage (%); specifies space between cell walls and content of cell

» **Cellspacing:** Value in pixels or percentage (%); specifies space between cells

Your tables also include a width attribute, which is a value expressed in pixels or a percentage (%). The width attribute specifies the width of the table in relation to the width of the browser window. Table rows and table columns have numerous attributes as well.

Tutorial
» Constructing a Table Template

A sequence of tags is required for every table. Rather than typing the tags and attributes over and over, which only leads to boredom and error, make a template. In this tutorial, you create a table template file to use in a similar fashion to the `basic.html` file that you built in Session 1. It makes constructing tables simpler. In fact, you start with the `basic.html` file. In the images of the code, note that the table tags are a different color.

1. **Open Notepad. Open `basic.html`, located in the Storage folder within your Sizzle site folder.**
   You start with the same declaration and use the same basic tags. Rather than starting again, reuse what you have already constructed.

2. **Save the file as `table.html`, and store it in the Storage folder.**
   You now have two template files in the storage folder—the basic file and the table file.

3. **In line 6, change the title. Between the <title> tags, type:** `Table Template`
   Always customize the title when you use copies of any page.

4. **Delete the placeholder text in line 11. Leave the line blank.**
   Separating the body tag from the table tags makes it easier for you to read the page and to select the table content for copying and pasting it to another page.

5. **On line 12, type:** `<table width="50%" border="2" cellspacing="0" cellpadding="0">`
   The four attributes in this line of code are used for your project's tables with some variation in the values. A table width of 50% means that the table is one-half the width of the browser window. The border is set to 2 pixels so you can see the outline of the table in the browser. The border has no color, and unless a border width is specified, you don't see anything in the browser.

```
6  <title>Table Template</title>  3
7  <meta http-equiv="Content-Type" content="text/html; charset=utf-8" />
8  </head>
9
10 <body>
11  4
12 <table width="50%" border="2" cellspacing="0" cellpadding="0">  5
```

< T I P >

Including the basic tag attributes when you construct a template is a good idea. When you use the template, it is easier to delete those attributes that you don't need than to manually type additional attributes.

< N O T E >

If you don't explicitly assign values for cellspacing and cellpadding, most browsers display the table as if you used a cellpadding value of 1 pixel and a cellspacing value of 2 pixels. For borders, if you don't assign a value, the table is displayed with a 1 pixel border. In tables where you want no cellspacing, cellpadding, or borders visible, type the value as "0".

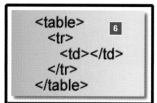

```
13    <tr>
14        <td>Cell A</td>    6
15        <td>Cell B</td>
16    </tr>
17    <tr>
18        <td>Cell C</td>
19        <td>Cell D</td>
20    </tr>
21    <tr>
22        <td>Cell E</td>
23        <td>Cell F</td>
24    </tr>
25 </table>    7
```

Table Template Microsoft Internet ... [screenshot]

```
Cell A    Cell B
Cell C    Cell D
Cell E    Cell F
```

6. Starting on line 13 and continuing to line 20, type:

```
<tr>
 <td>Cell A</td>
 <td>Cell B</td>
</tr>
<tr>
 <td>Cell C</td>
 <td>Cell D</td>
<tr>
 <td>Cell E</td>
 <td>Cell F</td>
</tr>
```

The basic table uses three rows, each row containing two columns for a total of six cells. Adding text to each table cell makes the structure of the table visible when you preview the page in a browser later in the tutorial.

< N O T E >

Instead of naming the cells, you can also use a non-breaking space. This character adds a space but doesn't add a return; it is written as `<td> </td>`. The cells in the table template are named to make it simpler for you to understand how to configure the cells and content in later tutorials.

7. On line 25, type: `</table>` **to close the <table> tag.**

8. Preview the page in Internet Explorer.
Drag the resize handle at the lower right of the browser window to see the table change size proportionally.

9. Save the file.
You have created a table template to use in your project. You can start a new page using a full copy of the `table.html` file or copy and paste the table code to other pages. Leave Notepad open to continue with the next tutorial.

How Big is an Image?

The images you place into pages have `height` and `width` attributes. To find the values for these attributes, follow these steps:

>> Open Windows Explorer; browse to the location of the image file.

>> Right-click the image, and choose Properties from the shortcut menu (the bottom option).

>> The Properties dialog box opens; click the Summary tab.

>> Locate the height and width of the image in the Summary, as shown in the image.

>> Click OK to close the dialog box.

main2.jpg Properties [screenshot]

Property	Value
Image	
File Type	Joint Photographic Experts Gro
Width	200
Height	300
Horizontal ...	30068
Vertical R...	16
Bit Depth	24
Color Repr...	True color RGB

Tutorial

» Using a Table on the Site's Main Page

In this tutorial, you add a table and some images to the `main.html` page and rearrange the text added in an earlier tutorial. You use three images to complete this tutorial.

1. **Copy these files from your CD or storage folder location into the Sizzle site's Images folder:**
   `main1.jpg`
   `main2.jpg`
   `main3.jpg`
   You add these three images to the table in this tutorial.

2. **Open Notepad, and then open the `table.html` file.**
   If you are continuing from the last tutorial, the file is already open.

3. **Click and drag to select the <table> tags that you added in the last tutorial on lines 12 to 25.**
   Select beginning with the first <table> tag through to the closing tag, </table>.

4. **Choose Edit→Copy to copy the text.**
   The text is stored on the system's clipboard; you add it to another page.

5. **Choose File→Open, and browse to your Sizzle site folder. Select `main.html`, and click Open.**
   The `main.html` page opens in Notepad.

6. **Choose Edit→Go To... In the dialog box, enter 20 and click OK.**
   The cursor moves to the start of line 20.

7. **Paste the text. Choose Edit→Paste, or use Ctrl + V.**
   The table tags are added to lines 20 through 33 and are located after the heading on the page.

8. **Move the text added to the `main.html` file in Session 1 into table cells.**
   Use the information in Table 2-1 for placing text. The tags are listed in the first column, the content is listed in the second column along with any additional tags. You add three images to the table that you are creating. You return to these tags and the <table> tag in the next steps.

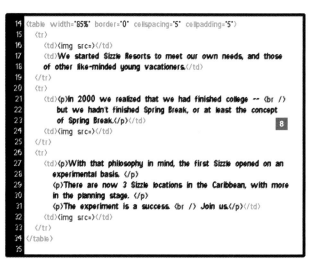

< N O T E >

The Go To command is not active if the Format→Word Wrap command is selected. Depending on how you are defining your location in the Notepad page, you must either deselect the Word Wrap feature or manually count to line 20.

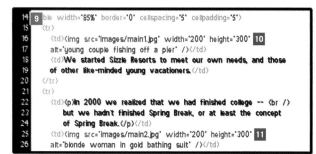

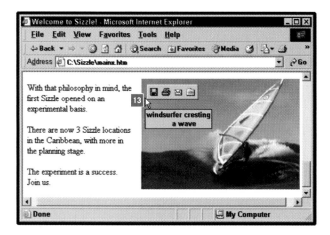

< N O T E >
The <tr> tags are included as reference; you don't need to type any code for these tags, indicated by NIL in the table. Replace the default table cell text with the text listed in the Move This Text and Add Tags: column of Table 2-1. Add the text tags as shown; when you preview the page in your browser, note how the text display differs depending on whether you add a <p> or <br /> tag. A <p> tag produces a larger gap between blocks of text than a <br /> tag, which merely starts the text after the break at the beginning of the next line.

9. **Change the attributes in the opening table tag. In line 14, type:**
   ```
   <table width="85%" border="0" cellspacing="5"
   cellpadding="5">
   ```
   The table has no borders; adding space and padding the cells and their content separates the images and blocks of text.

10. **In line 16, and wrapping to line 17, type:** `<img`
    ```
    src="Images/main1.jpg" width="200"
    height="300"
    alt="young couple fishing off a pier" /></td>
    ```
    The first image is added to the upper-left cell of the table. The image tag has four attributes. You define its source, the src attribute, by describing the location of the image. You add the width and height attributes as pixel values (you only type the numbers), and an alternate text attribute that displays on the browser window when the reader moves their mouse over the image.

11. **In line 25, and wrapping to line 26, type:** `<img`
    ```
    src="images/main2.jpg" width="200"
    height="300"
    alt="blonde woman in gold bathing suit" />
    ```
    The second image is added to the table in the right column.

12. **In line 34, and wrapping to line 35, type:** `<img`
    ```
    src="Images/main3.jpg" width="300"
    height="200" alt="windsurfer cresting
    a wave" />
    ```
    Split the `alt` attribute as shown. A third image is added to the lower-right cell of the table.

13. **Preview the page in Internet Explorer. Scroll down the page, and hold the cursor over the last image.**
    Note how the text that you added for the `alt` attribute splits over two lines according to how you wrapped it in the `html` file. Minimize the browser.

14. **In Notepad, move the beginning portion of the** `alt` **attribute from line 34 to line 35.**

View the page again in your browser. The `alt` attribute's content now extends over only one line.

15. **Save the file.**

You added a table to the `main.html` page. You defined attributes for the overall table and placed text and images. Leave Notepad open for the next tutorial.

Table 2-1: Text Placement for the `main.html` Table

Tag	Move This Text and Add Tags:
<tr>	NIL
<td>Cell A</td>	<img src=>
<td>Cell B</td>	We started Sizzle Resorts to meet our own needs, and those of other like-minded young vacationers.
</tr>	NIL
<tr>	NIL
<td>Cell C</td>	<p>In 2000 we realized that we had finished college — but we hadn't finished Spring Break, or at least the concept of Spring Break.</p>
<td>Cell D</td>	<img src=>
</tr>	NIL
<tr>	NIL
<td>Cell E</td>	<p>With that philosophy in mind, the first Sizzle opened on an experimental basis.</p> <p>There are now three Sizzle locations in the Caribbean, with more in the planning stage.</p> <p>The experiment is a success. Join us. </p>
<td>Cell F</td>	<img src=>
</tr>	NIL

Tutorial
» Using Tables on the Resorts' Main Pages

In the previous tutorial, you added a table to the introductory page of the Sizzle site. In this tutorial, you add a table and more images to each of the three Sizzle locations' pages. The set of three pages uses the same table structure and same layout. You need six images to complete this tutorial. The instructions use the `table.html` file that you constructed early in this session. Please note that the tables contain the information you need to add to the table code in your pages, and the breaks are listed according to how the lines are wrapped in the source html files; code indents are not shown in the tables.

```
19  the choice is yours.</p>
20
21  <table width="50%" border="2" cellspacing="0" cellpadding="0">
22    <tr>
23      <td>Cell A</td>
24      <td>Cell B</td>
25    </tr>
26    <tr>
27      <td>Cell C</td>
28      <td>Cell D</td>
29    </tr>
30    <tr>
31      <td>Cell E</td>
32      <td>Cell F</td>
33    </tr>
34  </table>
```

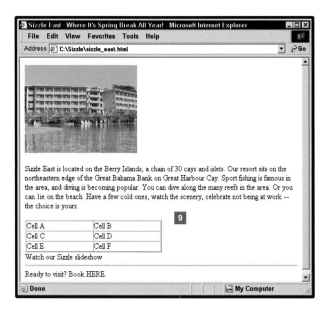

1. **Copy these files from your CD or storage folder location into the Sizzle site's Images folder:**
   `east2.jpg`
   `east3.jpg`
   `south2.jpg`
   `south3.jpg`
   `west2.jpg`
   `west3.jpg`
   You add these six images to the pages in this tutorial.

2. **Open the `table.html` file.**
   If you are continuing from the last tutorial, the file is already open.

3. **Click and drag to select the <table> tags on lines 12 to 25.**

4. **Choose Edit→Copy to copy the text.**

5. **Choose File→Open, and browse to your Sizzle site folder. Select `sizzle_east.html`, and click Open.**

6. **Choose Edit→Go To... In the dialog box, enter 20 and click OK.**
   The cursor moves to the start of line 20, the line following the <text> and <image> tags you added earlier in the session.

<TIP>
Remember to turn off the Word Wrap feature when you use the Go To command.

7. **Press Enter to add a blank line at line 20.**
   Use the blank line to separate the <table> tags that you are about to add from the existing <text> and <image> tags.

8. **Paste the text in line 21. Choose Edit→Paste, or use Ctrl + V.**
   The table tags are added to lines 21 through 34.

9. **Preview the file in Internet Explorer.**
   You see the table added to the page below the text and image added in Session 1. Minimize the browser.

10. **Make changes to the code in your file as outlined in Table 2-2.**
Move the existing text content on the page and add new content as indicated in the table. The entire content of the <table> tags is included in the table, including attributes and image information.

<NOTE>
You can never be sure how text is displayed in a browser. The paragraph and line breaks added in the table's text look different under different browser circumstances; the breaks added are used to define messages. Never try to format the text by adding empty lines and spaces to the text.

Table 2-2: Table Content for the `sizzle_east.html` Page

Tag	Move This Text and Add Tags:
<table>	<table width="85%" border="2" cellspacing="2" cellpadding="2">
<tr>	NIL
<td>Cell A</td>	<p>Sizzle East is located on the Berry Islands, a chain of 30 cays and islets.</p> <p> Our resort sits on the northeastern edge of the Great Bahama Bank on Great Harbour Cay. </p>
<td>Cell B</td>	<td align="center"><img src="Images/east1.jpg" width="240" height="180" alt="Sizzle East Resort - hotel and pool" /></td>
</tr>	NIL
<tr>	NIL
<td>Cell C</td>	<td align="center"><img src="Images/east2.jpg" width="200" height="300" alt="Couple walking to tennis courts." /></td>
<td>Cell D</td>	<td> </td>
</tr>	NIL
<tr>	NIL
<td>Cell E</td>	<td><p>Sport fishing is famous in the area, and diving is becoming popular. You can dive along the many reefs in the area.</p> <p> Or you can lie on the beach.</p> <p>Have a few cold ones, watch the scenery, celebrate not being at work — the choice is yours.</p></td>
<td>Cell F</td>	<td align="center"><img src="Images/east3.jpg" width="240" height="300" alt="Breakfast buffet" /></td>
</tr>	NIL
</table>	NIL

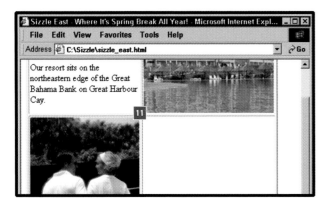

11. **Preview the page in Internet Explorer. Resize the page to see the table decrease in width only to the size of the largest image.**
    Note that the middle row has no text in the right column (Cell D). You added a space in Step 10. In the next tutorial, you combine cells in the table. Minimize the browser.

12. **Save the `sizzle_east.html` file.**
    Make sure that it is saved into the root of the Sizzle project folder.

13. **Open the `table.html` file located in the Storage folder in your Sizzle project folder.**
    You reuse the table code in the next resort page.

```
11
12  <table width="50%" border="2" cellspacing="0" cellpadding="0">
13      <tr>
14          <td>Cell A</td>
15          <td>Cell B</td>
16      </tr>
17      <tr>
18          <td>Cell C</td>
19          <td>Cell D</td>
20      </tr>
21      <tr>
22          <td>Cell E</td>
23          <td>Cell F</td>
24      </tr>
25  </table>
```

14. **Select and copy the table code from lines 12 to 25.**
    Your selection begins with the first <table> tag and ends with the closing </table> tag. This is the same step that you performed in the previous tutorial.

15. **Open `sizzle_west.html`.**
    You add a table and configure the content much the same way as the `sizzle_east.html` page.

< N O T E >
If you work carefully, you can copy the table code from the `sizzle_east.html` file and paste it into the `sizzle_west.html` page. Then replace the text and image information as necessary. Check Table 2-3 to make sure that you have the text distributed correctly.

16. **Go to line 20 and press Enter to add a blank line.**

17. **On line 21, paste the table code that you copied in Step 15.**

18. **Make changes to the code in your file as outlined in Table 2-3.**
    In Table 2-3, only those lines and tags changed from the `table.html` template file are listed along with their content.

```
12  <table width="85%" border="2" cellspacing="0" cellpadding="0">
13      <tr>
14          <td>Sizzle West caters to couples. Our resort, situated on the Dominican
15          Republic's Caribbean Coast, offers a romantic getaway near the secluded
16          coastal village of Juan Dolio.</td>
17          <td align="center"><img src="Images/west1.jpg" width="240" height="180"
18          alt="Sizzle West Resort - A Romantic Paradise" /></td>
19      </tr>
20      <tr>
21          <td align="center"><img src="Images/west2.jpg" width="200"
22          height="300" alt="View from the bungalows on land side." /></td>
23      </tr>
24      <tr> </tr>
25      <tr>
26          <td><p>Our suites open on to the beach or our pool area; each has a
27          private cabana area. </p>
28              <p>Enjoy romantic strolls along miles of beautiful coastline
29              and beaches.</p>
30              <p>Snorkel in the exotic reef-protected ocean lagoon in Boca Chica.</p>
31          <td align="center"><img src="Images/west3.jpg" width="200" height="300"
32          alt="Couple dancing outside bungalow" /></td>
33      </tr>
34  </table>
```

19. **Preview the page in your browser.**

    Again, note that the center row has a blank cell. Also note that the images are centered in their cells. Minimize your browser.

20. **Choose File→Save the** `sizzle_west.html` **page.**

    You modified and expanded the page's table.

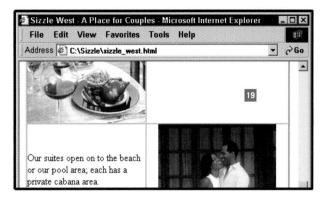

21. **Open the** `table.html` **template page, and copy the same table code as you did in Step 15.**

22. **Open the** `sizzle_south.html` **page from your Sizzle project folder.**

```
11
12  <table width="50%" border="2" cellspacing="0" cellpadding="0">
13    <tr>
14      <td>Cell A</td>
15      <td>Cell B</td>
16    </tr>
17    <tr>
18      <td>Cell C</td>
19 21   <td>Cell D</td>
20    </tr>
21    <tr>
22      <td>Cell E</td>
23      <td>Cell F</td>
24    </tr>
25  </table>
```

Table 2-3: Table Content for the `sizzle_west.html` Page

Tag	Move This Text and Add Tags:
<table>	<table width="85%" border="2" cellspacing="2" cellpadding="2">
<td>Cell A</td>	<td>Sizzle West caters to couples. Our resort, situated on the Dominican Republic's Caribbean Coast, offers a romantic getaway near the secluded coastal village of Juan Dolio.</td>
<td>Cell B</td>	<td align="center"><img src="Images/west1.jpg" width="240" height="180" alt="Sizzle West Resort - A Romantic Paradise" /></td>
<td>Cell C</td>	<td align="center"><img src="Images/west2.jpg" width="200" height="300" alt="View from the bungalows on land side." /></td>
<td>Cell D</td>	<td> </td>
<td>Cell E</td>	<td><p>Our suites open onto the beach or our pool area; each has a private cabana area. </p><p>Enjoy romantic strolls along miles of beautiful coastline and beaches. </p><p>Snorkel in the exotic reef-protected ocean lagoon in Boca Chica.</p></td>
<td>Cell F</td>	<td align="center"><img src="Images/west3.jpg" width="200" height="300" alt="Couple dancing outside bungalow" /></td>

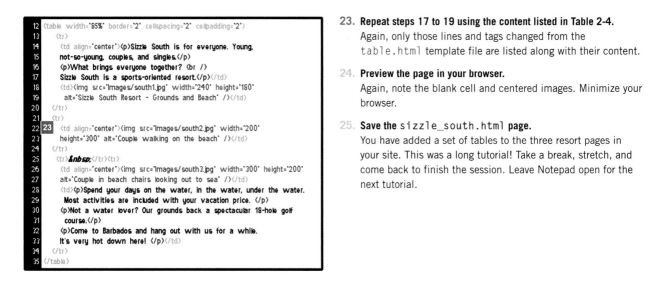

```
12  <table width="85%" border="2" cellspacing="2" cellpadding="2">
13    <tr>
14      <td align="center"><p>Sizzle South is for everyone. Young,
15      not-so-young, couples, and singles.</p>
16      <p>What brings everyone together? <br />
17      Sizzle South is a sports-oriented resort.</p></td>
18      <td><img src="Images/south1.jpg" width="240" height="180"
19        alt="Sizzle South Resort - Grounds and Beach" /></td>
20    </tr>
21    <tr>
22 23   <td align="center"><img src="Images/south2.jpg" width="200"
23      height="300" alt="Couple walking on the beach" /></td>
24    </tr>
25    <tr> </tr><tr>
26      <td align="center"><img src="Images/south3.jpg" width="300" height="200"
27      alt="Couple in beach chairs looking out to sea" /></td>
28      <td><p>Spend your days on the water, in the water, under the water.
29      Most activities are included with your vacation price. </p>
30      <p>Not a water lover? Our grounds back a spectacular 18-hole golf
31      course.</p>
32      <p>Come to Barbados and hang out with us for a while.
33      It's very hot down here! </p></td>
34    </tr>
35  </table>
```

23. **Repeat steps 17 to 19 using the content listed in Table 2-4.**
    Again, only those lines and tags changed from the
    `table.html` template file are listed along with their content.

24. **Preview the page in your browser.**
    Again, note the blank cell and centered images. Minimize your
    browser.

25. **Save the `sizzle_south.html` page.**
    You have added a set of tables to the three resort pages in
    your site. This was a long tutorial! Take a break, stretch, and
    come back to finish the session. Leave Notepad open for the
    next tutorial.

Table 2-4: Table Content for the `sizzle_south.html` Page

Tag	Move This Text and Add Tags:
<table>	<table width="85%" border="2" cellspacing="2" cellpadding="2">
<td>Cell A</td>	<td><p>Sizzle South is for everyone. Young, not-so-young, couples, and singles.</p> <p>What brings everyone together? Sizzle South is a sports-oriented resort.</p></td>
<td>Cell B</td>	<td align="center"><img src="Images/south1.jpg" width="240" height="180" alt="Sizzle South Resort - Grounds and Beach" /></td>
<td>Cell C</td>	<td align="center"><img src="Images/south2.jpg" width="200" height="300" alt="Couple walking on the beach" /></td>
<td>Cell D</td>	<td> </td>
<td>Cell E</td>	<td align="center"><img src="Images/south3.jpg" width="300" height="200" alt="Couple in beach chairs looking out to sea" /></td>
<td>Cell F</td>	<td><p>Spend your days on the water, in the water, under the water. Most activities are included with your vacation price. </p> <p>Not a water lover? Our grounds back a spectacular 18-hole golf course.</p> <p>Come to Barbados and hang out with us for a while. It's very hot down here! </p></td>

Tutorial

» Spanning Columns in Tables

In the previous tutorials, you added a table to the `main.html` page and then used the same table on the three resort pages. In this short tutorial, you change some of the tables' code in the set of resort pages to take care of the blank cell next to the second image on each page. Tables are composed of rows and columns; you combine the content of two cells horizontally (across the table) using the `colspan` (column span) attribute. In the next tutorial, you combine the content of cells vertically (down the table) using the `rowspan` attribute.

1. **Open** `sizzle_east.html` **in Notepad.**

2. **Go to line 22. Expand the** `<td>` **tag. Type** `colspan="2"` **after the opening <td tag.**
   The `colspan` attribute instructs the browser to combine the content of cells horizontally (across columns); the value "2" means the content of two cells is combined.

< N O T E >
In the image, the `height` attribute is moved to line 23 to display on the page correctly. In the html files for all three pages, the attribute is moved from line 22 to line 23.

3. **Go to line 24. The tag currently reads** `<td> </td>`. **Delete the row.**
   After a `colspan` attribute is included, you can't define a second cell in the row.

4. **Save the file.**

5. **Preview the page in Internet Explorer.**
   Note the second image's location. The image spans two cells, and it is centered according to the `align` attribute. Minimize your browser.

6. **Open** `sizzle_west.html`. **Repeat Steps 2 through 5.**
   You modify the column span and remove the extra cell from the center row of the table.

7. **Open** `sizzle_south.html`. **Repeat Steps 2 through 5 again.**
   You added a column span attribute and removed the blank cell. In this tutorial, you combined the content of a row in each of the resort pages' tables. Leave Notepad open for the next tutorial.

Tutorial
» Adding Tables to the Navigation Pages

In Session 1, you created the first of two navigation pages for your Sizzle site. Recall that the site's interface uses a navigation page at the left side of the browser window. In this tutorial, you add the table and text to the page that you built previously.

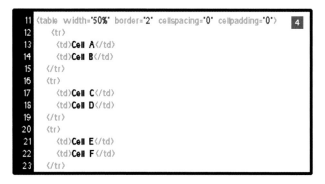

```
11  <table width="50%" border="2" cellspacing="0" cellpadding="0">   4
12    <tr>
13      <td>Cell A</td>
14      <td>Cell B</td>
15    </tr>
16    <tr>
17      <td>Cell C</td>
18      <td>Cell D</td>
19    </tr>
20    <tr>
21      <td>Cell E</td>
22      <td>Cell F</td>
23    </tr>
```

```
24    <tr>                6
25      <td>Cell E</td>
26      <td>Cell F</td>
27    </tr>
```

1. **In Notepad, choose File→Open. Browse to the Storage folder within your Sizzle site folder, and select the** `table.html` **template file.**

2. **Copy the <table> code from lines 12 to 25 as you did in the previous tutorial.**

3. **Choose File→Open. Select the** `nav_left.html` **file in your Sizzle root folder, and click Open.**

4. **Go to line 11. Paste the copied lines.**
   You add the standard <table> tags to the `nav_left.html` page.

5. **Press Enter to add a blank line 24, after the <table> tags. Copy lines 20 to 23 of the table.**
   The navigation tables use four rows; the template provides only three.

6. **Paste the copied lines into line 24.**
   You add a fourth row to the table. You have two copies of Cell E and Cell F.

7. **Modify the table content as you did in the previous tutorial. Use the information in Table 2-5.**
   The table width is described in pixels rather than a percentage as you used in the resort pages' tables. The navigation table must fit exactly on the page, and specifying a precise pixel value makes sure the table stays the same size regardless of how the user resizes the page.

Table 2-5: Table Content for the `nav_left.html` Page

Tag	Move This Text and Add Tags:
<table>	<table width="119" border="2" cellspacing="2" cellpadding="2">
<td>Cell B</td>	Replace "Cell B" with ABOUT US
<td>Cell D</td>	Replace "Cell D" with SLIDESHOW
<td>Cell F</td>	Replace "Cell F" with VIDEO
<td>Cell F</td> (second copy)	Replace "Cell F" with CONTACT US

8. **Preview the page in your browser. Drag the resize handle at the bottom right of the browser window.**

   You can see that the table doesn't change size. Also note the remaining cell labels in the first column. Minimize your browser.

9. **On line 13, replace** `<td>Cell B</td>`. **Type:**
   `<td rowspan="4"></td>`
   The `rowspan` attribute allows the first cell, originally named Cell A, to extend down four rows.

10. **Delete the three remaining `<td></td>` tags containing text for Cell C, Cell E, and Cell E (second copy).**

    The `rowspan` attribute added in Step 8 extends for the height of the entire table. The revised table's code is contained on lines 11 to 25.

```
11  <table width="119"  border="2"  cellspacing="0"  cellpadding="0">
12    <tr>
13      <td rowspan="4"></td>
14      <td>ABOUT US</td>
15    </tr>
16    <tr>
17      <td>SLIDESHOW</td>  10
18    </tr>
19    <tr>
20      <td>VIDEO</td>
21    </tr>
22    <tr>
23      <td>CONTACT US</td>
24    </tr>
25  </table>
```

11. **Preview the page again in Internet Explorer.**

    Look closely at the table; you can see a thin grey vertical line separating the two columns. In Session 3, you create a graphic image to use in the first column.

The column remains even when the content is removed.

<TIP>

If you want to see the first column more clearly, change the `cellspacing` and `cellpadding` attributes for the `<table>` tag in line 11.

12. **Save the `nav_left.html` file.**

    You added a table to the navigation page for your site. The table contains several labels to use as navigation links. You added a `rowspan` attribute to span the height of the table. You have added a table to both navigation pages for your site's interface. The tables each contain several labels to use as navigation links. You added a `rowspan` attribute to span the height of the table.

Tutorial
» Constructing a Slideshow Page Table

The final table you tackle in this session is the basic table for the slideshow pages. In the previous tutorial, you learned to use the `rowspan` attribute. In this tutorial, you use the `colspan` attribute. The slideshow table's tags are appreciably different from the `table.html` tags; you can either copy the tags from the template file and paste them into the `ss1.html` file, or enter the code line by line. The steps in the tutorial add the content line by line.

```
11  <table width="85%" border="2" cellpadding="0" cellspacing="0">
12   <tr>
13    <td colspan="2">Sizzle South</td>
14   </tr>
15   <tr>                                    2
16    <td>image ss1a</td>
17    <td>image ss1b</td>
18   </tr>
19   <tr>
```

1. **In Notepad, open** `ss1.html` **from your Sizzle site root folder.**
   You created the original file in Session 1.

2. **Starting in line 11, and continuing to line 19, type:**
   ```
   <table width="85%" border="2" cellpadding="0"
   cellspacing="0">
    <tr>
     <td colspan="2">Sizzle South</td>
    </tr>
    <tr>
     <td>image ss1a</td>
     <td>image ss1b</td>
    </tr>
    <tr>
   ```
   The title sits in a row spanning both columns of the table; text identifying the images' placement is added to separate cells in the second row of the table. The final line is the opening tag for the next row.

```
20  3  <td colspan="2"><p>This is some placement text. It will be set in a
21      table and centered below the images on the slide.</p></td>
22    </tr>  4
23    <tr>
24     <td colspan="2">button links</td>  5
25    </tr>
```

3. **In line 20, type** `<td colspan="2">` **and move the paragraph of placement text to follow the opening <td> tag in line 20, wrapping to line 21. Add the closing** `</td>` **tag.**

4. **In line 22, type:** `</tr>`
   Close the third row of the table.

5. **Add another row to the table. In line 23, and continuing to line 25, type:**
   ```
   <tr>
    <td colspan="2">button links</td>
   </tr>
   ```
   The third row is reserved for button links that you build, add, and code in several later sessions.

6. **Add a fourth row. Starting in line 26, and continuing to line 27, type:**
   ```
   <tr>
    <td colspan="2"><p> BACK | NEXT | EXIT </p></td>
   ```
   This moves the navigation text paragraph to line 27, placing it between the <td> tags.

7. **In line 28, type:** `</tr>`**, and in line 29, type:** `</table>`
   The fourth table row is closed, as is the entire table.

8. **Preview the page in Internet Explorer.**
   Notice how the text extends across both columns. Close your browser. You have added a table to the first of the slideshow pages using a number of attributes.

< N O T E >

The image of the page shown in the browser does not strictly use the content of your page. The bgcolor (background color) attribute from line 10 was removed to show the table. When you preview the page, the default black text displays against a dark blue background, which is difficult to see on your screen.

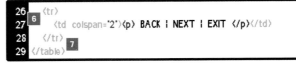

Working with Special Characters

In Session 1, you created a page template. The content written at the top of the page included a charset parameter, in this case UTF-8. The character set identifies a character encoding method, a portion of which converts a sequence of characters to symbols. You have seen the   character string that represents a non-breaking space. Here is how to write a few other popular characters:

>> “ — left quotation mark

>> ” — right quotation mark

>> — — em dash

>> © — copyright mark

>> ™ — trademark symbol

» Session Review

This session covered the process of building and adding basic tables to your project's pages. You added tables to the main page of the site and for each resort. You added tables to the navigation pages and built the first slideshow page's table.

You learned to build a table template to reuse, saving time and possible errors. The image at the start of this session shows the main page of your site, including the basic table template. You learned how tables are constructed. You also learned how to build tables that combine the content of rows or columns using attributes. The final image in this session shows the same introductory page for the Sizzle site. Adding and configuring the table and images certainly makes a difference in the page's impact!

Use these questions to review the information in this session. The answer to each question is in the tutorial noted in parentheses.

1. What does it mean when a tag is "deprecated"? (See Discussion: Looking at Tables.)

2. What are three basic attributes applied to an entire table? (See Discussion: Looking at Tables.)

3. What two measurement options can be used to define the width of a table? (See Tutorial: Constructing a Table Template.)

4. Is it necessary to define a table's attributes for every table? Why or why not? (See Tutorial: Constructing a Table Template.)

5. Is it necessary to use an attribute if the value is "0"? Why or why not? (See Tutorial: Constructing a Table Template.)

6. Can you use other tags inside <td> tags? (See Tutorial: Using a Table on the Site's Main Page.)

7. How is the text for an `alt` attribute affected by wrapping it in Notepad? What is the solution? (See Tutorial: Using a Table on the Site's Main Page.)

8. How does the `align` attribute work? Where is it added in a table's code? (See Tutorial: Using Tables on the Resorts' Main Pages.)

9. What does   mean? How is it used? (See Tutorial: Using Tables on the Resorts' Main Pages.)

10. What is the `colspan` attribute? How is it used? (See Tutorial: Spanning Columns in Tables.)

11. How does a column span affect the rest of a table? (See Tutorial: Spanning Columns in Tables.)

12. How do you use the `rowspan` attribute? (See Tutorial: Adding Tables to the Navigation Pages.)

13. How do you determine the value for the attribute? (See Tutorial: Adding Tables to the Navigation Pages.)

14. Can you use more than one `rowspan` or `colspan` attribute in the same table? (See Tutorial: Constructing a Slideshow Page Table.)

» Other Projects

Start a new page, and add a table with several rows and columns. Experiment with the table's configuration. Modify the column and row spans; combine and recombine both full rows and columns, as well as spanned rows and columns. Change the table's attributes. Experiment with different table sizes and border/cell attributes. Make copies of the project's pages if you want to experiment with those tables.

Hot Beaches - Hot Times

We started Sizzle Resorts to meet our own needs, and those of other like-minded young vacationers.

In 2000 we realized that we had finished college --
but we hadn't finished Spring Break, or at least the concept of Spring Break.

With that philosophy in mind, the first Sizzle opened on an experimental basis.

There are now 3 Sizzle locations in the Caribbean, with more in the planning stage.

The experiment is a success.
Join us.

Part III
Working with Graphics

Hot Beaches - Hot Times

We started Sizzle Resorts to meet our own needs, and those of other like-minded young vacationers.

Drawing Graphic Elements

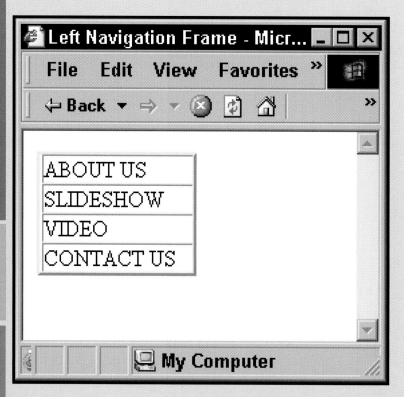

Session Introduction

One of the most powerful aspects of Web browsers is the ability to display images. The old saying "a picture is worth a thousand words" certainly applies. You may find dozens or even hundreds of images on one site. Imagine how difficult it would be to purchase products via the Web if you couldn't see the merchandise, or how difficult it would be to visualize a vacation if you couldn't see pictures of the location.

As you view sites on the Internet, you see that most sites use graphics in two different ways—as content and as a suite of graphical elements such as backgrounds and buttons. It is important to create a "look" for your site. One of the simplest ways to achieve this is to consistently use the same elements.

This is the first of two sessions devoted to working with graphics; a later session works with pictures, and you work on images occasionally in other sessions as well. In this session, you work with two images. You are already familiar with the first image, which is the striped background added to your site in Session 1. You use that image in this session as the basis for some of your site's other graphic elements. You also create a striped image to use for a tiled border on the navigation table of your Sizzle site. In this session, you create two of the navigation buttons used in the slideshow. Tutorials describe how to create one pair of the buttons. The CD contains four PhotoPlus files for each of the four buttons, as well as the four buttons in JPG format for use in your Web site.

Before you start the session, install the software. PhotoPlus 5.5 is on the HTML Complete Course CD. Follow the instructions in the CD Appendix for installing software.

TOOLS YOU'LL USE
Notepad, PhotoPlus 5.5 - Add Text dialog box, Adjust Color dialog box, Color Selection tool, Color Tab, Copy commands, Duplicate Layer command, Emboss effect , Gridlines, Layer Manager Tab, Layer opacity slider, Move tool, New Image dialog box, Paste commands, Preferences, Shape tools, Startup Wizard, Text tool, Zoom settings

CD-ROM FILES NEEDED (Artwork Folder)
blue_button.Spp, green_button.Spp

For reference, in the Artwork folder: exitA.Spp, exitB.Spp, nextA.Spp, nextB.Spp, stripe.Spp, color palette.bmp

For reference, in the Images folder: exitA.jpg, exitB.jpg, nextA.jpg, nextB.jpg, stripe.jpg

For reference, in the Session03 folder: nav_left_test.html

TIME REQUIRED
90 minutes

Discussion

Understanding Color

Web browsers display color based on the capabilities of your monitor. Although there are millions of colors in the universe, until recent years monitors could show only a 256-color palette. To complicate things even more, Windows and Macintosh systems have different color display systems, leaving a total of 216 colors that are referred to as the Web-safe palette. As you can see in the image, the Windows OS color palette (on the left) starts with white and ends with black; the Macintosh OS color palette (on the right) lists colors from black to white. The Web-safe palette colors display the same on monitors controlled by either operating system.

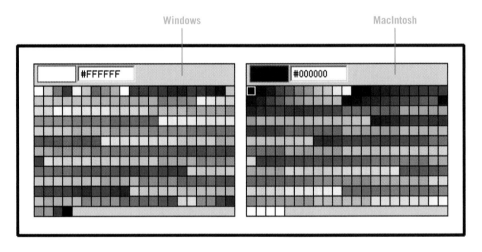

Modern browsers are capable of showing millions of colors. Browsers using Web-safe colors check for the color in the system's Web palette. A color displays if it is part of the palette. If the color isn't included in the palette, either the color is shifted to the closest palette color, or pixels from different colors are mixed

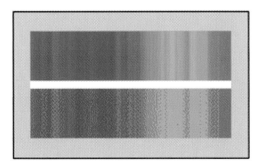

together to simulate the color using a process called *dithering*. In the image, you can see a portion of the background color bar used for the Sizzle site. The lower image is the same color bar set to display with far fewer colors. You can see pixels mixed in with other colors.

There are numerous color models. This book uses two ways to define color: the RGB color model and hexadecimal (hex) values. Additive color, which is the color shown on a screen, is composed of three colors—red, green, and blue, which is referred to as RGB. The Web-safe palette includes six shades each of red, green, and blue, as well as combinations (6 x 6 x 6 = 216).

Hex values and RGB values represent the same color using different notations. The hex system uses the values 00, 33, 66, 99, CC, and FF for each color (red, green, and blue). The value 00 is the most intense and FF is the least intense. In other words, black (the most intense) has a hex value of 000000 (00 as the darkest value for each of red/green/blue). On the other hand, white has a value of FFFFFF (FF as the lightest value for each of red/green/blue). Pure red is written as FF0000 (darkest red value, no green, no blue); pure green is written as 00FF00 (no red, darkest green, no blue). It likely comes as no surprise that pure blue is written as 0000FF (no red, no green, darkest blue).

In the RGB model, Web-safe colors are defined as absolute values or percentages. The absolute values can be 0, 51, 102, 153, 204, and 255. In percentages, colors can be written as 0%, 20%, 40%, 60%, 80%, and 100%. In this book, you use these color values.

How do the colors look? Here is the scale of green, starting with no color of any kind, and increasing in amount to pure green. The hex and RGB values are shown to the left of the color.

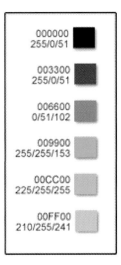

Monitors now generally support many more colors than either the Web-safe or basic Web palette. In your project, you use several Web palette colors.

The Sizzle site uses nine colors. The values of the colors and their uses on the Web pages are shown in Table 3-1.

Table 3-1: Color Values and Web Page Usage

Values	Color; Used For...
FF0033 255/0/51	Bright red; logos and table borders
003366 0/51/102	Dark blue; text and headings
FFFF99 255/255/153	Pale yellow; text and borders
E1FFFF 225/255/255	Pale blue; borders and backgrounds
D2FFF1 210/255/241	Pale green; borders and backgrounds
336633 51/102/51	Medium green; tables and Sizzle East identification
006666 0/102/102	Teal green; tables and Sizzle West identification
333366 51/51/102	Deep blue; tables and Sizzle South identification
009966 0/153/102	Grass green; tables

A copy of the figure is on the CD in the Sizzle site's Artwork folder and is named `color palette.bmp`.

Tutorial
» Constructing a Color Palette for Your Site

You are using a dark striped background image on some pages of your Sizzle site. The image is used as the basis for much of your site's color palette. In this tutorial, you create some custom colors in the PhotoPlus program's palette to use for constructing the artwork for the site. To provide a cohesive appearance in your site, the artwork uses the same color scheme as the Web pages. Building a palette not only makes for a more consistent site, it also saves time because you don't have to guess at colors.

1. **From your desktop, choose Start→Programs→Serif Applications→ PhotoPlus 5.0→ PhotoPlus 5.5.**
   The PhotoPlus 5.5 Startup Wizard opens.

<NOTE>
Refer to the CD Appendix for information on installing PhotoPlus 5.5.

2. **Move your cursor over the image named Create New Picture, and click when the image is highlighted.**
   The Startup Wizard closes, and the New Image dialog box displays.

3. **Click OK to close the Create New Image dialog box.**
   Leave the default settings. A new blank image displays on the screen.

<NOTE>
Your default settings may appear different than those in the figure.

<NOTE>
You don't work with an actual image in this tutorial; you work with the program's color palette. In the following tutorial, you start a new image.

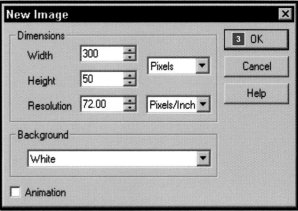

4. **Select View→Color Tab.**
   The Color Tab window opens, displaying the current foreground and background colors.

<TIP>
Click the double-ended arrow between the color swatches to swap the foreground and background colors.

5. **Double-click a color swatch at the upper left of the Color Tab.**
   The Adjust Color dialog box opens.

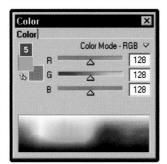

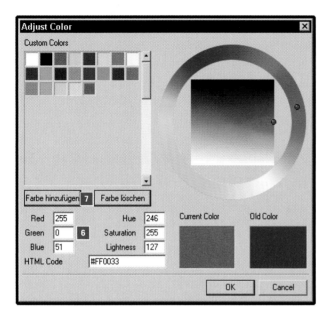

6. **At the left of the dialog box, type** 255 **in the Red box,** 0 **in the Green box, and** 51 **in the Blue box.**
   You see the bright red color display in the color swatch under the color wheel.

7. **Click Farbe hinzufugen (Add Color).**
   The red color swatch loads in the Custom Palette area at the top left of the Adjust Color dialog box. The color's hex value, FF0033, is listed in the box under the RGB values.

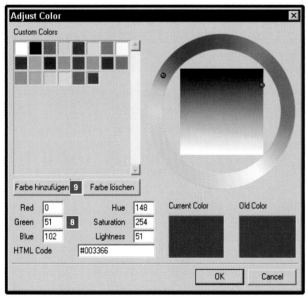

8. **At the left of the dialog box, type** 0 **in the Red box,** 51 **in the Green box, and** 102 **in the Blue box.**
   A dark blue color displays in the color swatch under the color wheel.

9. **Click Farbe hinzufugen (Add Color).**
   The blue color swatch loads in the Custom Color Palette area to the right of the red that you added in Steps 6 and 7. The color's hex value, 003366, displays in the box under the RGB values. Descriptions of the Adjust Color dialog box in the Help files show the buttons' labels in English.

10. **Repeat Steps 8 and 9 to add five additional colors to the palette.**
    Use the color values listed here. A description of each color follows the values in brackets:
    255/255/153 (pale yellow)
    51/102/51 (medium green)
    0/102/102 (teal green)
    51/51/102 (deep blue)
    0/153/102 (grass green)

<NOTE>
Other colors are used in the site as well, but they aren't used in the artwork.

11. **Click OK to close the Adjust Color dialog box.**
    You created a set of custom colors to use for your site's artwork. Close the unsaved image; leave PhotoPlus open for the next tutorial.

<NOTE>
You can also delete color from the Custom Color Palette area. Select a color, then click Farbe Loschen (Delete Custom).

Tutorial
» Choosing Settings and Preferences for Drawing

In the previous session, you started the table used for navigation in your site. The table includes an image in the left column of the table. In this tutorial, you set some program preferences, and get ready for drawing the image by choosing foreground and background colors. In Session 1 you created a new folder in your Sizzle site folder named Artwork; you use the folder to store source images and artwork files.

1. **In PhotoPlus, double-click the background color on the Color Tab. The Adjust Color dialog box opens.**
   You set a background color.

2. **Click the dark blue custom color that you set in the previous tutorial.**
   You use the dark blue background for the image.

<NOTE>
Choose the custom blue color with RBG values of 0/51/102.

3. **Click OK. The Adjust Color dialog box closes.**
   The dark blue color displays as the background color on the Color Tab.

4. **Double-click the foreground color on the Color Tab to reopen the Adjust Color dialog box.**
   You use a custom color for the foreground image.

5. **Select the pale yellow color that you added to the Custom Color palette in an earlier tutorial.**
   You use the pale yellow as one of the image's colors.

6. **Click OK. The Adjust Color dialog box closes.**
   The pale yellow color displays as the foreground color on the Color Tab.

7. **Choose File→New.**
   The Startup Wizard displays again.

8. **Click Create New Picture.**
   The Startup Wizard closes. The New Image dialog box opens.

9. **In the Width box, type: 25. In the Height box, type: 25.**
   The new image is set at the pixel dimensions specified.

10. **Click the drop-down menu to open the Background options list, and then select Background color.**
    You use the dark blue color set in Step 2.

11. **Click OK to close the New Image dialog box.**
    A new untitled image opens in the program.

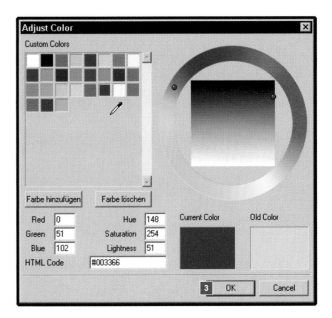

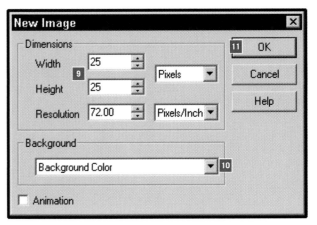

<NOTE>
You use the custom foreground and background colors in the next tutorial to draw an image.

12. **Choose File→Preferences.**

    The Preferences dialog box opens.

13. **Click the Layout Tab.**

    You set the grid dimensions and color used as you construct the image.

14. **Double-click the Grid Color color swatch to open the Adjust Color dialog box.**

    The default color for the grid is blue, which is difficult to see against the blue background used in the image.

15. **Click the bright green color in the top row of the color palette.**

    Green provides a contrasting color for the grid.

16. **Click OK. The Adjust Color dialog box closes.**

    The Grid Color color swatch displays the selected green color.

17. Change the Grid Spacing values. For both Horizontal and Vertical values, type 5.

The gridlines are set to display every five pixels.

18. Click OK to close the Preferences dialog box.

The grid preferences are reset.

19. Choose View➞Grid.

The horizontal and vertical gridlines display on the page.

<TIP>

You can also use a ruler for element placement; click View➞Ruler.

20. Choose View➞Zoom In➞8:1.

You need a larger view of the image to start the drawing.

<TIP>

You can also use the Magnification tool on the toolbar. Click the tool, and then move the tool over the image and click. Continue to click until the image is large enough to view clearly.

<NOTE>

If you increase the magnification, the image may become larger than the image window. Drag from any side of the image window to resize it and display the entire image.

21. Choose File➞Save.

The Save As dialog box opens.

22. Select the Artwork folder inside the Sizzle site folder.

Store source artwork files in the Artwork folder you created in Session 1.

23. Name the file stripe.Spp.

The PhotoPlus file format is .Spp.

24. Click Save.

The file is saved, and the dialog box closes. You modified the image's size and color. You saved your first .Spp file, and reset some preferences. In the next tutorial, you add the foreground drawing, so leave the program and image file open.

Tutorial
» Drawing a Striped Image

In the previous tutorial, you constructed the background for the tiled image and set some program preferences. In this tutorial, you add a new layer and draw the stripes image. You use one of the PhotoPlus shape tools to construct the basic shape and then modify the settings to produce several wide stripes. You export the file as a JPG file, suitable for use on your Web site. PhotoPlus does not allow for GIF format file export, also a common format for images used on Web sites.

1. **Click New Layer on the Layer Manager Tab.**
   The Layer Properties dialog box opens.

   <NOTE>
   If you closed the Layer Manager Tab, reopen it. Choose
   View→Layer Manager Tab.

2. **In the Layer Properties dialog box, type** stripe **in the Name field.**
   The layer name is changed from the default name of *Layer 1*.

3. **Click OK.**
   The Layer Properties dialog box closes and the layer is added to the image.

4. **Select the *stripe* layer on the Layer Manager Tab.**
   You add the drawing to the new layer.

5. **Click the drop-down arrow to the right of the shape tool. A sub-palette opens displaying a variety of shapes. Click the Rectangle shape.**
   The subpalette closes, and the rectangle shape displays as the current shape tool.

6. **Move the cursor over the drawing. The tool displays as an angled arrow and a lightbulb. Click the image at the upper-left corner of the second grid column.**

7. **Click and drag down and to the right.**
   This creates a rectangle on the grid.

8. **Release the mouse when the rectangle extends across the grid segment and to the bottom of the image.**
   The image must cover the entire area in order to create a seamless tile.

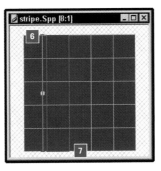

<**TIP**>
Don't click the tool outside the outline of the drawing—the shape is deleted and you must start again.

9. **Move the cursor (the angled arrow and lightbulb) over the shape. When it turns into the crossed-arrow icon, double-click the shape.**
   The shape is complete, and the rectangle fills with the pale yellow foreground color.

10. **Double-click the foreground color swatch on the Color Tab to open the Adjust Color dialog box.**
    You set a new foreground color.

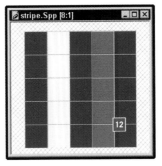

11. **Select your custom red color, and click OK.**
    The Adjust Color dialog box closes, and the foreground color changes to bright red.

12. **Repeat Steps 6 through 9 using the fourth grid segment.**
    A bright red rectangle is added to the image.

13. **Choose File→Export to open the Export dialog box.**
    You save a copy of the file to use on your Web page.

<**CAUTION**>
Don't choose File→Save. That saves the image as the PhotoPlus .Spp file format, which can't be used in your Web site.

14. **Open the Images folder within your Sizzle site folder.**
    You store the finished image ready for use on your Web site.

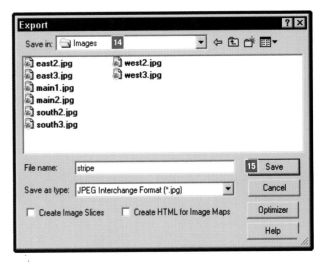

<**TIP**>
The file is automatically named, and the JPG image format is selected.

15. **Click Save.**
    The file is saved; the dialog box closes. Close the file.

Tutorial
» Testing the Navigation Tables' Tiled Image

The striped tile image you completed in the previous tutorials is officially added to the project in a much later session (Session 9) when it is included as part of the site's style sheet. That is far too long to wait to see if it tiles correctly! In this short tutorial, you add the image to one of the navigation tables for testing.

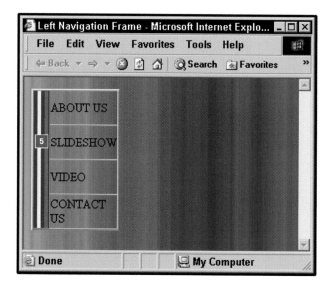

<NOTE>
If your image doesn't tile correctly, that is, if you see uncolored areas, check the original image again. Make sure the color bars extend completely from the top to bottom of the image.

<NOTE>
You can see the effects of the attribute settings when you look at the page in your browser. In correct XHTML, the attributes are part of a style sheet and not an attribute for a specific table row. If you test this page using the W3C Validator, you receive XHTML errors regarding the attributes.

1. **Open Notepad. Open** `nav_left.html`, **located in your Sizzle site folder.**
   You make a copy of the file to use for testing.

2. **Go to line 13. Add width and image attributes. Change the text to read:** `<td width="25 rowspan="4" background= "Images/stripe.gif">`
   The cell is given a width of 25 pixels, and the background image is named.

3. **In line 14, type** `height="45"` **within the** `<td>` **opening tag.**
   A height is defined for the row.

<NOTE>
When the table is complete in Session 10, that is, when the rows have styles defining height, the image tiles several times. Setting the height attributes simulates the styles that you use for the table cells in Session 10.

4. **In lines 17, 20, and 23, change the** `<td>` **tag to read:** `<td height="45">`
   This ensures that all four rows of the table share the same height attribute.

<NOTE>
A Web page background can also contain a tiled image. You don't have to define a size for the page.

5. **Open Internet Explorer. Choose File→Open, and select the** `nav_left_test.html` **file. Click OK to load the file in your browser.**
   Look at the image stripes. The image tiles several times vertically along the left side of the table. Close your browser.

6. **Save the file.**
   You tested the tiling image for your site. You can keep this file for future reference or delete it from your project folder. It is used for experimentation only.

Tutorial
» Building a Navigation Button

Much of the navigation in your Sizzle site is done with text. In the slideshow, you use text navigation as well as a pair of buttons. The buttons are used to navigate from slide to slide and also to exit from the slideshow. When the user passes a mouse over a button, it looks different to indicate it is active and responding to the mouse. You often seen buttons that appear to glow, or get larger or smaller. In this tutorial, you adjust the program's settings and add the text to the first navigation button.

1. **In PhotoPlus, choose File→Open. Browse to the location on your hard drive where you stored the CD Tutorial Files. Select the** green_button.Spp **file from the Artwork folder. Click Open to load the image into the program.**
   You use the image for the button's background.

<NOTE>
If you didn't download the Tutorial Files from the CD, insert the HTML Complete Course CD into the CD-ROM drive. Open Explorer. Open the CD drive (usually the D drive). Open the Tutorial Files folder and then the Image Storage folder. Select the green_button.Spp file. Ctrl+drag the file from the folder on the CD to your Sizzle site folder.

2. **Choose View→Zoom In→2:1.**
   The view doubles in size. The larger size makes it simpler for you to place the text later in the tutorial.

3. **Choose File→Preferences. Click the Layout Tab.**
   You reset the gridlines.

4. **Reset the horizontal and vertical gridlines to 10 pixels.**
   You use the gridlines to assist in text placement.

5. **Click OK to close the Preferences dialog box.**
   The preferences are reset.

6. **Choose View→Grid.**
   The gridlines overlay the image.

7. **Double-click the foreground color swatch on the Color Tab.**
   The Adjust Color dialog box opens.

8. **Click the custom dark blue color that you added to the color palette early in the session.**
   The color's RGB values are 0/51/102.

9. **Click OK to close the Adjust Color dialog box.**
   The dark blue is set as the foreground color.

10. **Click the Text tool on the toolbar to select it, and click the image with the tool.**
    The Add Text dialog box opens, and you see the blinking cursor in the text field.

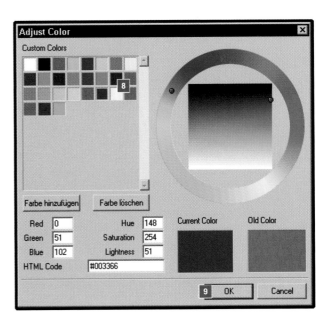

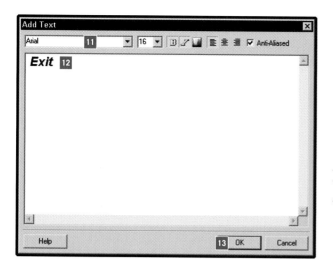

11. **Click the drop-down arrow, and choose Arial from the font drop-down list. Set the size to 16 (points is the default), click the _I_ icon to select italic, and click the B icon to select bold for the text.**

12. **Type** Exit **in the text field.**
    The text for the button displays in the dialog box.

13. **Click OK to close the Add Text dialog box.**
    The text is added to the image.

    <NOTE>
    When you add text to the image, a separate layer is automatically added to the file.

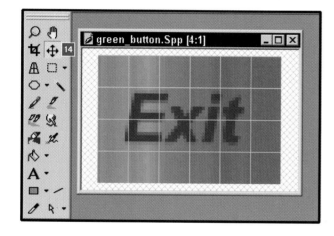

14. **Select the Move tool in the toolbar, click the text on the image, and drag upward. Release the mouse when the text is centrally located on the image.**
    Use the gridlines to assist you in placing the text.

15. **Choose File→Save As. Save the file as** exitA.Spp **in the Artwork folder.**
    You added a text layer to the first button for the site. Leave the file open for the next tutorial.

Tutorial
» Finishing the Navigation Button

You added text to the first navigation button for the site. In this tutorial, you duplicate and modify the text layer. After applying effects, the button's text appears to have a shadow and highlights. You also export the first finished button in this tutorial.

1. **Select the *Exit text* layer on the Layer Manager Tab.**
   You use a copy of the layer for the shadow.

2. **Choose Layers→Duplicate.**
   A second copy of the text is added to the image.

< T I P >
The text layer, because it was the last layer worked with in the image, is the active layer.

3. **Click Hide/Show for the *Copy of Exit* layer to toggle the layer's visibility to off.**
   The eye icon appears closed. The layer is hidden to work on the underlying layer.

4. **Right-click the *Exit text* layer on the Layer Manager to open the shortcut menu, and click Render Text Layer.**
   The shortcut menu closes; the *Exit text* layer is converted from editable text to a bitmap image. When it becomes a bitmap image you can manipulate it like any other type of drawing.

< T I P >
A text layer contains editable text; after text is rendered, it cannot be edited and the T indicator is removed from the layer. Rendering is the process of changing the content on the layer from editable text (meaning you can change the letters, font, and so on) to an image of text.

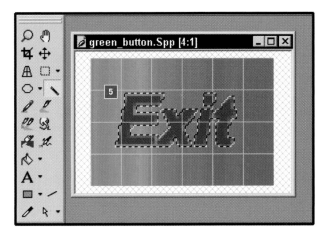

5. **Click the Color Selection tool in the toolbar, and then click the text. Shift+click the other blue areas until the text is selected.**
   You modify the blue text areas on the layer.

< T I P >
Press the Shift key and hold it as you click other areas to add them to the selection; to remove a selection, press the Alt key and click the area to remove it from the selection.

6. **Choose Image→Other→Emboss.**
   The Emboss Filter dialog box opens.

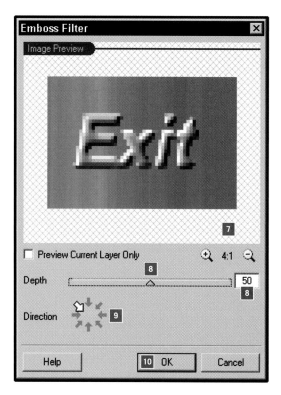

7. **Click the (+) magnification tool to increase the magnification to 4:1.**
   The original image is small; magnifying it shows the content clearly.

8. **Increase the depth to 50.**
   Drag the depth slider right to the center of the slider bar; or type the value in the field.

9. **Click the arrow to reset the shadow direction.**
   You see the shadow/highlight areas of the image change as you change the direction of the effect. Adjust the shadow direction to the arrow left of upper center.

10. **Click OK.**
    The dialog box closes, and the effect is applied to the image.

11. **Choose Select→Deselect, or use the shortcut keys Ctrl+D.**
    The selection marks are removed from the image.

12. **On the Layer Manager Tab, click the *Copy of Exit text* layer to make it active.**
    You make final adjustments to the text.

13. **Toggle the Hide/Show icon to visible.**
    You had the layer hidden when you were working with the rendered text layer.

14. **Click the drop-down arrow next to the opacity level to display the slider.**
    You decrease the opacity of the text.

15. **Drag the opacity slider left until the level shows 80%.**
    You decrease the opacity of the text layer to allow some of the underlying effects layer to be visible. Watch the effect on your image as you adjust the opacity.

<TIP>
Rather than using the slider, you can type the value directly in the field.

16. **Choose File→Export. Save the image as** exitA.jpg **in the Sizzle site's Images folder.**
    You exported the first button to use in the slideshow.

17. **Choose File→Save. Save a finished copy of the PhotoPlus file in the Artwork folder.**
    You finished the first navigation button for the slideshow. Leave the green_button.Spp image open to continue with the next tutorial.

<NOTE>
As you work on the images, save finished copies of the PhotoPlus files along with the exported versions that you use on the Web site. If you decide to change or update the images at a later time, you have the original artwork preserved to reuse or modify.

Tutorial
» Duplicating and Modifying the Navigation Button

You finished the first navigation button, green_button.Spp. In this tutorial, you use layers from that finished button as well as another background image to create the second navigation button.

1. **Choose File→Open. In the Artwork folder, select** blue_button.Spp **and click Open.**
The second navigation button file opens. You swap the background used in the first button for the second.

2. **Choose Edit→Copy.**
The blue background layer is copied to the clipboard.

3. **Click the** green_button.Spp **file to make it active.**
You add the copied background layer.

4. **Choose Edit→Paste→As a Layer.**
The copied background is added to the green_button.Spp file.

5. **Drag the new layer, *Layer 2*, to the bottom of the layer stack in the Layer Manager Tab.**
The blue background layer moves to the background of the image.

6. **Delete *Layer 1*.**
You remove the original green background layer, leaving the blue background, the text layer, and the rendered text layer.

7. **Double-click the *Exit text* layer.**
The Add Text dialog box opens.

8. **Click Adjust Color to open the Adjust Color dialog box. Select the custom pale yellow color in the Custom Color Palette. Click OK to close the Adjust Color dialog box.**
You change the text color.

9. **Click OK to close the Add Text dialog box.**
The text color on the text layer is changed to pale yellow.

10. **Choose File→Export. Save the image as** exitB.jpg **in the Sizzle site's Images folder.**
You finished the second navigation button for the slideshow.

11. **Choose File→Save As. Save the image file as** exitB.Spp **in the Artwork folder.**
Keep a finished copy of the image file for future use or modification. You completed the pair of buttons for the site.

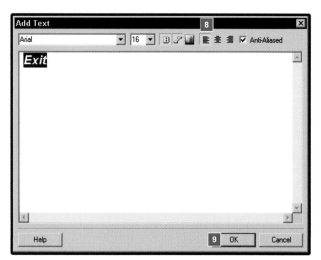

<NOTE>
The Layer Manager controls the layout of the image's elements. Layers are stacked from bottom to top; the topmost layer that appears on the image is also the topmost layer listed in the Layer Manager.

<NOTE>
You need another pair of buttons for the site as well. They are available on the CD in the Images folder named nextA.jpg (blue text on a green background) and nextB.jpg (yellow text on a blue background). Source files for the two images are on the CD in the Artwork folder named nextA.Spp and nextB.Spp.

» Session Review

This session introduced you to the PhotoPlus program. You built a color palette for your Web site in the program to make choosing color simple and consistent. You constructed and tested a repeating (or tiled) image for later use in your navigation tables. The image at the start of this session shows the navigation table for your site. The final image shows the same table with the tiled image applied. You used the site's striped background image as the source for creating some navigation buttons. You learned how to construct images and text and then composite them in layers. You learned how to reuse text as a rendered image and how to use layers to create shadow effects.

Here are some questions to help you review the information in this session. The answer to each question is in the tutorial noted in parentheses.

1. What are two common ways to identify color? What is each used for? (See Discussion: Understanding Color.)

2. In hexidecimal values, what does 00 represent? What does FF represent? (See Discussion: Understanding Color.)

3. Why should you formally construct a color palette, or define the colors, when constructing the elements for a Web site? (See Tutorial: Constructing a Color Palette for Your Site.)

4. How do you quickly swap foreground and background colors in PhotoPlus? (See Tutorial: Constructing a Color Palette for Your Site.)

5. How do you specify a background color for a new file? (See Tutorial: Choosing Settings and Preferences for Drawing.)

6. How do you reset the gridline settings in PhotoPlus? What other guides are available? (See Tutorial: Choosing Settings and Preferences for Drawing.)

7. How do you modify drawn shapes? (See Tutorial: Drawing a Striped Image.)

8. Why is it important to consider the appearance of the edges when creating a tiling image? (See Tutorial: Drawing a Striped Image.)

9. Can you use a tiled image on a Web page? Is the process the same as tiling in a table cell? (See Tutorial: Testing the Navigation Tables' Tiled Image.)

10. Do you have to create a new layer before adding text to a PhotoPlus image file? Why or why not? (See Tutorial: Building a Navigation Button.)

11. What is the difference between a text layer and a rendered text layer? (See Tutorial: Finishing the Navigation Button.)

12. How can you make contents of underlying layers visible through an overlying layer? (See Tutorial: Finishing the Navigation Button.)

13. Can you have more than one file open at the same time in PhotoPlus? (See Tutorial: Duplicating and Modifying the Navigation Button.)

14. Can you see color changes applied to text in the Add Text dialog box? (See Tutorial: Duplicating and Modifying the Navigation Button.)

» Other Projects

Experiment with different colors and shapes for the tiling image. Instead of using stripes, try using curves or a geometric shape.

Rather than using the button images from the CD, create the nextA.jpg and nextB.jpg images from scratch using the blue_button.Spp and green_button.Spp files on the CD in the Artwork folder.

Building the Web Site's Logos

Session Introduction

In the last session, you started working with PhotoPlus. You learned to use the program, built a simple graphic for your site, and created a pair of navigation buttons. You learned to work with text and image layers and how to apply effects. You also learned how to export files for use on your Web site.

In this session, you continue with graphics development work. You make the main logo for the Sizzle Web site using several layers of text and graphic elements. You work with more of the program's tools, including selection and fill tools. You make smaller logos for each of the resorts' main pages. In the next session, you have a chance to look at your completed work when you add the logos to their respective pages.

TOOLS YOU'LL USE
Internet Explorer, PhotoPlus Add Text dialog box, Adjust Color dialog box, Blur Effects, Color Tab, Deform tool, Duplicate command, Expand selection command, Feather command, Gradient fill tool, Gridlines, Hide/Show toggle command, Layer Manager Tab, Layer opacity setting, Motion blur, Preferences, Rulers, Select similar command, Selection tools, Soften blur effect, Startup Wizard, Tool Properties Tab, Zoom tool

CD-ROM FILES NEEDED (Artwork folder)
bar.Spp, bar2.Spp, palm.Spp

FILES CREATED (Artwork folder)
logo.Spp, sizzle_east.Spp, sizzle_west.Spp, sizzle_south.Spp

FILES CREATED (Images folder)
logo.jpg, sizzle_east.jpg, sizzle_west.jpg, sizzle_south.jpg

TIME REQUIRED
90 minutes

Tutorial

» Assembling Layers for the Sizzle Logo

The Sizzle logo uses six layers. The logo has a stylized palm branch at its left side, text, graphic, and background layers. In this tutorial, you create the logo file and add the image elements. The two files required for the logo construction are in the Artwork folder on the CD. Start construction from the Startup Wizard. If you want to start from the program's interface, click the "X" at the bottom left of the Startup Wizard to deselect the option. The next time you open the program, the Startup Wizard won't display.

1. **Open PhotoPlus, and choose File→New.**
   The Startup Wizard opens.

2. **Click Create New Picture.**
   The New Image dialog box opens.

3. **Type** 500 **for the Width, and type** 120 **for the Height.**
   You create a banner-shaped image.

4. **Click the drop-down arrow, and select White from the Background options.**
   You assemble the components against a white background.

5. **Click OK.**
   The New Image dialog box closes; the Startup Wizard window closes, and a new image opens.

<NOTE>

The windows in the program stay organized in the last configuration saved. Each time you open the program, the windows are displayed in the same way.

6. **Choose File→Preferences to open the Preferences dialog box. Click the Layout Tab.**

7. **Set the horizontal gridline value. Type** 150 **to set the horizontal gridline value, and type** 30 **to set the vertical gridline value.**
   Gridlines are spaced according to the image's dimensions in pixels.

8. **Click OK.**
   The Preferences dialog box closes.

9. **From the main program menu, choose View→Gridlines.**
   The gridlines overlay the image.

10. **Choose View→Ruler.**
    The vertical and horizontal rulers frame the image.

11. **Choose File→Open. Browse to the Artwork folder, select bar.Spp, and click Open.**
    The bar image opens in a new window.

12. **Choose Edit→Copy.**
    The bar image is copied.

13. **Click the logo image to select it. Choose Edit→Paste→As New Layer.**
    A copy of the bar is pasted to the upper left of the logo image.

14. **Select the Move tool in the toolbar. Drag the bar image downward until the top of the image is at the 100-pixel mark on the ruler.**
    You see a small arrow marker on the ruler identifying the location of the Move tool. The first logo element is in position.

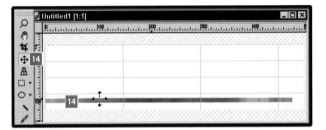

15. **Choose File→Open. Browse to the Artwork folder, select palm.Spp, and click Open.**
    The palm fronds image opens in a new window.

16. **Repeat Steps 12 and 13 to paste the palm image to the top left of the logo image.**
    Check the palm image's location. By default, it pastes to the upper-left margins of the image.

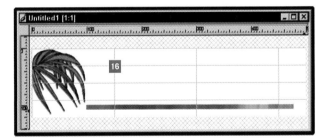

17. **Close the bar.Spp and palm.Spp files.**
    You are finished with the two source files. You do not need to save them because you made no changes to them.

18. **Choose File→Save. The Save As dialog box opens. Name the file logo.Spp, and save it in the Artwork folder.**
    Your logo file has a white background layer and two image layers added so far. Leave the image open to continue with the next tutorial.

Tutorial
» Adding More Layers to the Logo File

You added and positioned two images that are used for the composite logo image. The logo file has three layers at this point. The palm fronds image is the top layer named Layer 2, the bar image is the middle layer named Layer 1, the bottom layer is the background. In this tutorial, you modify the palm fronds image and add more layers to the image. You also organize the layers in the composition. When you added layers to the image in the previous tutorial, the Layer Manager Tab displayed. If you closed the tab, reopen it for this tutorial. Choose View→Layer Manager Tab from the main program menu.

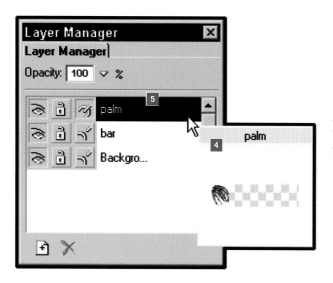

1. **Right-click the layer named *Layer 1* on the Layer Manager Tab to open a shortcut menu. Click Properties.**
   The Layer Properties dialog box opens.

2. **In the Layer Properties dialog box, name the layer** bar.
   Always use a descriptive name for layers.

3. **Click OK to close the dialog box.**
   The layer is renamed on the Layer Manager Tab.

4. **Move the cursor over the *Layer 2* name on the Layer Manager Tab.**
   A popup window opens showing a thumbnail of the layer's contents.

<TIP>
Whenever you are unsure of what is on a layer, hold the cursor over the layer name to show the content in the thumbnail.

5. **Right-click the *Layer 2* name to open the shortcut menu. Repeat Steps 1 through 3, naming the layer** palm.
   The layer's name is changed.

6. **In the Layer Manager, toggle the Hide/Show status for the *bar* and *background* layers to Hide.**
   You work with the *palm* layer.

7. **From the main menu, choose View→Zoom In→3:1.**
   Reposition the content to display the palm leaves image. You need to see the *palm* layer's content clearly.

8. **Select the Color Selection tool in the toolbar.**
   You use the tool to select segments of the layer.

9. **From the main menu, choose View→Tool Properties.**
   The Tool Properties dialog box opens, displaying the settings for the Color Selection tool.

<TIP>
You can open and close the Tool Properties Tab, or leave it open in a corner of the screen for reference as you use the tools.

10. Set the Tolerance to 50 pixels.

The higher the Tolerance level, the wider the color range selected with the Color Selection tool.

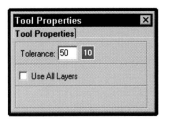

11. Click anywhere in the white background area on the image.

The selection is framed by a dashed line called a marquee. If you look closely at the image, you see that only white areas that physically touch one another are selected.

12. Choose Select→Modify→Similar.

All pixels on the image within the specified tolerance are selected, including the white areas between palm fronds.

<TIP>

If you aren't pleased with the outcome of an edit, choose Edit→Undo. You can continue to choose the same command to go backward through your edits until you reach the last saved version of the file.

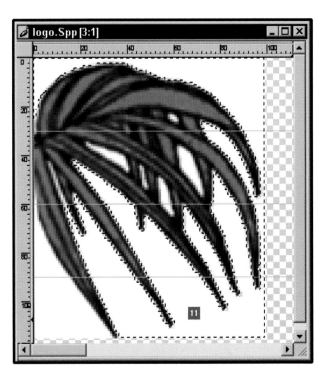

13. Press Delete.

All the selected pixels are removed from the image, and the transparent background is revealed.

14. Choose Select→Deselect.

The selection marquee is removed.

15. Choose View→Normal Viewing.

The image returns to its regular size.

16. Choose Layer→Duplicate.

A copy of the *palm* layer is added to the Layer Manager Tab above the original *palm* layer, and named *Copy of Palm*.

<TIP>

When you add a new layer, it automatically becomes the active layer in the image.

17. **Toggle the Hide/Show icons to show all layers.**
You can see the arrangement of the image's content as you continue in the tutorial.

18. **Double-click the new *Copy of Palm* layer.**
The Layer Properties dialog box opens.

19. **Rename the layer *shadow*, and click OK.**
The layer is renamed.

20. **Drag the *palm* layer down one level.**
The layer is now second from the bottom of the image's layer stack.

21. **Click the *bar* layer to select it.**
You add a text layer in the next steps. When you add a layer, it is always added to the composition above the layer selected in the Layer Manager Tab, in this case the *bar* layer.

22. **Select the Text Tool in the toolbar, and click the image.**
The Add Text dialog box opens.

23. **In the Add Text dialog box, click the drop-down arrow to display the Fonts list. Choose the Century Gothic font.**

24. **Click the font size displayed, and type 96 in the field.**
You set the font size to a larger size than the default values in the list.

25. **Click B to make the font bold, and click *I* to make it italic.**
The text uses both bold and italic font face settings.

26. **Click Adjust Color to open the Adjust Color dialog box. Select your site's custom red color, and click OK.**
The dialog box closes. You see the blinking cursor in the text field of the Add Text dialog box.

27. **Type Sizzle in the text field of the Add Text dialog box.**
The text displays in the large font, using the font face settings of bold and italic.

28. **Click OK to close the Add Text dialog box.**
The text layer is added to the image.

29. **Choose File→Save.**
You removed the background from the *palm* layer, duplicated the layer, and rearranged the content. You added a text layer. Leave the image open. In the next tutorial, you manipulate the text and add the final layers to the logo.

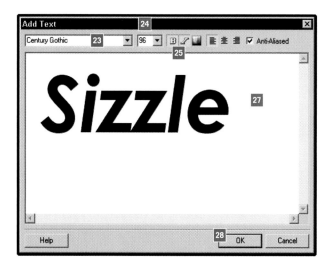

Tutorial
» Manipulating and Organizing the Logo's Layers

Your logo image now has five layers. You added two copies of the palm fronds image and added a text layer. In this tutorial, you manipulate the text layer to resize it using the Deform tool. The tool is used for resizing an image, and can also rotate and move the image on the layer. You also create another text layer to use for an effect.

1. **In the Layer Manager Tab, click the *Sizzle* text layer.**
   You activate the layer to work with its contents.

2. **Click the Deform tool in the toolbar.**
   The text on the image is framed with a solid box containing resize handles.

3. **Drag the top edge of the deform frame upward until the dot on the letter "i" is at about 10 pixels.**
   You resize the image vertically.

4. **Drag a right handle on the deform frame right until the right edge of the frame is at approximately 450 pixels.**
   Measure along the horizontal ruler at the top of the image.

5. **Drag a left handle on the deform frame left to approximately 80 pixels.**
   The "S" overlays some of the palm leaves on the left and touches the gridline on the right.

6. **Drag a bottom handle on the deform frame down to approximately 100 pixels.**
   The bottom edges of the letters "S" and "e" slightly overlap the striped bar.

<TIP>
You can use a different combination of adjustments to achieve the same outcome. For example, instead of using a font size of 96 for the text, use a larger size. The finished layout is much wider than the font specifies; you need to use the Deform tools to adjust width regardless of font size.

7. **Click any other tool on the toolbar to remove the Deform frame.**
   You are finished adjusting the text. The text layer remains selected in the Layer Manager Tab until you click another layer to select it.

<NOTE>

Although you have manipulated the text, it still behaves as text. If you double-click the text layer in the Layer Manager Tab, the Add Text dialog box opens and displays the typed text. You see the font size remains at 96 points, even though the text appears resized on the image.

8. **With the text layer still selected in the Layer Manager Tab, choose Layer→Duplicate.**
   A second copy of the *Sizzle* text layer is added to the image.

9. **Double-click the *Copy of Sizzle* text layer to open the Layer Properties dialog box. Name the layer *highlight,* and click OK to close the dialog box.**
   The layer's name is changed.

10. **Right-click the *highlight* text layer to display the shortcut menu. Click Render Text Layer.**
    The text is converted to a rendered image layer, and the text icon is removed from the Layer Manager Tab.

11. **Drag the *highlight* layer down in the stacking order below the *Sizzle* text layer.**
    The *highlight* layer is used for a highlight effect for the text and must appear to be behind the text.

12. **Choose File→Save.**
    You manipulated the text layer and added an additional layer to the image. You named and reordered the layers. Leave the image open to continue to the next tutorial.

Tutorial
» Finishing the Sizzle Logo

All the layers for your site's logo are added and organized. In this tutorial, you add effects to two layers to finish the logo design. You also export the finished file for later use in your Sizzle Web site. In this tutorial, you render all the text layers.

1. **Toggle Hide/Show to hide the *shadow*, *Sizzle* text, and *palm* layers.**
   You work with the *highlight* and *background* layers, and you use the *bar* layer for placement.

2. **Click the *highlight* layer in the Layer Manager Tab to make it active.**
   You modify the layer.

3. **Click the Color Selection tool in the toolbar.**
   You select the red letters on the layer.

4. **Click a red text area on the image to select it.**
   All contiguous (touching) pixels are selected.

5. **Choose Select→Modify→Similar.**
   The rest of the red letters are selected.

6. **Choose Select→Modify→Feather.**
   The Feather Selection dialog box opens.

7. **Type 2 in the Number of Pixels field.**
   The higher the pixel value, the wider the feathering.

<NOTE>
Feathering is a type of selection used to modify the sharpness of a selection's edges. At a feathering value of 2 pixels, the edges of the letters are slightly rounded; at a high value, such as 20 pixels, the feathered selection is a large oval shape, with no individual letter distinction.

8. **Click OK to close the dialog box.**
   The edges of the selection on the image are feathered by 2 pixels.

9. **Double-click the foreground color swatch in the Color Tab to open the Adjust Color dialog box. Select the custom yellow color, and click OK.**
   The foreground color is set to yellow.

10. **Double-click the background color swatch in the Color Tab to open the Adjust Color dialog box. Select the medium green custom color, and click OK.**
    The background color is set to green.

11. **Click the drop-down arrow to the right of the Flood Fill tool on the toolbar to open its subpalette. Click the Gradient Fill tool.**
    The Gradient Fill tool is active.

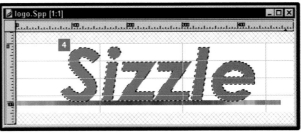

12. **Click above the image with the tool, and drag vertically across the image while holding the mouse button. Release the mouse when the indicator line extends completely through the image.**
The selection is filled with a yellow-green gradient.

13. **Choose Select→Deselect.**
The gradient-filled areas are deselected.

14. **Select the *Sizzle* text layer in the Layer Manager Tab. Right-click the layer, and choose Render Text Layer.**
The text is converted to a rendered layer. Instead of being a series of letters, it is converted to a bitmap image so it can be manipulated. Once rendered, you can't change the letters.

<TIP>
If you aren't sure whether you want to render a text layer or leave it as editable text, make a duplicate. Render one layer, and hide the other layer. This way, if you decide you don't want to use a rendered layer, you still have a copy of the original text to use.

15. **Click the Color Selection tool in the toolbox. Click a red text area on the image.**
The red area is selected.

16. **Choose Select→Modify→Similar.**
The rest of the red text areas are selected.

17. **Choose Image→Blur→Blur Effects.**
The Blur Effects Filter dialog box opens.

18. **Click Motion to set the blur type.**
A motion blur softens the edges of a selected area and creates a sense of motion.

19. **Drag the intensity slider to 8.**
The blur is applied to the image preview.

20. **Click at the left center of the dial to set the directional arrow.**
The arrow moves left. The blur appears to start at the left of the letters.

<TIP>
Click the dial at different locations to see how the direction affects the look of the blur.

21. **Click OK to close the Blur Effects Filter dialog box.**
The blur is applied to the layer.

22. **In the Layer Manager Tab, click Show/Hide to display all layers.**
You finish the layers' settings in preparation for export.

<NOTE>
The Copy of Sizzle layer is a "spare" text layer. It is shown on the
Layer Manager Tab image; its visibility is set to Hide. This layer
can be used for experimentation as noted in the Other Projects at
the end of the session.

23. **Click the *shadow* layer to make it active.**
You adjust its visibility.

24. **In the opacity field, set the opacity to 50%.**
The overlying palm fronds layer becomes semi-transparent.

25. **Choose Edit→Blur→Soften.**
The harsh edges of the shadow image are smoothed.

26. **Click the *palm* layer to make it active.**
You adjust its softness.

27. **Choose Edit→Blur→Soften.**
The edges of the palm image are smoothed.

28. **Choose File→Preview in the browser.**
Internet Explorer opens, and the logo is displayed at full size.
Close the browser.

29. **Choose File→Export to open the Export dialog box.**
Export a copy of the file as `logo.jpg`; save it in the Sizzle
site's Images folder.

30. **Choose File→Save.**
You finished the main logo for your project's Web site. You
added multiple layers, manipulated the layers' content, and
added color and other effects to enhance the final image.
Close the `logo.Spp` file.

31. **Take a break.**
Drawing on a computer is physically tiring. Roll your eyes,
stretch out your neck and shoulders, or go for a walk. Come
back in a few minutes to create the resort pages' logos.

Working with Gradient Fills

You can add a linear gradient in PhotoPlus 5.5. A gradient is a
type of fill where color changes gradually according to specified
colors. In the tutorial, you set the foreground color to yellow, and
the background color to green. The starting color for the gradient
is the same as the foreground color; the ending color for the gradient is the green chosen for the background color. You can vary
the direction of the color change by dragging the tool from a different location in relation to the image. When you click and drag
across the image, you define the start and end locations for the
gradient fill. If you start and stop outside the margins of the image,
the gradient is applied evenly across the entire area. If you drag
from the outside of the image and stop partway across the image,
more of the gradient uses the foreground color. If you start partway across the image and drag outside the image, more of the
gradient uses the background color.

Tutorial

» Starting the Resort Pages' Logos

The individual resort pages are important pages in the site and warrant a heading more significant than a text heading. One of the goals of good Web site design is consistency. The resorts' logos are similar to the main logo, but less complex. The same general appearance aids in consistency, while the decreased complexity means that the logos act like subheadings for the site. In this tutorial, you create one logo file. The three logos are very similar, having different text and using a custom color specific to each resort.

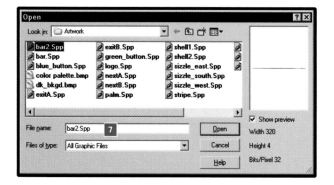

1. **In PhotoPlus, choose File→New to open the Startup Wizard. Choose Create New Image.**
   The New Image dialog box opens.

2. **Set the dimensions for the new image; type** 320 **pixels for width and** 45 **pixels for height.**
   The size for the resort pages' logos is smaller than the main site logo.

3. **Click the background drop-down arrow to open the background options. Select white.**

4. **Click OK.**
   The New Image dialog box closes. The Startup Wizard closes. The new image displays in the program.

5. **Click View→Zoom In→2:1.**
   Zoom in to see the image more clearly.

6. **Click View→Rulers.**
   The vertical and horizontal rulers display on the image window.

7. **Choose File→Open. Browse to the Artwork folder location. Select** bar2.Spp, **and click Open.**

8. **Choose Edit→Copy.**
   The content of the bar2.Spp file is copied.

9. **Click the blank image to select it. Choose Edit→Paste→As New Layer.**
   The bar image is pasted to the new image.

10. **Select the Move tool on the toolbar.**
    You move the bar into its final position.

11. **Click and drag the _bar_ layer downward.**
    Release the mouse when the top of the bar is at approximately 40 pixels (measure using the vertical ruler).

12. **Double-click the foreground color swatch on the Color Tab.**
    The Adjust Color dialog box opens.

13. **Click the medium green custom color in the Custom Color swatch area.**
    The color has RGB values of 51/102/51.

14. **Click OK to close the Adjust Color dialog box.**
    The foreground color is set to the custom green color.

15. **Click the Text tool on the toolbar to select it.**
    Click the image to open the Add Text dialog box.

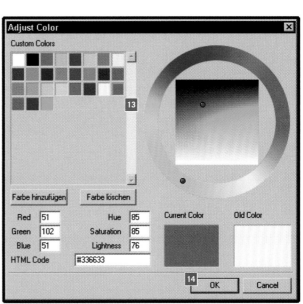

16. **Choose the Century Gothic font from the Fonts drop-down list.**
    Use the same font as the main logo for consistency.

17. **Type** 42 **in the font size field.**
    The required point size is not one of the default font sizes.

18. **Click B, and then click I.**
    The text has the bold and italic face settings.

19. **Type** Sizzle East **in the text field.**
    You add the text for the layer.

20. **Click OK to close the Add Text dialog box.**
    The text is added to the image.

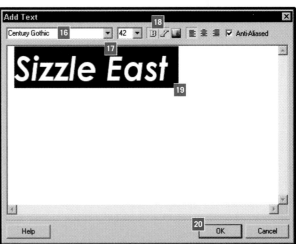

21. **Click the Move tool on the toolbar. Drag the text to start at approximately 80 pixels.**
    Position the text slightly above the horizontal striped bar.

22. **Choose File→Save. The Save As dialog box opens.**
    Name the file sizzle_east.Spp. Save the file in the Artwork folder. You created the first logo for the Sizzle resorts' pages. Leave the file open to continue with the next tutorial.

Tutorial
» Creating the Resort Pages' Logos

In the previous tutorial, you built the first logo for the Sizzle East resort's page. In this tutorial, you create the other two logos using the completed file. The three logos are very similar, having different text and using a custom color specific to each resort. Start the tutorial with the `sizzle_east.Spp` file open in PhotoPlus.

1. **With the `sizzle_east.Spp` file open, choose File→Save As.**
   The Save As dialog box opens.

2. **Name the file `sizzle_west.Spp`, and save the file in the Artwork folder.**

3. **Repeat Steps 1 and 2; name the file `sizzle_south.Spp`.**
   You have a set of three files, each with the same content. The `sizzle_south.Spp` file is open in the program.

4. **Double-click the text layer in the Layer Manager Tab to open the Add Text dialog box.**
   You change the text and text color.

5. **Type Sizzle South in the text field.**
   This changes the text for the Sizzle South resort's page.

6. **Click the Adjust Color icon to open the Adjust Color dialog box.**
   You set the custom color for the text.

7. **Click the dark blue custom color in the bottom row of the Custom Color swatches.**
   The color's RGB values are 51/51/102.

8. **Click OK.**
   The Adjust Color dialog box closes.

9. **Click OK to close the Add Text dialog box.**
   The dark blue text for the Sizzle South logo displays on the page.

10. **Choose File→Save.**
    The `sizzle_south.Spp` file is saved.

11. **Choose File→Open.**
    In the Open dialog box, select the `sizzle_west.Spp` file and click Open.

12. **Repeat Steps 4 and 5. Type:** Sizzle West **in the text field instead of Sizzle South.**

    You change the text for the final resort logo.

13. **Click Adjust Color to open the Adjust Color dialog box.**

    You change the text color.

14. **In the Adjust Color dialog box, choose the custom teal color.**

    The color's RGB values are 51/102/102.

15. **Click OK.**

    The Adjust Color dialog box closes.

16. **Click OK to close the Add Text dialog box.**

    The teal text for the Sizzle West logo displays on the image.

17. **Choose File→Save.**

    The sizzle_west.Spp file is saved. You created three logo files for the three resorts' Web pages. Each logo contains a similar layout and uses a custom color for the text.

Tutorial
» Completing and Exporting the Logos

The images that you constructed in the previous tutorials are similar, using the same layouts and text. In this tutorial, you add a highlight to each logo's text similar to that used in the main site's logo. You export the logos for use in your Sizzle site. As in other tutorials, zoom in to the image to see your work more closely.

1. **In PhotoPlus, choose File→**`sizzle_east.Spp.`
   Select the file from the listing at the bottom of the File menu. You start work with the Sizzle East logo.

2. **In the Layer Manager Tab, click the *Sizzle* text layer.**
   You use two copies of the text in the image.

3. **Choose Layer→Duplicate.**
   A second copy of the text layer is added to the image.

4. **Toggle Show/Hide to hide the *Copy of Sizzle* text layer.**
   You work with the underlying text layer first. Leave the copy of the text layer as the final, overlying text layer, and manipulate the original text layer.

<TIP>
It isn't necessary to rearrange layers in the image. Remember the layer stacking order—a layer listed higher in the stacking order displays on top of layers lower in the stacking order.

5. **Double-click the *Sizzle* text layer.**
   The Add Text dialog box opens.

6. **Click the Adjust Color icon. The Adjust Color dialog box opens.**
   Select the custom yellow color, and click OK to close the Adjust Color dialog box.

7. **Click OK to close the Add Text dialog box.**
   The text turns yellow.

<NOTE>
You can change the text color independently of the foreground/ background colors set for the image using the Adjust Color dialog box through the Add Text dialog box. The color is applied to the text in the text box only.

8. **Click the top text layer, *Sizzle East*, in the Layer Manager to select it.**
   The layer contains the green text.

9. **Toggle the Hide/Show icon to Show.**
   You previously turned off the layer to work with the underlying text layer.

10. **Right-click the text layer to open the shortcut menu. Click Render Text Layer.**
    The layer is changed from text to an image.

11. **Click the Color Select tool on the toolbar, and then click a colored text area on the image.**
    The color area is selected.

12. **Choose Select→Modify→Similar.**
    All the colored areas on the image are selected.

13. **Choose Image→Blur→Blur Effects.**
    The Blur Effects Filter dialog box opens.

14. **Click the Zoom tool (+) to zoom in to 4:1.**
    The image is small; zooming in shows you the effect clearly.

15. **Click Motion to set the blur type.**

16. **Drag the intensity slider to 4.**
    The blur is applied to the image preview.

17. **Click the left center of the dial to set the directional arrow.**
    The arrow moves left. The blur appears to start at the left of the letters.

<TIP>
Click the dial at different locations to see how the direction affects the look of the blur.

18. **Click OK to close the Blur Effects Filter dialog box.**
    The blur is applied to the layer.

19. **Choose File→Save.**
    The sizzle_east.Spp file is complete.

20. **Choose File→Export.**
    The Export dialog box opens.

<NOTE>
The Export dialog box has been used previously in this session, so it defaults to the most recent folder used for export, which is the Images folder within your Sizzle site folder.

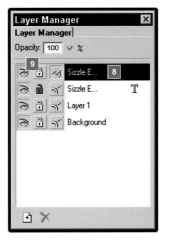

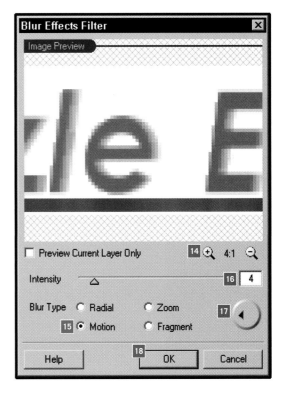

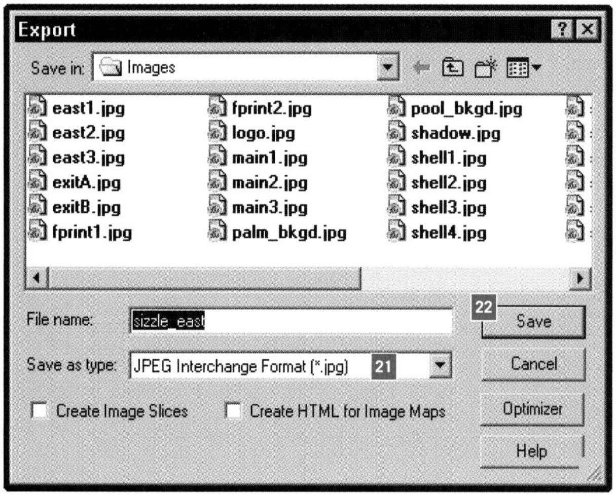

Export ? ×

Save in: [📁 Images ▼] ← 🔁 📑 ▦▾

📄 east1.jpg	📄 fprint2.jpg	📄 pool_bkgd.jpg
📄 east2.jpg	📄 logo.jpg	📄 shadow.jpg
📄 east3.jpg	📄 main1.jpg	📄 shell1.jpg
📄 exitA.jpg	📄 main2.jpg	📄 shell2.jpg
📄 exitB.jpg	📄 main3.jpg	📄 shell3.jpg
📄 fprint1.jpg	📄 palm_bkgd.jpg	📄 shell4.jpg

File name: [sizzle_east]   **22** → Save

Save as type: [JPEG Interchange Format (*.jpg) **21** ▼]   Cancel

☐ Create Image Slices   ☐ Create HTML for Image Maps   Optimizer

Help

21. **Leave the default settings.**

The file is named sizzle_east by default; the .jpg file format is selected by default.

22. **Click Save.**

The Export dialog box closes. The sizzle_east.jpg file is saved in the Images folder for use in your Web site.

23. **Choose File→sizzle_west.Spp.**

The second resort page's logo opens.

24. **Repeat Steps 2 through 22.**

The second file is saved as sizzle_west.Spp in the Artwork folder and exported as sizzle_west.jpg to the Images folder.

25. **Choose File→sizzle_south.Spp.**

The third resort page's logo opens.

26. **Repeat Steps 2 through 22.**

The third file is saved as sizzle_south.Spp in the Artwork folder and exported as sizzle_south.jpg to the Images folder. You completed the set of three resort pages' logos for your Web site. Close PhotoPlus.

» Session Review

This session introduced more uses of the PhotoPlus program's tools and also described how to construct sophisticated images. You built the Sizzle Web site's logo using several elements. You constructed the logos for each of the three Sizzle resorts using similar methods and processes, finishing with a set of three coordinated but slightly different logos. You also learned to work with PhotoPlus effects.

The first image in this session shows the Sizzle East resort's page in its current state of development. The final image in the session shows the same page with the logo added. In the next session, you add the logos to their pages.

Answer these questions to review the information in this session. The answers are in the tutorial noted in parentheses.

1. Is it necessary to use the Startup Wizard in PhotoPlus? (See Tutorial: Assembling Layers for the Sizzle Logo.)

2. With rulers displayed, can you see when a layer is moved? (See Tutorial: Assembling Layers for the Sizzle Logo.)

3. How does increasing the tolerance level of color selection tools affect the pixels selected? (See Tutorial: Adding More Layers to the Logo File.)

4. How do you work with the Deform tool? What are its uses? (See Tutorial: Manipulating and Organizing the Logo's Layers.)

5. What is the difference between a text layer and a rendered text layer? (See Tutorial: Manipulating and Organizing the Logo's Layers.)

6. Does manipulating text with the Deform tool affect how you edit the text? (See Tutorial: Manipulating and Organizing the Logo's Layers.)

7. Why do you feather a selection? (See Tutorial: Finishing the Sizzle Logo.)

8. What colors of background can you set for a new image? How do you choose the background? (See Tutorial: Starting the Resort Pages' Logos.)

9. How can you change the color of text from the Add Text dialog box? (See Tutorial: Starting the Resort Pages' Logos.)

10. Can you use text sizes other than the sizes listed in the Add Text dialog box? (See Tutorial: Creating the Resort Pages' Logos.)

11. How do the layers stacked in the Layer Manager Tab relate to the layers visible in an image? (See Tutorial: Completing and Exporting the Logos.)

12. How do you add additional areas of similar color to a selected area on a layer? (See Tutorial: Completing and Exporting the Logos.)

» Other Projects

Modify the text layers that you added to the logos. You may want to try other effects, such as adding noise and other types of blurs. The copy of the `logo.Spp` file on the CD contains an extra text layer for you to use for experimentation. The layer is added below the background and set to Hide. The layer doesn't appear in the finished and exported versions of the image.

Add a gradient to the logos' text or backgrounds, or try drawing a graphic image to use for the resort pages' logos.

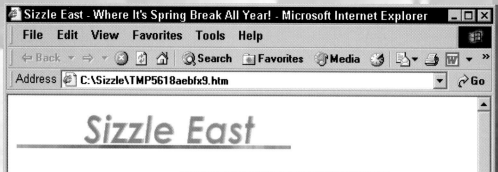

Sizzle East

Sizzle East is located on the Berry Islands, a chain of 30 cays and islets.

Our resort sits on the northeastern edge of the Great Bahama Bank on Great Harbour Cay.

Part IV

Adding Graphics and Images to Pages

Customizing Tables Using Styles

Booking Your Visit - Microsoft Internet Explorer

File   Edit   View   Favorites   Tools   Help

Address   C:\Sizzle\booking.html   Go

Staying at Sizzle

Visit Sizzle when YOU want to visit.

For a long weekend, for a month -- the choice is yours!

Give us a few days' notice. For many parts of the year, call during the week to book a weekend. Unlike most resort locations, you don't have to arrive on Wednesday and leave the following Tuesday.

Like other "hot" spots, we tend to get overbooked at certain times of the year.

You have to prebook during these times: last week of December first week of January Spring Break week

Done   My Computer

Session Introduction

Your Sizzle Web site is not quite finished from the image-manipulation perspective. In the interests of preserving your eyesight, the remaining image session comes later. In this session, you make the tables on many of your site's pages more visually interesting. You also add the resort logos to their pages and create a new file for the main Sizzle logo.

In Session 3, you experimented with tiling the navigation table's image. You altered the <table> tags in the Web page to see the image tile. In this session, you start a style sheet for your site that describes some of the tables' attributes as styles.

In correct XHTML, many table attributes are not included in the XHTML code. Instead, they are described in styles, which are attached to the Web page in several ways. You work with the site's main pages—the intro page (main.html) and the three resort pages. You also construct a new page and add tables, images, and styles to it.

The pages that you work with in this session are XHTML validated; the style sheet is CSS2 validated.

TOOLS YOU'LL USE
Notepad, Web browser, W3C CSS Validator, W3C XHTML Validator

CD-ROM FILES NEEDED (Images Folder)
pool_bkgd.jpg, air_bluestar.gif, air_seawinds.gif, air_global.gif, air_td.gif

CD-ROM FILES NEEDED (Storage Folder)
booking_text.txt

FILES CREATED
logo.html, sizzle.css, booking.html

FILES MODIFIED
main.html, sizzle_east.html, sizzle_west.html, sizzle_south.html

TIME REQUIRED
90 minutes

Tutorial

» Constructing a New Page for the Sizzle Logo

You have built the logos for your Web site. In this tutorial, you add the main Sizzle logo to its own page. In Session 7, when you construct framesets, the logo's page displays at the top left of the screen.

```
6  <title>Sizzle Resorts</title>  3
7  <meta http-equiv="Content-Type" content="text/html; charset=utf-8" />
8  </head>
9
10 <body>
11 <img src="Images/logo.gif" width="520" height="120" alt="Sizzle site logo" />  4
12 </body>
13 </html>
```

1. **Open Notepad. Choose File→Open. Select the** basic.html **file in the Storage folder of your Sizzle site, and click Open.**
   The basic page layout file opens.

2. **Choose File→Save As. Name the file** logo.html, **and save it in the Sizzle site folder.**
   Do not save it in the Storage folder.

3. **Go to line 6. Replace the placeholder page name. Type:** Sizzle Resorts
   Each page of your site must be named; browsers use the page title as the text when a user adds a bookmark to the page.

4. **Go to line 11. Delete the placeholder text. Type:** <img src="Images/logo.jpg" width="500" height="120" alt="Sizzle site logo" />
   The site logo is added to the page.

<NOTE>
You finished the logo in the last session and saved it in the Images folder.

5. **Open Internet Explorer. Choose File→Open. Click Browse to open an Explorer window.**

6. **Locate your** logo.html **file, and click the file to select it.**

7. **Click Open.**
   The dialog box closes, and your page loads.

8. **Check the page in the browser. Move the cursor over the image to read the alternate text that you added in Step 3.**
   Note the page name at the top of the browser window. Close your browser.

9. **Save the** logo.html **file in Notepad.**
   Leave Notepad open for the next tutorial. You just added another page to your site for the main logo image.

Discussion
Styles and Cascading Style Sheets

Style sheets can be applied in several ways. You can write a style for an entire page or inline by including it with a line of HTML code. An external style sheet is a separate file, saved with the file extension .css which identifies the page as a cascading style sheet file, that is then linked to your pages. Most of the styles constructed for your Sizzle site are added to the site's external style sheet.

Cascading Order

The order of styles determines the style used for each element on a Web page. It isn't necessary to write styles for everything on a page. For example, you can write a style to use for paragraphs, and use the default browser styles for the headings. In this case, the browser default and custom styles both contribute to the finished page's appearance in the browser. All styles use the following rules where inline styles have the highest priority:

» Browser default

» External Style Sheet

» Internal Style Sheet (inside the <head> tag)

» Inline Style (inside HTML element)

The layered sequential assignment of styles is referred to as "cascading." For example, an inline style (inside an HTML element) has the highest priority, which means that it overrides every style declared inside the <head> tag, in an external style sheet, and in a browser (a default value).

You can create styles that replace default HTML formatting, such as identifying a font, size, and color to replace the default characteristics of a <heading> tag. These tags are generally used throughout an entire page. You can define a specific tag several times by defining classes. For example, if you set a style for a table, whenever that tag is read anywhere in your site (if the style sheet is linked to the page), the same attributes are assigned to the table. And, if you create several style classes for the same tag, you can specify on a page-by-page basis which of the tags to modify.

Formatting Styles

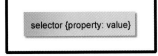

selector {property: value}

Regardless of how or why you attach a style, use the same format for writing (as shown in the figure). The selector is the HTML element or tag that you want to define. The property is the attribute that you want to specify, and the property is assigned one or more values. The property and value are separated by a colon and surrounded by curly braces.

A simple example is `body {color: #003366}`. This means that the <body> tag is selected, its color attribute is specified, and a value (the color) is assigned.

Use these basic rules for working with styles:

» If the value has more than one word, enclose it in quotes, such as `p {font-family: "sans serif"}`

» If you want to specify more than one property, separate each property with a semicolon and describe each property on a separate line. In the example, the paragraphs are right aligned and have red text.
```
p {
text-align:right;
color:#FF0000;
}
```

» One property can have multiple values. Save space and time by combining them on one line. For example, a bottom border that is dotted, has a width of 8 pixels, and is red in color can be written as follows:
`border-bottom: 8px dotted #FF0000;`
The values can be combined into one string; don't add any additional punctuation.

» You can group selectors to save time and confusion. Separate each selector with a comma. In this example, the heading elements listed are blue in color.
```
h1,h2,h3 {
color: #0000FF;
}
```

The Class Selector

In this session, you define five classes for the <table> tag. One class is defined for each of the tables on the main Sizzle page, the three resort pages, and a new page that you add to the site. With the class selector, you can define different styles for the same type of HTML element.

To construct a class-specific style, you must expand the selector portion of the CSS script. In your tutorials, you use two-part selectors, such as `table.mainborders` that refers to a style for the <table> tag named `mainborders`. The attribute(s) and value(s) portions of the style remain the same. After the styles are defined and saved in the style sheet, the style sheet is attached to your pages using anchor tags in the <head> portion of the page. Using the class-specific styles also requires an additional attribute set for the <table> tag that you add later in the session.

Tutorial
» Starting the Sizzle Site's Cascading Style Sheet

In this tutorial, you start the style sheet for your site. The first styles that you define are borders for your main pages' tables. Many of the attributes that you use for tables are not specific to tables, but can be used with a variety of page elements. Borders, for example, can be used with other elements such as headings, text, or images.

1. **In Notepad, choose File→New.**
   A new blank window opens.

2. **In line 1, type:** `table.mainborders {`
   The selector is defined in two parts: table, which refers to the HTML tag <table> and `.mainborders`, which is a custom name for the style that you are defining. The description for the style is enclosed within curly braces; add the opening brace following the selector name.

3. **On lines 2 to 5, type:**
   ```
   border-top: 8px solid #003366;
   border-right: hidden;
   border-bottom: hidden;
   border-left: 4px solid #FF0033;
   ```
   A style can have numerous properties, each having one or more values.

```
1  table.mainborders { 2
2  border-top: 8px solid #003366;
3  border-right: hidden;            3
4  border-bottom: hidden;
5  border-left: 4px solid #FF0033;
6  } 4
```

< T I P >
The top and left borders of the table are given a border size, type, and color. The right and bottom borders have a "hidden" value. Specifying a border width of 0px produces the same results.

4. **In line 6, type:** `}`
   Define the end of the list of properties with the closing curly brace.

< N O T E >
You can combine the values for the same property into one string. The border-top property, for example, lists a width, a border type, and a color.

5. **Choose File→Save.**
   Save the file as `sizzle.css` in your Sizzle site folder.

6. **Choose File→Open. Browse to your Sizzle site folder, select** `main.html`, **and click Open.**
   You attach the style sheet to the page and specify the first style.

HTML versus CSS

Look at this HTML tag: **<p right-align></p>**

Now look at this CSS style:

```
p {

text-align:right;

}
```

The two processes are actually very similar, which makes sense if you remember that styles are removed from the content in XHTML. Earlier HTML versions included visual information as part of the tags.

The components are named differently, but they mean much the same thing. In (X)HTML, a tag is named, and then its attributes are defined and given a value. In CSS, the tag is referred to as the selector, the attribute is called a property, and it still has a value.

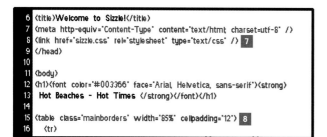

```
 6  <title>Welcome to Sizzle!</title>
 7  <meta http-equiv="Content-Type" content="text/html; charset=utf-8" />
 8  <link href="sizzle.css" rel="stylesheet" type="text/css" />  7
 9  </head>
10
11  <body>
12  <h1><font color="#003366" face="Arial, Helvetica, sans-serif"><strong>
13    Hot Beaches - Hot Times </strong></font></h1>
14
15  <table class="mainborders" width="85%" cellpadding="12">  8
16    <tr>
```

7. Go to line 8. Press Enter to add a blank line, and then type:
`<link href="sizzle.css" rel="stylesheet" type="text/css" />`
The style sheet is linked to your page. Within the <link> tag, the style sheet is named (the `href` or hypertext reference attribute); the relationship is defined as a style sheet; and the `type` attribute is set for a style sheet.

8. Go to line 15. Modify the table tag to read: `<table class= "mainborders" width="85%" cellpadding="12">`
The new style, `mainborders`, is identified as a class for the <table> tag. Delete the `border` and `cellspacing` attributes used to help you place and visualize the initial table; increase the padding for the current layout. The table's width remains the same.

9. Open Internet Explorer. Choose File→Open, and load the main.html page.
Look at the table's layout. The top border is one of your site's blue shades, the same shade of blue as the heading on the page; the left border is your site's custom red color. Also note the difference in width between the two borders.

10. Close the browser.

11. Save the main.html file in Notepad.
You created a style sheet. You attached the style sheet to the page and attached a style to the table.

Tutorial

» Adding Borders and Logos to the Resort Pages' Tables

In the last tutorial, you started a style sheet for your site. You learned how to write a style, how to attach the style sheet to the page, and how to attach the particular style to the table. In this tutorial, you write three more styles and then attach them to the three resort pages.

1. **In Notepad, reopen** `sizzle.css`.
   You add three more styles to the file.

2. **Select the text in lines 1 through 6. Copy the text.**
   The new styles are very similar to the existing style; save time by reusing the existing content.

3. **Go to line 7. Press Enter to add a blank line, and then paste the text in line 8.**
   You have a second copy of the style.

4. **Go to line 14. Press Enter to add a blank line, and then paste the text in line 15.**
   You have a third copy of the style.

5. **Go to line 21. Press Enter to add a blank line, and then paste the text in line 22.**
   You have a fourth copy of the style.

6. **Save the file.**
   You now have four copies of the same style in your style sheet.

```
 1  table.mainborders {
 2  border-top: 8px solid #003366;
 3  border-right: 0px;                    [2]
 4  border-bottom: 0px;
 5  border-left: 4px solid #FF0033;
 6  }
 7
 8  table.mainborders {
 9  border-top: 8px solid #003366;
10  border-right: 0px;                    [3]
11  border-bottom: 0px;
12  border-left: 4px solid #FF0033;
13  }
14
15  table.mainborders {
16  border-top: 8px solid #003366;        [4]
17  border-right: 0px;
```

7. **Go to line 8. Modify the text to read:** `table.eastborders {`
   You use the style for the table in the Sizzle East page.

8. **Go to line 9. Change the color number to:** #336633.
   The Sizzle East resort page uses a medium green accent color.

```
 7
 8  table.eastborders { [7]
 9  border-top: 8px solid #336633; [8]
10  border-right: 0px;
11  border-bottom: 0px;
12  border-left: 4px solid #FF0033;
13  }
14
```

<**N O T E**>

In this book you write a color's name as hexadecimal or using RGB values. It is also possible to use descriptive color names. Consult online sources for lists and descriptions of color names. They are not recommended as they are difficult to remember and hard to quantify in comparison to hexadecimal or RGB values.

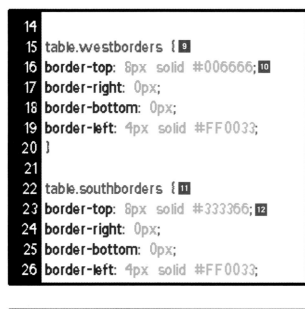

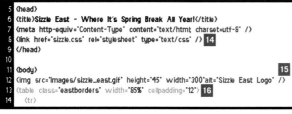

9. **Go to line 15. Modify the text to read:** `table.westborders {`
The style is used for the table in the Sizzle West page.

10. **Go to line 16. Change the color number to:** #006666.
The Sizzle West resort page uses a teal accent color.

11. **Go to line 22. Modify the text to read:** `table.southborders {`
The style is used for the table in the Sizzle South page.

12. **Go to line 23. Change the color number to:** #333366.
The Sizzle South resort page uses a royal blue accent color.

13. **Choose File→Open. Browse to your Sizzle site folder, and open** `sizzle_east.html`.
You are prompted to save the `sizzle.css` file. Click Yes. Your first resort page opens in Notepad.

14. **Go to line 8. Press Enter to add a blank line and then type:**
`<link href="sizzle.css" rel="stylesheet" type="text/css" />`
The style sheet is linked to your page.

15. **Go to line 12, and type:** `<img src="Images/sizzle_east.jpg" height="45" width="320" alt="Sizzle East Logo" />`
The Sizzle East logo is added to the page.

16. **Go to line 13, and modify the table tag to read:**
`<table class="eastborders" width="85%" cellpadding="12">`
The table style specific to the Sizzle East page is attached to the table.

17. **Preview the page in Internet Explorer. Drag from the right-bottom corner of the browser window to resize it.**
Note that the upper green border of the table resizes as the table resizes. Minimize the browser.

18. **Open the** `sizzle_west.html` **page.**
When prompted to save the `sizzle_east.html` page, click Yes.

19. **Go to line 8. Press Enter to add a blank line, and then type:**
    `<link href="sizzle.css" rel="stylesheet"`
    `type="text/css" />`
    This is a repeat of Step 14. The style sheet is linked to the
    sizzle_west.html page.

20. **Go to line 12, and type:** `<img`
    `src="Images/sizzle_west.jpg" height="45"`
    `width="320"alt="Sizzle West Logo"/>`
    The Sizzle West logo is added to the page.

21. **Go to line 13, and modify the table tag to read:** `<table class=`
    `"westborders" width="85%" cellpadding="12">`.
    The table style specific to the Sizzle West page is attached to
    the table.

22. **Preview the page in Internet Explorer. Drag from the right-bottom
    corner of the browser window to resize it as you did in Step 17.**
    Review the layout of the page in your browser. Note that the
    upper border of the table resizes as the table resizes. Minimize
    the browser.

23. **Open the** sizzle_south.html **page. Save the**
    sizzle_west.html **page when prompted.**

24. **You guessed it. Repeat Steps 14 through 16.**
    Use the sizzle_south.jpg image; label its alt
    attribute Sizzle South Logo; name the table's class
    southborders.

25. **Preview the** sizzle_south.html **page in your browser.**
    Close the browser.

26. **Save the** sizzle_south.html **file.**
    You added three more styles to your style sheet and applied
    the styles to the three resort pages. You also added the resort
    logos to their pages.

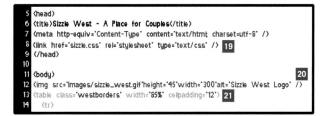

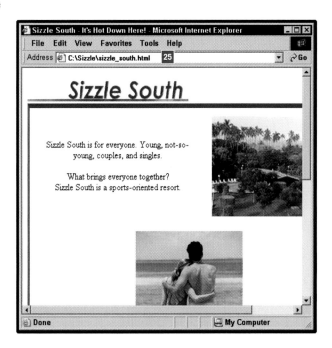

Tutorial

» Validating Page and Style Sheet Content

You have added logos and set the borders for the tables on the main page and resort pages. In the next tutorial, you create a new page and more styles. Before continuing, you need to take a few minutes to validate your work. It is very frustrating to think that you have designed proper styles and used them throughout a site, only to discover errors. In this tutorial, you add comments to the style sheet, validate the styles, and validate one of the pages completed earlier.

1. **In Notepad, open** `sizzle.css`.
   You add comments to the page before validating.

2. **Go to line 1. Insert an empty line, and then type:** `/* borders for main tables */`
   Your site's style sheet contains numerous styles; adding comments helps keep track of what you have to work with and where it is used in your site.

<NOTE>
In the code figure, comments are shown in gray.

3. **Save the file.**
   Leave Notepad open for the next tutorial.

4. **Open your browser. In the browser address bar, type:**
   `http://jigsaw.w3.org/css-validator`
   The W3C CSS Stylesheet Validation page displays.

5. **Scroll down the page to the W3C CSS Validation Service. Click on the "by upload" portion of the Validate Service section.**
   The validation information page loads.

<TIP>
It is a very good idea to regularly check your progress in terms of writing valid style sheet and XHTML code. Add a bookmark to the validation site pages in your browser. If you are using an uploaded file to test your CSS, add a bookmark to the page that you display after completing Step 5, the Validation Service Page. Choose Favorites→Add to Favorites, or press Ctrl + D.

Using Comments

In the tutorial, you added comments to your style sheet. You can also add comments to a Web page (which you do in several later sessions). Just as there are similarities between assigning characteristics to elements and tags in HTML and style sheets, there are similarities between adding comments in a style sheet and an (X)HTML page. Comments in style sheets are identified with the opening and closing `/* */` characters. Comments on Web pages are enclosed in `<!— —>` tags. The content of comments, regardless of source, are for your benefit and that of anyone else reading or working with your site's code, and they don't display in a browser.

6. **Scroll down the page. Click Browse, locate the** `sizzle.css` **file on your hard drive, and click Open.**

   Your page location displays in the field.

7. **Click the drop-down arrow to display the Profile menu.**

   Select CSS Version 2. The version is set as the Profile.

<N O T E>

Validation is done according to the version or type of style sheet selected.

8. **Click Submit this CSS File for Validation.**

   The file is processed. The results are displayed on a new page.

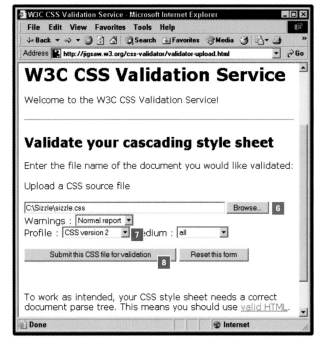

Reading Validation Errors

The first style you wrote for the main page's table was placed into its own file and errors were added. The style reads:

```
/* borders for main tables */

table.mainborders {

border-top: 8px solid #003366

border-right: 0px;

border-bottom: 0px;

border-left: 4 solid #FF0033;
```

In the second line, the semi-colon for the end of the border-top style is missing, and the closing curly brace is missing.

The file was tested using the W3C Validator. The results are shown in the image.

The results identify the error in line 5, and states a semi-colon is missing from the border-top property in line 4. As a result of the second error, the missing curly brace to close the style, the validator decides that this isn't a style sheet at all.

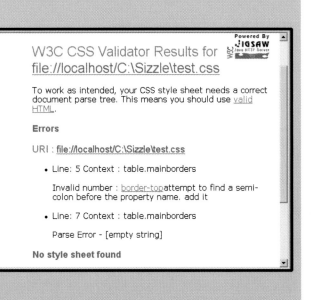

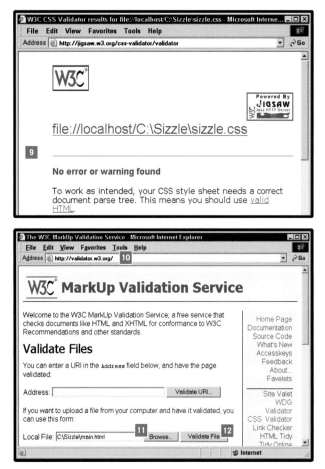

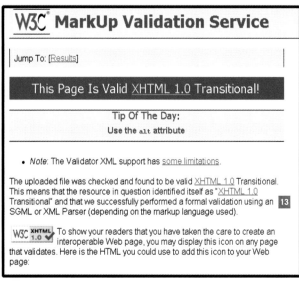

9. Scroll through the results page.

The `sizzle.css` style sheet that you constructed so far in this project is valid CSS. If errors are detected or warnings are necessary, they are listed and identified on this page.

10. In the browser address bar, type:

`http://validator.w3.org/`

You need to validate one of the set of pages that you worked on earlier in the session. The Markup Validation Service page opens.

< T I P >

Add a bookmark to this page. It is a good practice to test your pages as you develop them, and having the page bookmarked makes it easy to run the Validator.

11. Click Browse, locate the `main.html` file on your hard drive, and click Open.

Your page location displays in the field.

12. Click Validate File.

The file is processed, and a new page opens to display the results.

13. Scroll through the results page.

The `main.html` page is valid XHTML 1.0. If errors are detected or warnings are necessary, they are listed and identified on this page.

< N O T E >

You can validate the other pages that you worked on in this session as well. If you have correctly typed the styles, the pages will validate. The resort pages are very similar to the main page; you duplicated and then modified the content as you worked on the pages. Still, it is never a bad thing to check your work!

14. Close your browser.

You added a comment to your style sheet. You validated the style sheet as valid CSS Version 2.0, and you validated one of your latest Web pages as valid XHTML 1.0.

Tutorial

» Adding a New Page for Booking Information

You have added logos and set the borders for the tables on the main page and resort pages. Now add another new page to the site. This page is used for booking information. It describes how and when to visit the resorts. It has links to a number of fictitious airlines. In Session 8, you add specific anchor tags within the page to link to text on the navigation tables. In this tutorial, you construct the basic page, add the text, and then divide the text into paragraphs.

1. **In Notepad, choose File→Open. Open the Storage folder in your Sizzle site folder. Select the** `basic.html` **file, and click Open.**
   You start a new page with a copy of the basic page information.

2. **Go to line 6, and replace the page title placeholder text. Type:**
   `Booking Your Visit`
   The page's name displays at the top of the browser window for identification.

3. **Go to line 8. Insert a blank line, and type:** `<link href= "sizzle.css" rel="stylesheet" type="text/ css" />`
   You use the style sheet for this page; attaching it at this point is convenient because you are working with the basic information at the top of the page.

<NOTE>
The styles applicable to the page are constructed and added later in this session.

4. **Save the file as** `booking.html` **in your Sizzle site folder.**
   Store the page with your other site pages.

5. **Choose File→Open. Open the Storage folder in your Sizzle site folder again. Select the** `booking_text.txt` **file, and click Open.**
   Use the text in the file for the Web page.

6. **Select all the text in the file, and then copy the text.**

7. **Open the** `booking.html` **file again.**
   You add the pre-supplied text to the page.

8. **Go to line 12. Delete the placeholder text, and then paste the copied text.**
   The pasted text is added to lines 12 to 39.

<CAUTION>
Your line numbering may differ slightly from that shown in the tutorials. Use the line numbers as references to different areas of a page, but read the content of the line carefully as you follow the steps to ensure you are modifying or adding code to the correct line.

```
5  <head>
6  <title>Booking Your Visit </title> 2
7  <meta http-equiv="Content-Type" content="text/html; charset=utf-8" />
8  <link href="sizzle.css" rel="stylesheet" type="text/css" /> 3
9  </head>
10
```

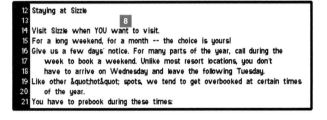

```
12  Staying at Sizzle
13             8
14  Visit Sizzle when YOU want to visit.
15  For a long weekend, for a month -- the choice is yours!
16  Give us a few days' notice. For many parts of the year, call during the
17      week to book a weekend. Unlike most resort locations, you don't
18      have to arrive on Wednesday and leave the following Tuesday.
19  Like other &quot;hot&quot; spots, we tend to get overbooked at certain times
20      of the year.
21  You have to prebook during these times:
```

< T I P >

In line 19, you see a string of text that reads "Like other "hot" spots..." When you look at the page in the browser in Step 9, look for the text. " translates to quotation marks when read in a browser.

9. **Open your browser. Preview the page.**

   Note that the text appears in a constant, difficult-to-read string, and wraps as you resize the page. It isn't particularly attractive at this point! Minimize the browser.

10. **In Notepad, add <p> tags to the text. Insert the opening tag at the locations identified in Table 5-1.**

< T I P >

The text in booking_text.txt is arranged in paragraphs; the beginning of each new paragraph starts flush with the left margin of the page. After transferring the text to the booking.html page, you can easily identify locations to add paragraph tags.

< C A U T I O N >

If you preview the page with the opening <p> tags, you see the content divided into paragraphs. However, if you attempt to validate the page using the W3C Validator, you receive a large number of errors—each opening tag is required to have a closing tag in correct XHTML.

11. **Add the closing </p> tags to the text.**

   Each paragraph needs a closing </p> tag prior to the opening <p> tag for the following paragraph.

12. Preview the page in Internet Explorer.

You see that the text is much more legible now that it is divided into paragraphs. Close the browser.

<NOTE>

If you scroll through the page, you see the paragraph beginning "You have to prebook…" This paragraph eventually becomes a bulleted list, and each item moves to separate lines.

13. Save the file.

You built another page for your site. You attached the style sheet to it, added text, and divided the text into paragraphs. Leave the file open in Notepad for the next tutorial.

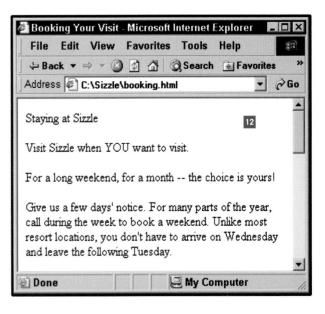

Table 5-1: Paragraph Tags for the Booking Page

Line	Text starts with...
12	Staying at Sizzle
14	Visit Sizzle when YOU want to visit.
15	For a long weekend,
16	Give us a few days' notice.
19	Like other "hot" spots,
21	You have to prebook
25	Rooms are reserved during
28	Spring Break is another story.
33	Call and check with us.
34	Room Rates vary according to location and date.
36	Getting Here
37	Click a link to book flights from these North American airlines:
39	Book local flights in the Caribbean from:

Tutorial

» Placing Tables on the Booking Information Page

You started a new page in the last tutorial. In this tutorial, you add two tables to hold logos from different airlines, which are used as links to the airlines' flight information. You also add the airlines' logo images.

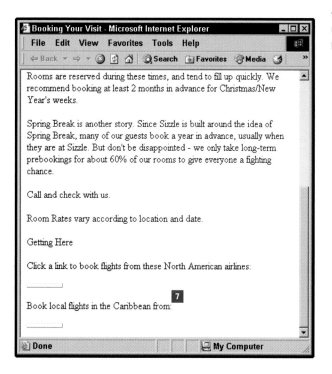

1. **Open your Sizzle site folder. Open the Image Sources folder. Select these four images; copy and paste or move the images into your site's Images folder:**
   ```
   air_bluestar.gif
   air_seawinds.gif
   air_global.gif
   air_td.gif
   ```
   The images are used as links in the tables that you add to the booking.html page.

< N O T E >

The set of airline logo files are named in a similar way starting with the same prefix. This is a convenient way to name files for ease of use. Select all the files starting with "air," and you have the complete set of images.

2. **In Notepad, go to line 37.**
   You add table tags.

3. **On lines 37 to 42 type:** `<table border="1" cellpadding="12">`
   `<tr>`
   `<td></td>`
   `<td></td>`
   `</tr>`
   `</table>`
   You add a table with one row and two cells. The table has a border and padding.

4. **Copy the <table> tags that you added in Step 3.**
   You add a second table.

5. **Go to line 44, and paste a copy of the tags.**
   You have a second table added to the page to use for Caribbean airline logos.

6. **Save the booking.html page.**
   You added two tables.

7. **Open your browser, and preview the page.**
   Note the two tables separated by the last paragraph of text. Close the browser.

8. **Go to line 39.**
   You add <image> tags to the cells of the first table.

9. **Starting in line 39, wrapping to line 40, and within the <td> tags, type:** `<img src="Images/air_global.gif" width="200" height="45" alt="Global Airlines logo" />`
   You add the first image tag.

10. **Go to the second pair of <td></td> tags in the first table, starting at line 41. Within the <td></td> tags, type:** `<img src= "Images/air_td.gif" width="200" height="45" alt="TD International Airlines logo" />`
    You add the second image tag.

11. **Go to line 48.**
    You modify the content for the second table starting at this line.

12. **Starting in line 48, continuing to line 49, and within the <td> tags, type:** `<img src="Images/air_bluestar.gif" width="200" height="45" alt="BlueStar Airways logo" />`
    You add the first image tag to the second table.

13. **Go to the second pair of <td></td> tags in the first table, starting at line 50. Within the <td></td> tags, type:** `<img src="Images/air_seawinds.gif" width="200" height="45" alt="Seawinds Airline logo" />`
    You add the second image tag.

14. **Save the** `booking.html` **file. Preview the page in your browser. Resize the page using the resize handle at the bottom right of the window.**
    Note that the text resizes, but the tables do not. The tables have definite widths associated with the image attributes and won't resize. You added two tables and four images to the page. Close your browser.

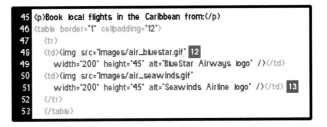

```
36  <p>Click a link to book flights from these North American airlines:</p>
37  <table border="1" cellpadding="12">
38    <tr>
39    <td><img src="Images/air_global.gif" width="200" height="45"  9
40    alt="Global Airlines logo" /> </td>
41    <td><img src="Images/air_td.gif" width="200" height="45"  10
42      alt="TD International Airlines logo" /></td>
43    </tr>
44    </table>
```

```
45  <p>Book local flights in the Caribbean from:</p>
46  <table border="1" cellpadding="12">
47    <tr>
48    <td><img src="Images/air_bluestar.gif"  12
49      width="200" height="45" alt="BlueStar Airways logo" /></td>
50    <td><img src="Images/air_seawinds.gif"
51      width="200" height="45" alt="Seawinds Airline logo" /></td>  13
52    </tr>
53    </table>
```

Tutorial

» Attaching Styles to the Booking Information Page

The booking information page is developing. You have textual information, tables, and a collection of images. In the final tutorial for this session, you create two styles for this page—a table style and one for the page background. Before you start, add another image to your site's Image folder.

```
29
30   /* booking information page */ [5]
31   table.booking {
32   border-top: 4px solid #009966; [6]
33   }
34
35   body.bookingbkgd {
36   background-image: url(Images/pool_bkgd.jpg); [7]
37   background-repeat: no-repeat;
38   }
```

1. **Open the Image Sources folder, and select** `booking_bkgd.jpg`.
   The folder is within your Sizzle site folder (if you copied the files) and is also on the CD.

2. **Move or copy the image to your site's Images folder.**
   The image is used as a background for the page.

3. **In Notepad, open the** `sizzle.css` **file.**
   You add two additional styles.

4. **Go to line 28. Press Enter twice to add two blank lines.**
   Leave space between the styles for clarity.

5. **In line 30, type:** `/* booking information page */`
   Add a comment before you start the styles specific to the `booking.html` page.

6. **Starting in line 31, and continuing to line 33, type:**
   ```
   table.booking {
   border-top: 4px solid #009966;
   }
   ```
   The style is applied to the <table> tags later in this tutorial. You establish a class of style for the <table> tag that uses a 4-pixel top border in a medium green color.

7. **Leave a blank line in line 34. Starting in line 35, and continuing to line 38, type:**
   ```
   body.bookingbkgd {
   background-image: url(Images/pool_bkgd.jpg);
   background-repeat: no-repeat;
   }
   ```
   The style is applied to the <body> tag in the page. The style attaches a background image to the body of the page. The image's repeating property has a value of "no-repeat," meaning that the image is displayed once on the page.

8. **Save the** `sizzle.css` **file. Open the** `booking.html` **page.**
   You attach your new styles to tags on the page.

<TIP>
Be careful when writing references to images in your styles, which is quite different from referencing images in (X)HTML. The image is included as part of a value based on a URL (or location). Enclose the image's file location in angle brackets.

<NOTE>
You return to the `body.bookingbkgd` style again in Session 9 to add some positioning properties.

9. **Go to line 11, and expand the <body> tag to read:** <body class="bookingbkgd">

   The style is attached to the page's <body> tag.

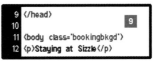

10. **Go to line 37. After "table," type:** class="booking"

    The tag now reads: <table class="booking" border="1" cellpadding="12"> The table border style is attached to the <table> tag.

11. **Go to line 46, and repeat Step 10.**

    The table border style is attached to the second table's tag.

12. **Open your browser, and preview the page.**

    You see the background image (placed at the upper left of the page by default). Close your browser.

13. **Save the** booking.html **file.**

    You constructed two new styles and attached them to the page.

» Session Review

This session returns to the site's pages and introduces you to working with styles. The visual display information from the Web page and place was removed in a style sheet conforming to current Web development standards.

You constructed a style sheet file and designed styles to apply to the tables on the site's main pages. You learned how to construct a style appropriately and how to link a style sheet to a Web page. You validated both your style sheet and one of the site's main pages. You also learned how to create specific styles, referred to as classes, that modify tags on the Web pages.

You added a new page to your site. The basic text page is shown at the introduction to this session. You placed a great deal of text on the page and added two tables. You applied styles to both the tables and the page itself. The final figure in this session shows the page completed to this point.

The questions below help you review the information in this session. The answer to each question is in the tutorial noted in parentheses.

1. Why is it important to title Web pages? (See Tutorial: Constructing a New Page for the Sizzle Logo.)
2. What types of styles can be added to a Web page? (See Discussion: Writing Styles.)
3. What does "cascading" refer to? (See Discussion: Writing Styles.)
4. What are some basic rules for writing styles? (See Discussion: Writing Styles.)
5. Can a style have more than one property assigned? (See Tutorial: Starting the Sizzle Site's Cascading Style Sheet.)
6. How do you attach an external style sheet to a Web page? (See Tutorial: Starting the Sizzle Site's Cascading Style Sheet.)
7. What are the different ways to identify color values? What's the difference in how the values are written? (See Tutorial: Adding Borders and Logos to the Resort Pages' Tables.)
8. Why should you add comments to a style sheet? Is it required? (See Tutorial: Validating Page and Style Sheet Content.)
9. Are all style sheets validated the same way? What determines how a page is evaluated? (See Tutorial: Validating Page and Style Sheet Content.)
10. What does the text string " mean? (See Tutorial: Adding a New Page for Booking Information.)
11. Is it correct coding to use a <p> opening tag but not the closing tag? Why or why not? (See Tutorial: Adding a New Page for Booking Information.)
12. Why is it useful to add <p> tags to a page, even if you eventually change some of the tags? (See Tutorial: Placing Tables on the Booking Information Page.)
13. What is a good way to name a collection of graphic images that are used in a similar way or similar location in your Web site? (See Tutorial: Placing Tables on the Booking Information Page.)
14. Do you refer to an image the same way in CSS as in (X)HTML? Why or why not? (See Tutorial: Attaching Styles to the Booking Information Page.)

» Other Projects

Experiment with other styles for the site's tables. Try different border arrangements. Refer to an online attributes list for a complete list of border attributes.

Experiment with other attributes for the site's pages. Try different configurations for background images, for example.

Staying at Sizzle

Visit Sizzle when YOU want to visit.

For a long weekend, for a month -- the choice is yours!

Give us a few days' notice. For many parts of the year, call during the week to book a weekend. Unlike most resort locations, you don't have to arrive on Wednesday and leave the following Tuesday.

Like other "hot" spots, we tend to get overbooked at certain times of the year.

You have to prebook during these times: last week of December first week of January Spring Break week

Rooms are reserved during these times, and tend to fill up quickly. We recommend booking at least 2 months in advance for Christmas/New Year's weeks.

Spring Break is another story. Since Sizzle is built around the idea of Spring Break, many of our guests book a year in advance, usually when they are at Sizzle. But don't be disappointed - we only take long-term prebookings for about 60% of our rooms to give everyone a fighting chance.

Call and check with us.

Room Rates vary according to location and date.

Getting Here

Click a link to book flights from these North American airlines:

Book local flights in the Caribbean from:

Working with Pictures

Sizzle South	
image ss1a	image ss1b
This is some placement text. It will be set in a table and centered below the images on the slide.	
button links	
BACK | NEXT | EXIT	

Session Introduction

This session is predominantly a work session. You learn some new HTML and CSS code, write some different types of styles, and work with some pictures. You also build another page for your site.

Much of the work in this session relates to pictures. You learn how to resize an image for use in a Web page and how to separate an image into smaller images, which you sprinkle throughout your site's pages. Rather than placing the images and text into tables, you learn to align and size the pictures using styles.

You revise the slideshow page for your site in this session as well, and add images, text, and styles to the page. To complete this session's work with the slideshow page, you work with both new style properties and a new HTML tag.

TOOLS YOU'LL USE
Internet Explorer, Notepad, **PhotoPlus:** Canvas Size settings, Crop handles, Crop tool, Export Optimizer, Freehand Selection tool, Image Size settings, Paste as New Image command, Rulers, Zoom tool

CD-ROM FILES NEEDED (Image Folder)
fprint2.jpg, seashell.jpg, shell3.jpg, shell4.jpg, xfprint1.jpg, xss2a.jpg, xss3a.jpg

For reference, in the Artwork folder: shell1.Spp, shell2.Spp, xfprint1.jpg, xss2a.jpg, xss3a.Spp

For reference, in the Storage folder: basic.html, fine_print_text.txt

FILES CREATED
fine_print.html, fprint1.jpg, shell1.jpg, shell2.jpg, ss2a.jpg, ss3a.jpg

FILES MODIFIED
booking.html, sizzle.css, ss1.html

TIME REQUIRED
90 minutes

Tutorial
» Separating an Image into Segments

The Sizzle site uses several small seashell images for visual interest. Two of the seashell images are part of a larger image. In this tutorial, you isolate and resize the first image.

1. **From the desktop, choose Start→Programs→Serif Applications→PhotoPlus 5.-→PhotoPlus 5.5.**
   The program opens, displaying the Startup Wizard.

2. **Click the X at the bottom left of the Startup Wizard.**
   You deselect the Wizard. The next time the program opens, you start from the program's interface.

< T I P >
If you turn off the Startup Wizard, but realize that you'd prefer to use it, you can restore it. Choose File→Preferences. Click the Startup tab, and select the Startup Wizard option.

3. **Click Open Saved Work.**
   The Open Saved Work dialog box appears.

4. **Click Browse. In the Explorer window that opens, locate the seashells.jpg image in the Image Sources folder and click Open.**

   The Open Saved Work dialog box closes, and the image opens in the program.

If the file you want to work with is listed in the dialog box, click the file to select it and then click Finish. The Open Saved Work dialog box closes, and the image opens in the program.

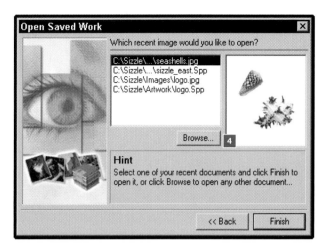

5. **Click the drop-down arrow to open the Selection Tools subpalette.**

   You choose a different tool.

6. **Click the Freehand tool to activate it.**

   The subpalette closes, and the Freehand tool is the active Selection tool.

7. **Drag a selection marquee around the upper-left seashell.**

   The selection appears as a blue line; double-click when you get back to the starting point to close the selection and deselect the tool.

<TIP>
Using the Freeform Select tool lets you select unusually shaped objects, such as the seashell, without selecting portions of any other image. Another Freeform tool, the Polygon Select tool, allows you to select an object by adding linear segments to draw around the area.

8. **Choose Edit→Copy.**

   You copy the seashell selection.

9. **Choose Edit→Paste→As New Image.**

   A new image opens, and the selected area is pasted to the new image.

<NOTE>
The background is transparent. You export the image as a JPG file, and the transparent areas are automatically flattened and colored white.

10. **Select the crop tool in the Toolbar.**

    You crop the image to remove excess blank space around the seashell.

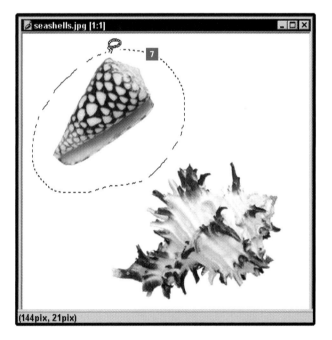

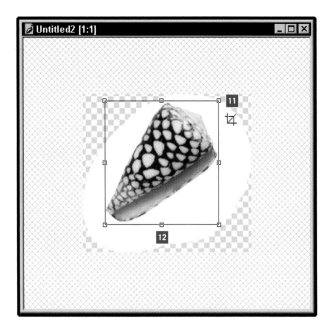

11. **Click above the image at one corner, and drag to draw a box around the entire seashell. Release the mouse.**
    This is the cropping frame.

12. **Resize the crop frame using the resize handles and the corners and sides of the box.**
    Crop as close to the image as you can.

< T I P >
Loading images on a Web page can take lots of time; crop the image as small as possible to create the smallest file size possible.

13. **Double-click the image with the Crop tool.**
    The image is cropped and excess space around the seashell is removed.

14. **Choose Image→Image Size.**
    The Image Size dialog box opens. You reset the resolution and size of the image here before saving.

< N O T E >
You usually want to maintain *aspect ratio* when you resize images. Aspect ratio refers to the relationship between the width and height of the picture. If you want to reshape your image, deselect Maintain Aspect Ratio at the top of the Image Size dialog box.

15. **Type** 100 **in the Width field, and then click another field on the dialog box.**
    The Height field is automatically resized because the Maintain aspect ratio box is checked.

< T I P >
The values shown in your image may differ slightly from those shown in the figure depending on how the image was cropped. The final image sizes will be the same.

< N O T E >
The default values are pixels; you can also resize based on percentage. Click the drop-down arrow to the right of the Height and Width fields, and select Percentage.

16. **Type** 72 **in the Resolution field. Keep the default pixels/inch.**
    Monitors display images at 72 dpi (dots per inch). A higher resolution adds to the file size, but it doesn't increase the quality of the image on screen.

17. **Click OK to close the Image Size dialog box.**
    The picture is resized. You separated the first seashell image from the original image and resized it. Leave the file open to continue to the next tutorial. You have to test the image quality and export it.

Tutorial

» Testing Image Quality

In this tutorial, you test the image quality and export the image that you created in the previous tutorial for use on your Web site. You also prepare and export a second seashell image. The finished sizes of your images may vary slightly from those used in the tutorials because of the cropping frame's dimensions. As you learn later in the session, the exact measurements aren't critical because the shell images are sized for the final Web page using styles.

1. **Choose File→Export Optimizer.**
   The Export Optimizer dialog box opens.

2. **Click Double View to split the screen and show two copies of the image.**
   You test the image for size versus quality. The goal is to export the highest quality image with the lowest file size possible.

3. **Click the Zoom tool to magnify the shell image.**

<NOTE>

The JPEG file format doesn't allow for transparency, so any transparent areas are automatically colored white.

4. **Click the bottom image to select it.**

5. **Drag the quality slider left. Look at the effect of decreasing quality on the selected image version.**
   The image is less clear and random colored pixels are added to the image. Decreasing the quality also decreases the file size.

6. **Click the upper image to select it.**
   You export the original. There is no advantage to decreasing quality; the file is small, and changes in quality are very obvious.

7. **Click Export to open the Export dialog box.**

8. **Name the image** shell1.jpg. **Click Save to save the file in the Images folder of your Sizzle site.**
   The Export dialog box closes. The first seashell image is ready for use on your Web site.

9. **Close the pasted image.**
   You exported the image and don't need to keep the original .Spp file.

<NOTE>

For reference, the file used in the tutorial is on the CD in the Artwork folder and is named shell1.Spp.

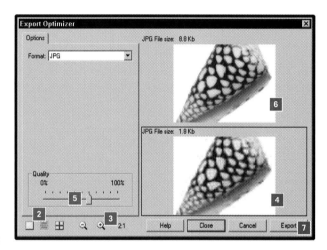

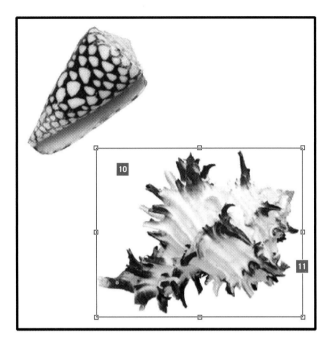

10. **Click the original** `seashells.jpg` **image to activate it. Frame the lower seashell with the cropping tool.**
    You isolate the second image for export.

11. **Adjust the cropping frame to closely outline the seashell image. Double-click the image with the cropping tool.**
    The image is cropped.

12. **Choose Image→Image Size to open the Image Size dialog box.**
    The cropped size is 273 x 214 pixels.

<TIP>
Your image's values may differ depending on how you crop the image.

13. **Click the Height field to activate it. Type:** 100.
    The image height is reset to 100 pixels. The image width is automatically reset to maintain aspect ratio.

<NOTE>
In the Sizzle site, the seashell images used are roughly the same size. The width of the image varies slightly as they are different sized shells, but all use the same 100-pixel height. So, if the initial image is 150 pixels wide and 200 pixels high, setting the height to 100 makes the image 75 pixels wide (maintaining aspect ratio.) If the initial image is 160 pixels wide and 200 pixels high, setting the height to 100 makes the image 80 pixels wide when aspect ratio is maintained.

14. **Click OK to close the Image Size dialog box.**
    The image is resized.

15. **Choose File→Export.**
    The Export dialog box opens.

<NOTE>
You don't have to reuse the Export Optimizer to test the second image because you used it for the first image and didn't find an advantage to modifying the image quality.

16. **Name the image** `shell2.jpg`. **Click Save to save the file in the Images folder of your Sizzle site.**
    The Export dialog box closes.

17. **Choose File→Close to close the** `seashells.jpg` **image.**
    When prompted to save, click No. The file closes. You exported the second seashell image for your Web site. The two seashells are added to the site's pages later in the session. Leave PhotoPlus open to continue with the next tutorial.

<NOTE>
For reference, the file used in the tutorial is on the CD in the Artwork folder and is named `shell2.Spp`.

Tutorial
» Resizing Pictures

In this tutorial, you resize three of the images used in your project. You already learned how to crop an image and use the Image Settings dialog box to resize images. In this tutorial, you use more tools to resize images. The three pictures used in this tutorial are in the Image Source folder on the CD (or your hard drive if you copied the folders); save the modified images in your site's Images folder.

1. **Choose File→Open.**
   Browse to your Image Source folder.

2. **Select** xss2a.jpg, **and click Open.**
   You resize this image for use in your Web site.

3. **Choose Image→Canvas Size.**
   The Canvas Size dialog box opens. The original image dimensions are 320 x 200 pixels.

<NOTE>
There are a number of anchors surrounding the miniature image shown on the dialog box. Click an anchor around the margins of the white area or the center to move the image. When you change the canvas size, the image is anchored to the specified location and cropped according to the meaurements that you set. The default location, shown in the figure, is the upper-left area of the canvas.

4. **Click the Width field, and type:** 300.
   The original width is 320 px; you trim the image from the right side.

5. **Click OK.**
   The dialog box closes, and the image is resized. The additional pixels are removed from the right side of the image.

<NOTE>
Resizing the canvas is not the same as resizing the image. Use the canvas to shave off portions of the image from different sides; use the image size to resize the entire picture.

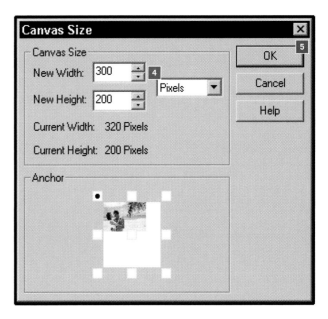

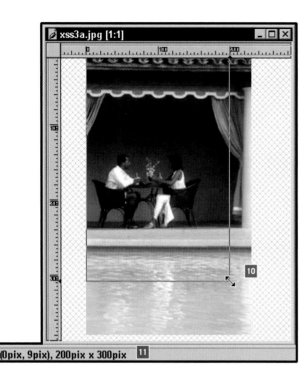

(0pix, 9pix), 200pix x 300pix

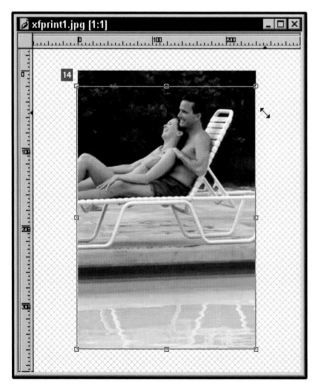

6. **Choose File→Export.**
   Browse to the location of your Sizzle site folder, and open the Images folder.

7. **Name the file** `ss2a.jpg`. **Click Save.**
   The file is saved, and the dialog box closes. You resized one of the slideshow images.

<N O T E>
The image modified in this tutorial is in the Artwork folder and is named `xss2a.Spp`.

8. **Open the** `xss3a.jpg` **file from the Image Sources folder.**
   You resize two dimensions on this image.

9. **Choose View→Rulers.**
   You crop the image from two directions. Using the rulers makes the cropping process simpler.

10. **With the Crop tool, drag a cropping frame around the image. Position the frame at the top-left corner of the image.**
    Adjust the bottom-right crop frame resize handle.

11. **Watch the dimensions in the lower area of the PhotoPlus window.**
    Stop when the picture's dimensions are 200 x 300 pixels.

11. **Choose File→Export.**
    Browse to the location of your Sizzle site folder.

12. **Name the file** `ss3a.jpg`. **Click Save to close the dialog box.**
    You modified another slideshow image.

<N O T E>
The image modified in this tutorial is in the Artwork folder and is named `xss3a.Spp`.

13. **Open the** `xfprint1.jpg` **file from the Image Sources folder.**
    The image size is 240 x 360 pixels. You crop this image from all four sides.

14. **With the Crop tool, draw a cropping frame around the image.**
    Using the left ruler as a guide, carefully drag the top frame down to approximately 10 pixels.

15. **Double-click the Crop tool on the image to complete the crop.**
    The image is resized.

16. **Choose Image→Canvas Size.**
    The Canvas Size dialog box opens.

17. **Click the New Width field, and type** 200; **click the New Height field, and type** 300.
    Set the trim size for the canvas.

18. **Click the upper-middle anchor.**
    The thumbnail moves right.

19. **Click OK to close the dialog box.**
    The image is trimmed from both sides and the bottom.

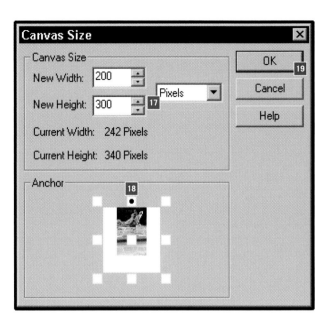

<TIP>
Sometimes it is simplest to use a combination of the cropping tool on the image and the Canvas Size dialog box. The top of the image is cropped to an approximate location, so use the cropping tool. When you have an intermediate size for the image, use the Canvas Size dialog box. The sides and final height of the image must be precise measurements, which can be accomplished only in the Canvas Size dialog box.

<NOTE>
The image modified in this tutorial is in the Artwork folder and is named xfprint1.Spp.

20. **Choose File→Export.**
    Browse to the Images folder in your Sizzle site folder.

21. **Name the file** fprint1.jpg. **Click Save to close the dialog box. Close PhotoPlus.**
    You resized three images using different cropping techniques.

Tutorial
» Adding the Fine Print

You can't have a commercial Web site without some fine print! In this tutorial, you construct another page for your site. Use the presupplied text file and the `basic.html` file as a starting point. In this tutorial, you add two regular images as well as two small seashell images. Before you start, add some images to your site's Images folder. Copy and paste or move the `seashell3.jpg`, `seashell4.jpg`, and `fprint2.jpg` images from the Image Sources folder into your site's Images folder. You now have four seashell images in total, and two `fprint.jpg` files.

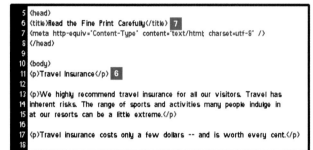

1. **Open Notepad, and then open** `basic.html`.
   The file is in your site's Storage folder. Use the file as the basis for the page in this tutorial.

2. **Choose File➡Save As. Name the file** `fine_print.html`.
   Save the page in your Sizzle site folder.

3. **Open the** `fine_print_text.txt` **file.**
   The file is on the CD in the Storage folder.

<TIP>
If you have copied all the project folders, the text file is in the copy of the Storage folder on your hard drive.

4. **Select the text in the file, and copy it.**

5. **Choose File➡Open. Select the** `fine_print.html` **file from your Sizzle site folder, and click Open.**
   The `fine_print_text.txt` file closes, and the `fine_print.html` file opens.

6. **Go to line 11. Select the placeholder text, "Add the page content here."and delete it. Paste the new text.**
   The content for the page is added.

<CAUTION>
Your line numbering may differ slightly from that shown in the tutorials. Use the line numbers as references to different areas of a page, but read the content of the line carefully as you follow the steps to ensure you are modifying or adding code to the correct line.

<TIP>
Unlike the text supplied for the `booking.html` page, this page's text is complete with <p> tags. As with the `booking.html` page, some of the tags remain as paragraph tags, and others are replaced with a variety of heading, list, and other tags.

<TIP>
Notepad doesn't show line numbers, but they are tracked and you can use the Edit➡Go To command to find a particular line on a page.

7. **Go to line 6. Select the placeholder text, and type:** Read the Fine Print Carefully
   The page is titled.

8. **Save the page.**
   The `fine_print.html` page is created.

9. **Go to line 13. On line 13, wrapping to line 14, type:** `<img src="Images/fprint1.jpg" width="200" height="300" alt="couple on lounge chair by the pool"/>`
   You add the first image to the page.

10. **Go to line 22. After the opening <p> tag, type:** `<img src="Images/shell2.jpg" alt="seashell image" />`
    The first seashell image is added to the page. Make sure that the image tag is placed after the opening <p> tag.

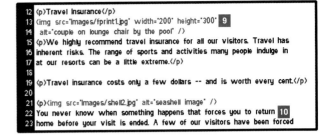

< N O T E >

There are no height and width attributes added for the seashell images. The attributes are not required for XHTML-compliant code, but are identified to allow the page's content to load more quickly in a browser. You control the size with styles added later in the session.

11. **Go to line 38. On line 38, wrapping to line 39, type:** `<img src="Images/fprint2.jpg" width="300" height="200" alt="couple on the beach" />`
    Place the image tag after the closing </p> tag. You add the third image to the page.

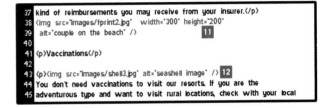

12. **Go to line 43. After the opening <p> tag, type:** `<img src="Images/shell3.jpg" alt="seashell image" />`
    You add the second seashell image to the page. Make sure that the image tag is placed after the opening <p> tag.

13. **Preview the page in your browser. Note the image placement, and the size and placement of the seashell images. Close the browser.**

14. **Save the file.**
    You added one more page to your site. You added text and four images to the page. Close the file, but leave Notepad open to continue with the next tutorial.

We highly recommend travel insurance for all our visitors. Travel has inherent risks. The range of sports and activities many people indulge in at our resorts can be a little extreme.

Travel insurance costs only a few dollars -- and is worth every cent.

You never know when something happens that forces you to return home before your visit is ended. A few of our visitors have been forced to return home early, missing out on some of the sun and fun they were entitled to. Don't let it happen to you.

Tutorial
» Configuring the Seashell Images

In the previous tutorial, you added two seashell images without height and width attributes. In this tutorial, you define a style for the seashell images and attach it to the page. You also add seashells to the `booking.html` page.

1. **In Notepad, open `sizzle.css`.**
   You create a new style for placing the seashells on the Web pages.

2. **Leave a blank line below the last style. Starting in line 42, type:**
   ```
   img.shells {
      margin-right: 4px;
      vertical-align:text-bottom;
      height: 50px;
      width: 50px;
   }
   ```
   The properties and values for the new style are added. All five properties (or rules) in this style are new to you. A breakdown of the properties and what they mean is included in Table 6-1.

3. **Save the `sizzle.css` file.**
   You have added another style written for a particular image class.

4. **Reopen the `fine_print.html` page.**

<TIP>

When this style is applied to the images, they are resized to 50 x 50 pixels regardless of their original dimensions. The only image that is not virtually square is the brown and white feathery-appearing shell; compressing the width to produce a square image doesn't deform the image. If you are using styles to resize images, test them first to be sure they do not distort.

Table 6-1: Components of the Style Used for the Seashell Images

Selector or Property	Means ...
img.shells {	The selector is the <img> tag. Because the style isn't applicable to all images in your site, create a class named "shells." Open the style description with the curly brace.
margin-right: 4px;	This property sets the right margin between the image and the text at 4 px.
vertical-align:text-bottom;	This property aligns the picture even with the bottom of the first line of text in the paragraph containing the image. If the image is not within paragraph tags, this setting has no effect.
height: 50px;	This property sets the image's height at 50 px.
width: 50px;	This property sets the image's width at 50 px.
}	Use the closing curly brace to end the style description.

5. **Go to line 8. Insert a blank line, and then type:** $<$link href="sizzle.css" rel="stylesheet" type="text/css" /$>$
   The style sheet is attached to the page.

6. **Go to the first seashell <image> tag, now on line 22, which starts:** $<$p$><$img src="Images/shell2.jpg" . **After the** src **attribute, type:** class="shells"
   The image style is attached to the seashell image.

7. Go to the second seashell image tag on line 44, and repeat Step 6.
   You attached the image style to the second seashell image.

< T I P >

Develop a method for writing tags and attributes that makes sense to you. Note that the class attribute is added after the source attribute. This is my method of writing the tags—the src attribute, then any other attributes, and the alt attribute is always last. It is simpler to review what is written and also simpler to troubleshoot if you use a standardized approach.

8. **Save the** fine_print.html **page.**
   You attached a style sheet and modified two images using styles.

9. **Open your browser, and preview the file.**
   Scroll down the page. Note that both seashell images have the same dimensions. Close your browser.

10. **Open the** booking.html **page.**
    You add two seashell images to this page as well.

< N O T E >

You attached the style sheet to this page in an earlier tutorial.

```
13  <p>Visit Sizzle when YOU want to visit.</p>
14  <p>For a long weekend, for a month -- the choice is yours!</p>
15  <p><img src="Images/shell1.jpg" class="shells" alt="seashell image"/> 11
16      Give us a few days' notice.
17      For many parts of the year, call during the week to book a weekend. Unli
18      resort locations, you don't have to arrive on Wednesday and leave the foll
19      Tuesday. </p>
```

```
26  <p><img src="Images/shell4.jpg" class="shells" alt="seashell image"/> 12
27  Spring break is another story
```

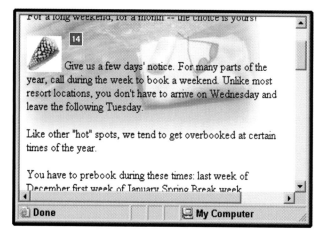

11. **Go to line 15. After the opening <p> tag, type:** <img
    src="Images/shell1.jpg" class="shells"
    alt="seashell image" /> **Press Enter to move the
    paragraph's text to the next line.**
    A seashell image and its style are added to the page. Moving
    the text for the paragraph to the next line makes the tag more
    distinctive and clearly shows where the text starts.

12. **Go to line 26. After the opening <p> tag, type:** <img
    src="Images/shell4.jpg" class="shells"
    alt="seashell image"/> **Press Enter to move the
    paragraph's text to the next line.**
    The second seashell image (although technically a starfish)
    is added to the page.

13. **Save the** booking.html **file.**
    You added two images and attached styles to the images.
    Leave Notepad open for the next tutorial.

14. **Preview the page in your browser. Note the size and locations of
    the images.**
    In the figure, you can see the first of the two images that you
    just added to the booking.html page. Close your browser.

< N O T E >
You see the white background of the seashell where it overlays the
background image. You define a background location for the image
in Session 9 that moves the background image on the browser
page.

Tutorial

» Writing Styles for the Slideshow

You constructed the first slideshow page in Session 2 and added a table to the page. In this tutorial, you create five styles to use for the slideshow pages. The styles include two for the pages' images, two for table rows, and the body background. You initially created the slideshow page with a colored background and a table displaying borders. In this tutorial, you replace the background attribute with a style and leave the borders intact for reference.

1. **In Notepad, open** `sizzle.css.`
   You add several new styles to the style sheet.

2. **Leave a blank line after the last style's closing bracket in line 49.**

3. **In Line 51, type:** `/* slideshow pages */`
   Add a comment to the page to identify the styles that follow.

4. **Leave another blank line. In line 53, type:** `body.ssbkgd {`
   You add a style class used for the <body> tag. The name of the style reflects what it is used for (bkgd) as well as where it is used (ss = slideshow).

5. **In lines 54 to 56, type:** `background-color: #003366;`
   `color: black;`
   `}`
   The background color is the same dark blue color that you originally added to the page as an attribute for the <body> tag. Because you are defining a background color, you must also define a text color—in this case, black text. Close the style with the curly bracket.

6. **Leave a blank line. In lines 58 to 60, type:** `tr.imagerow {`
   `height: 310px;`
   `}`
   The style is applied to a table row, specifically the row below the heading where the two images are placed on each slide.

7. **Leave a blank line. In lines 62 to 64, type:** `img.sslayout {`
   `padding: 5px;`
   `}`
   Your project uses a number of image classes. This style is written for the images on your slideshow. Padding around the images allows a border of the background color to display around the images and separate them visually in the table cell.

8. **Leave a blank line. In lines 66 to 68, type:** `tr.textrow {`
   `background-image: url(Images/dk_bkgd.gif);`
   `}`
   The style is used for the row below the images containing text. The value for the background-image property is the striped image used throughout your site.

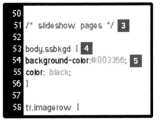

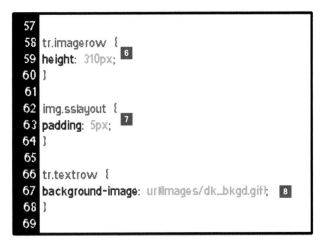

< N O T E >
If you set the background color only, the page displays correctly. However, the CSS Validator produces a warning if no color for the body is identified (the color applied to text).

< N O T E >
The images used throughout the slideshow are either 200px or 300px in height. Setting the style's height at 310px allows some padding applied to the images themselves in an image class style.

```
69
70  div.center {
71  text-align: center;
72  margin: auto;
73  padding: 3px;         [9]
74  }
```

<NOTE>

In Session 9, you add a class for the <p> tag to configure the text in the table row.

9. **Leave a blank line. In lines 70 to 74, type:** div.center {
   text-align: center;
   margin: auto;
   padding: 3px;
   }

   The style is used for a new tag you add to the page in the next tutorial. A <div> tag is like a container that holds other tags and elements. You use the tag to align the pair of navigation buttons on your slideshow page using a combination of the align and margin properties. Like the main images on the slideshow, padding is added to visually separate the two buttons.

10. **Save the file.**

    You added five styles for your project. These styles are used on the slideshow pages. Leave Notepad open for the next tutorial.

Naming Styles

Naming styles can be very confusing. One way to keep track of what you are writing is to add comments. Another way is to construct names that make sense. You create five styles for the slideshow in this session. The image shows where each style is applicable in the slideshow table.

The heading at the top of the page doesn't have a style, nor do the two text blocks. They are styled in later sessions.

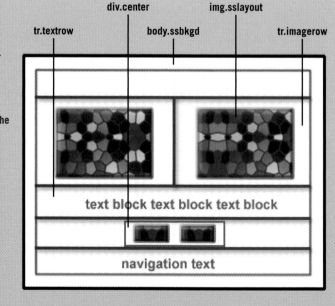

Tutorial

» Adding Images and Text to the Slideshow Page

In this tutorial, you add two of the slideshow images to the page, as well as one version of each of the navigation buttons that you built in Session 3.

1. **Open your Sizzle site folder, and then open the Image Sources folder. Copy and paste or move the** `ss1a.jpg` **and** `ss1b.jpg` **images into your site's Images folder.**
   You add the two images to the slideshow page.

2. **Open** `ss1.html` **in Notepad.**
   The file is in your Sizzle site folder.

3. **Go to line 16. Replace the placeholder text within the <td> tags reading image ss1a; type:** `<img src="Images/ss1a.jpg" width="300" height="200" alt="windsurfer riding rough waves" />`
   The first image is added to the slideshow page.

4. **Go to the second <td> tag for the row, now located in line 18. Replace the placeholder text between the <td> tags reading image ss1b; type:** `<img src="Images/ss1b.jpg" width="300" height="200" alt="young woman in blue bathing suit on a pink pool float" />`
   The second image is added to the slideshow page.

5. **Go to line 22. After the <td colspan="2"> tag, replace the placeholder text within the <p> tags which reads This is some placement text. It will be set in a table and centered below the images on the slide; type:** `Whether your interest in water is riding the rough waves or riding a pool float, <br /> Sizzle is the place to be!`
   Make sure that the text is within the <p> tags. Use the <br /> tag to divide the sentence over two lines.

6. **Go to line 28.**
   The current line reads: `<td colspan="2">button links</td>`

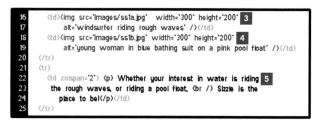

< T I P >
Make sure to add the text between the start and end <td> tags.

< N O T E >
It isn't necessary to start a new line on your page to use the <br /> tag; it displays a break when you preview the page in your browser.

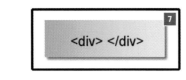

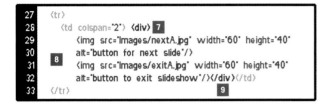

```
27    <tr>
28        <td colspan="2"> <div> 7
29            <img src="Images/nextA.jpg" width="60" height="40"
30    8       alt="button for next slide"/>
31            <img src="Images/exitA.jpg" width="60" height="40"
32            alt="button to exit slideshow"/></div></td>
33    </tr>                                              9
```

7. **Delete the placeholder text reading button links;**
   type ⟨div⟩
   Add the opening <div> tag to identify the content within the tag as a single unit.

8. **Go to line 28. From lines 29 to 32, type:**
   ⟨img src="Images/nextA.jpg" width="60"
   height="40"
   alt="button for next slide"/⟩
   ⟨img src="Images/exitA.jpg" width="60"
   height="40"
   alt="button to exit slideshow"/⟩
   Copies of the two navigation buttons that you created in Session 3 are added to the page. They are both placed in the same cell of the table.

9. **Following the end of the text added in line 32, type:** ⟨/div⟩
   Make sure this tag appears before the closing </td> tag. The <div> tag must be closed to signify to the browser where the container tag ends.

10. **Save the** ss1.html **file.**
    You added four images to the page, as well as a text caption. You also added a new tag. Leave the file open for the next tutorial.

11. **Preview the page in your browser.**
    You see the images in the page, filling their cells vertically. The caption text is added to its row and wraps to the second line where you added the <br /> tag. The two button images are added to the row below the caption and aligned with the left margin of the table. Close the browser.

<NOTE>
Open and close tags in sequence. The first tag added to a segment of your page should be the last tag closed. The second tag added to a segment should be the second-to-last tag closed, and so on.

Using the <div> Tag to Control the Images' Locations

Images are considered in-line elements—elements that are added to a page without disrupting the flow of a line. In-line elements appear on the page at the location where you add them, and not at the beginning of a line.

Block-level elements, such as paragraphs, headings, and forms, usually begin on a new line. A block can be aligned horizontally on a page using a style. To center your images in the table, you must wrap them in a <div> tag, which is a block element.

Tutorial

» Attaching Styles to the Slideshow Page

You constructed five styles for the slideshow page that you apply to the page in this tutorial. One of the styles that you created is for the <div> tag. The <div> tag defines a division/section in a document—in this case, a table row. It is used as a container to hold other elements and tags.

1. **Open `ss1.html` in Notepad.**
   The page hasn't been modified since Session 2.

2. **Go to line 8. Press Enter to add a new line, and then type:**
   `<link href="sizzle.css" rel="stylesheet" type="text/css" />`
   The style sheet is attached to the page.

3. **Go to line 11. Expand the <body> tag to read:** `<body class="ssbkgd">`
   You replaced the background color attribute with a body style name having the same color value.

<NOTE>
Although not "illegal" to use a background color attribute in the HTML code, the attribute is deprecated in XHTML and should be included in a style instead. Browsers are capable of displaying either; eventually, they will only display XHTML.

4. **Go to line 16. Expand the <tr> tag to read:** `<tr class="imagerow">`
   The style written for the table row containing the images is attached to the page. The style contains a vertical height property for the row.

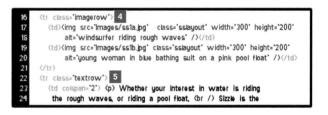

<NOTE>
The `tr.imagerow` style is used to develop a consistent presentation. Although the two images that you see on this slide look well aligned when you preview the page, the site includes other pages that use images that are 300px high. When your reader views the slideshow, the table size jumps to accommodate the image sizes unless a single consistent height is defined. Now when your reader views the slideshow, the images and captions change, but the rest of the table remains static.

5. **Go to line 22. Expand the <tr> tag to read:** `<tr class="textrow">`
   The style written for the table row containing the image captions is attached to the page. The style contains a background image for the row.

```
27   <tr>
28     <td colspan="2"> <div class ="center"> 6
29        <img src="Images/nextA.jpg" width="60" height="40"
30        alt="button for next slide"/>
31        <img src="Images/exitA.jpg" width="60" height="40"
32        alt="button to exit slideshow"/></div></td>
33   </tr>
```

< N O T E >

Styles for the text on this page, and the other pages on the site, are written and applied in Session 9.

6. **Go to line 28. Expand the <div> tag to read:** `<div class = "center">`

   The style applies to both button images added to the table. The style centers the pair of images horizontally, and adds margins and padding to make the buttons visually distinct.

7. **Save the** `ss1.html` **page.**

   You added styles to different elements on the page.

8. **Preview the page in your browser. Note the effect of the styles.**

   The background remains the same because the change is made only to the code, not the values; the images are centered vertically in a larger cell; the caption has a striped background; the buttons are centered and spaced. Close your browser.

< N O T E >

The table contains borders at this point. When you are finished working with the slideshow page, the last element changed is removing the borders. A visible border is much simpler to work with as you develop the pages.

Planning Your Site Design Strategy

In this session, you created slideshow styles and applied the styles and images to one slideshow page. Why not create all the slideshow pages now? The simple answer is that it is too much work. Develop one page and add its structure, style, and content. After the first page is complete to your satisfaction, it is simple to duplicate the page five times and modify each page as necessary. If you build all six pages now, each time you decide to alter something, you have to change all the pages. This can lead to errors and adds lots of time to your development process.

» Session Review

In this session, you did a variety of tasks and learned some new code for both your page and your style sheet. You learned how to resize some images in PhotoPlus, working with image and canvas sizes, as well as cropping and selection tools. You added several images to your site's pages. You added seashell images to the booking and fine print pages, and used styles to size the images.

The first image in this session shows the slideshow as it appeared before you started adding images and text. You also built a number of styles for the slideshow's table rows, content, and the page's background. You added a <div> tag to the page and learned how the tag is used as a container to control some of your page's content. After adding content and styles, the slideshow page now looks like the final image in the session.

Here are some questions to help you review the information in this session. The answer to each question can be found in the tutorial noted in parentheses.

1. When do you use the Freeform Select tool? (See Tutorial: Separating an Image into Segments.)

2. What happens to transparent areas of an image when exporting as a JPEG file? (See Tutorial: Separating an Image into Segments.)

3. What does "aspect ratio" mean? Why is it important? (See Tutorial: Separating an Image into Segments.)

4. Do you have to use the Export Optimizer each time you export an image? Why or why not? (See Tutorial: Testing Image Quality.)

5. What is the difference between image size and canvas size? (See Tutorial: Resizing Pictures.)

6. How do you use anchors for setting canvas size? (See Tutorial: Resizing Pictures.)

7. Are pictures placed inside or outside <p> tags? What is the difference? (See Tutorial: Adding the Fine Print.)

8. Are height and width properties required for an image tag? (See Tutorial: Adding the Fine Print.)

9. An image is vertically aligned with what element on a page? (See Tutorial: Configuring the Seashell Images.)

10. If you set a style for the <body> tag's background color, what other property should also be defined? Why? (See Tutorial: Writing Styles for the Slideshow.)

11. Do you write a color name the same way as you write a color's hex value? (See Tutorial: Writing Styles for the Slideshow.)

12. What is the padding property? What is it used for? (See Tutorial: Writing Styles for the Slideshow.)

13. What is a <div> tag? How is it used? (See Tutorial: Writing Styles for the Slideshow.)

14. To display a line break on your browser, is it necessary to have a line break in your HTML file? Why or why not? (See Tutorial: Adding Images and Text to the Slideshow Page.)

15. Is there a specific way to add opening and closing tags to a page? (See Tutorial: Adding Images and Text to the Slideshow Page.)

16. Is an image considered an in-line element or a block element? What is the difference? (See Tutorial: Adding Images and Text to the Slideshow Page.)

» Other Projects

There is an additional seashell image in the Image Sources folder named `shellx.jpg`. Use the shell on another page of the site, or add it to one of the pages that you worked with in the session.

Part V
Organizing the Site

Constructing Frames and Links

Session Introduction

Have you visited a Web site and seen a portion of the window that remains stationary while other parts of the window move? Or maybe you've clicked a link on one part of the window and changed the display of the page in another portion of the window. You were likely visiting a site using frames, or separate browser window divisions. In this session, you learn to use frames for your Sizzle site.

From a design perspective, frames are a useful method for arranging content on your site. Rather than having to use the Web site's logo on each page, for example, the logo can be added to a frame that remains visible regardless of what page the reader is viewing in other parts of the screen display. The same ease-of-construction applies to having navigation elements of the site arranged in frames.

After your frames are in place and pages assigned, it's time to make some links. You learn to link the text in the navigation frame's table to different pages in your site, which are loaded into one of the frames. You also learn different ways to make frame links and how to link to a specific page location.

You need to consider some issues when working with frames, aside from the obvious structural issues. Many readers don't use browsers that support (display) frames, or they prefer not to use frames. In addition, readers with disabilities use screen readers and other assistive devices that don't work with framed sites.

You learn to add a variety of tags in this session for working with frames, including an option for the user to access an alternate version of your site's pages without frames. You set one page as the start page for the frames-free, or noframes, version of your site; more noframes pages are constructed in Session 14 when you learn to create an accessible Web site.

TOOLS YOU'LL USE
Notepad, Internet Explorer

CD-ROM FILES NEEDED (Storage Folder)
basic.html

FILES CREATED
contact.html, index.html, n_main.html, store.html, video.html

FILES MODIFIED
booking.html, nav_left.html

TIME REQUIRED
90 minutes

Discussion

Using a Frameset

A frameset page is different from a regular (X)HTML page. In a frameset page, no page is visible in a browser. Instead, the frameset page describes the name and location of pages to load into defined areas of the screen and how each section appears. When you originally built the Sizzle pages, you started with a DTD statement that identified the page as using the Transitional standard for XHTML. Framesets have their own standard, named XHTML 1.0 Frameset.

One of the obvious differences between regular pages and a frameset page when you view them in Notepad is the use of basic tags. Your frameset doesn't need a <body> tag because it has no body. In fact, if you do accidentally add a <body> tag, you won't see anything in your browser! Your frameset page uses a <frameset> tag as well as a <noframes> tag for alternate content. The Sizzle site uses one frameset page to control the content of the three frames on your site. You can use different configurations to have frameset pages branch from different pages in your site or even embed a page within another frame.

You can assign a size to each page element by specifying the column width or row height. Your frameset page also includes source information. You use the src attribute to define the name and URL for the frame content, just as you used the src attribute with images to point to a storage location. Your site loads the frameset page, named index.html, that defines the sections on the browser page and loads the applicable pages into the sections.

You don't have to make changes to an individual Web page to use it in a frameset, but you do have to make changes in your navigation links. As you learn in Session 8, you define a target frame along with a hyperlink page. A link clicked on a page in one frame loads the linked page into the targeted frame, which can be any of your frames or a new page.

Configuring a Frameset

A frameset page contains descriptions of its contents. Each frame holds a separate document. A frameset can have either a column (vertical) or a row (horizontal) configuration, but not both, set with the cols or row attribute of the <frameset> tag. The order of the frame tags sets the order of the frames. If the frames are configured in rows, the first frame element is the top window, the second frame element is second from the top, and so on. For the columns configuration, the order is left to right. In the figure, you can see how a page can be structured either way with an equal numbers of frames.

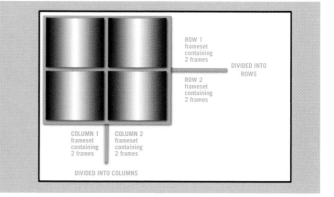

ROW 1
frameset
containing
2 frames

DIVIDED INTO
ROWS

ROW 2
frameset
containing
2 frames

COLUMN 1
frameset
containing
2 frames

COLUMN 2
frameset
containing
2 frames

DIVIDED INTO COLUMNS

Tutorial
» Creating the Frameset Page

Frames are described from top to bottom and left to right. Your Sizzle site uses three frames that you create in this tutorial. Across the top of the screen, the Sizzle logo and the map of the Caribbean display during a visitor's stay on your site. The navigation table remains at the left of the screen, and the other content for your site loads into the third frame.

1. **Open Notepad. Locate the** `basic.html` **page in your Storage folder, and open it.**

2. **Select all the text in the page, and copy it.**
   You use the text from the page to start the frameset.

3. **Choose File→New, and open a new page.**
   Paste the copied text to the page.

4. **In line 1, replace the text Transitional//EN. Type:**
   `Frameset//EN`
   This defines a different form of XHTML.

5. **Go to line 2, and replace the text "DTD/xhtml1-transitional.dtd">.**
   Type: `"DTD/xhtml1-frameset.dtd">`
   This defines the document type used for the page.

6. **Go to line 6, and delete the placeholder text. Type:** `Welcome to`
   `Sizzle!!`
   Your frameset page is named.

7. **Save the file as** `index.html`.
   You saved the initial frameset page. Leave the file open for the next tutorial.

```
1 <!DOCTYPE html PUBLIC "-//W3C//DTD XHTML 1.0 Frameset//EN"
2 "DTD/xhtml1-frameset.dtd">
3 <html xmlns="http://www.w3.org/1999/xhtml">
4
5 <head>
6 <title>Welcome to Sizzle!!</title>
7 <meta http-equiv="Content-Type" content="text/html; charset=utf-8" />
8 </head>
```

<NOTE>

You may wonder why the page is named `index.html` instead of something more descriptive of the site, such as `sizzle.html`. You need to define the starting page for your site when it is uploaded to a server. Often, you are required to name the initial page `index.html`. Using the name is also a simpler choice if you create lots of Web sites. Regardless of the site or its complexity, if you see a file named `index.html` you know where to start. Check with your Web service provider for information on naming your starting page.

Approach Frames Design with Caution

Frames can be overused! There is no maximum number of frames that you can add to a page, but a maximum is certainly a good idea from a practical standpoint. The key issue is how usable the page is for your reader. If your reader is faced with a dozen small frames that require scrolling to view or read any of your site's content, you won't likely have many repeat visitors.

Tutorial

» Splitting a Browser Window Display into Frames

In the previous tutorial, you created the initial frameset document. So far, you have declared the document type and added some of the basic information to the page. In this tutorial, you add the initial frameset and frame tags, and you define the rows and columns for your site's interface.

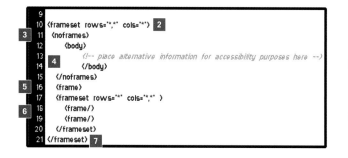

1. **In the** `index.html` **page, go to line 9. Press Enter twice to add two blank lines.**
   The <body> tag moves to line 12.

2. **In line 10, type:** `<frameset rows="*,*" cols="*">`
   You add the opening tag for the frameset. You also define the frameset as having two rows and a single column.

3. **In line 11, type:** `<noframes>`
   You need to define a page or content for your reader's browser to display if she is not using frames.

4. **In lines 12 through 15, change the original body text and add text to read:**
   ```
   <body>
   <!- place alternative information for
   accessibility purposes here ->
   </body>
   </noframes>
   ```
   The <body> tag sits within the <noframes> tag. The text in the <body> tag is converted to a comment by using the opening and closing characters. In the figure, comment text appears in gray.

5. **In line 16, type:** `<frame>`
   The <frame> tag is used to describe what appears in the top frame of the page. The frame's content is added in the next tutorial.

6. **Go to line 17. In lines 17 through 20, type:**
   ```
   <frameset rows="*" cols="*,*" >
   <frame />
   <frame />
   </frameset>
   ```
   The nested frameset is added, and tags for the individual frames are added.

7. **Go to line 21, and type:** `</frameset>`
   The first frameset is now closed.

<TIP>
You can't use a <body> tag before adding the <frameset> tag, but you can use it within the <frameset> tag to define alternate material, as described in this tutorial.

<NOTE>
Like other attributes, the values are enclosed in quotation marks. Because the frameset has two rows, the values are separated by a comma.

<NOTE>
Later in this session, you modify a page to use as the opening page for the no-frames version of your site, but you make changes throughout in Session 14.

<TIP>
XHTML requires that you include separate closing tags for each frameset that you add to a page.

8. **Choose File→Save and save the** `index.html` **file.**

9. **Preview the page in your browser.**
   You see that the window is divided into two rows, and the bottom row is divided into two columns based on the values you added. The rows and columns are divided proportionally. The frames are surrounded by borders and scroll bars.

<NOTE>
You don't see anything in the frames except for error pages. You add pages in the next tutorial.

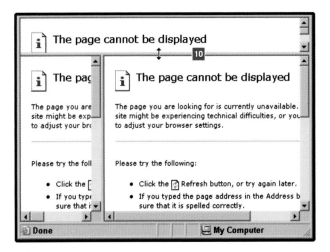

10. **Move your mouse over the frame borders. You see the cursor change to a double-ended arrow.**
    Drag the arrow to resize the frames. Dragging the arrow resizes the frames horizontally or vertically, depending on which frame border you drag. Close the browser. You created the structure for your site's frames. Leave the file open in Notepad to continue with the next tutorial.

<NOTE>
The browser displays the default configuration for your frameset page. The defaults include automatic scrollbars and resizing of the frames, as well as borders around all frames.

Defining Columns and Rows

The rows attribute sets the number of row frames and the cols attribute sets the number of column frames. The attribute is written as a comma-separated list of values instead of writing the number of rows or columns. Each value specifies the width of a frame; the number of values in the list determines the number of frames. Your site uses two rows, defined in the first frameset. The second frameset uses two columns, also defined with comma-separated values. Values can be a percentage of the window's width, a number of pixels, or an asterisk (*). You can use the asterisk with percentage or integer values as well, which you have used in the Sizzle frameset page.

Tutorial
» Setting Frame Attributes and Content

In the last tutorial, you saw the constructed framesets in the browser window. The frames are all proportional, all bordered, and all resizable, and they contain no content. In this tutorial, you define page sources for the frames and set some attributes.

```
10  <frameset rows="160,*" cols="*">
11    <noframes>
12      <body>
13        (!-- place alternative information for accessibility purposes here --)
14      </body>
15    </noframes>
16    <frame src="logo.html" id="logo" scrolling="no" noresize="noresize"
17      frameborder="1" />
18    <frameset rows="*" cols="145,*">
19      <frame src="nav_left.html" id="nav" noresize="noresize" frameborder="0" />
20      <frame src="main.html" id="main" frameborder="0" />
21    </frameset>
22  </frameset>
```

1. **Go to line 10 in the** `index.html` **file. Modify the** rows **value to read:** `="160,*"`
   You define a specific vertical dimension for the first row of the frameset, so regardless of the window size a reader uses, the first row uses 160px of the total vertical display available.

2. **Go to line 16, and expand the frame's tag. Type:** `<frame src="logo.html" name="logo" id="logo" scrolling="no" noresize="noresize" frameborder="1" />`
   The attributes and their values are explained in Table 7-1.

3. **Go to line 18. Modify the cols value to read:** `="145,*"`
   The second frameset uses two columns. Your navigation page uses the first column. Make sure that your reader can see the names of the links by defining the column width.

4. **Go to line 19, and expand the frame's tag to read:** `<frame src="nav_left.html" name="nav" id="nav" noresize="noresize" frameborder="0" />`
   The source file is defined for the frame. The frame is given a name and an id. The `noresize` attribute prevents hiding the content of the frame. The frame border is hidden.

5. **Go to line 20, and expand the frame's tag to read:** `<frame src="main.html" name="main" id="main" frameborder="0" />`
   Your site's main page is defined as the content for the frame. The frame is given an identification, and the borders are set to invisible.

6. **Save the** `index.html` **file in Notepad.**

7. **Preview the page in your browser.**
   The top logo frame has a border around it; the two lower frames do not. The lower-right frame now has scrollbars.

8. **Drag the resize handle from the lower-right corner of the browser window toward the upper left of the window.**
   The upper frame and the lower-left frame do not resize, while the main frame resizes in both directions. Close the browser. You assigned content and defined characteristics of the frames of your site.

<NOTE>
In the figure, the top frame's tag wraps over lines 16 and 17.

<NOTE>
The value of the `id` attribute must start with a letter or an underscore. The rest of the value can contain any alpha/numeric character. The unique value of the `id` means that it can be the target of a URL or used to define a style rule.

Tutorial
» Adding More Pages to the Sizzle Site

Now you have a set of three frames for your Sizzle site used for identifying the site, providing navigation, and displaying content. A number of pages are still missing from your site. In this tutorial, you create two more pages for the site in preparation for adding links later in the session, and you add a third page that is used as a placeholder page until a later session. You also save a copy of the `main.html` page to use as the introductory page for the no-frames version of your site.

1. **Open** `basic.html` **in Notepad.**
   The file is stored in your Storage subfolder in the Sizzle site folder.

2. **Save the file as** `contact.html`.
   The new file is used for a survey.

3. **Go to line 6, and delete the placeholder title text. Type:** We want to hear from you. Complete our Sizzle survey.
   This names the page using a descriptive sentence.

4. **Go to line 11. Type:** Sizzle Survey
   When you establish links on your site, you see text identifying the page and the link correctly.

5. **Choose File→Save As. Save the file as** `video.html`.
   You create another new file used to display a video about the Sizzle resorts.

6. **Go to line 6, and delete the title added in Step 3. Type:** See our resorts - watch the video!
   The page is titled.

7. **Go to line 11, and delete the text added in Step 4. Type:** Sizzle Video
   Again, you add text that displays on the page to test your site links.

<NOTE>
You don't see a page's title when viewing it in a frame; instead, you see the frameset's title. Adding some text to the page makes it simple for you to test your site's links.

Table 7-1: Frame Tag Attributes and Values

Attribute and Value	Means...
src="logo.html"	The source file used in the frame is the site's logo file.
name="logo"	This is the name for the frame, an identification of the frame used by many browsers.
id="logo"	This is a unique identification for the frame. In earlier HTML versions, a frame used a `name` attribute only.
scrolling="no"	The frame doesn't scroll, regardless of the browser window size.
noresize="noresize"	The frame and its contents will not resize based on the browser window size.
frameborder="1"	The global styles used by the browser attach borders automatically to the frame; defining a value "1" means that the border is visible (a value "0" means that the border is not displayed).

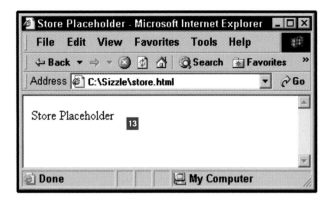

8. **Save the** video.html **file.**
   You create another new page for your site.

9. **Repeat Step 5, and name the file** store.html.

10. **Repeat Step 6. Type:** Store Placeholder
    The page is titled.

11. **Repeat Step 7. Type:** Store Placeholder
    When you complete Session 12, you replace the placeholder page with a PDF file. The page is used to test your site's link structure.

12. **Save the** store.html **file. Open** main.html **in Notepad.**
    You make an alternate copy to modify for the no-frames version of your site.

13. **Open your browser. Preview the pages.**
    You see the placeholder text and the page title. Close your browser.

14. **Go to line 10, and add a blank line. In line 11, type:** <!--no frames main page-->
    A comment is added to the page. Later in this session, you link the page from your navigation table; in Session 14, you modify the content of the page.

15. **Insert another blank line.**
    The <body> tag moves to line 13, and the comment is clearly visible.

16. **Save the file as** n_main.html.
    You added four more pages to your site. One page is used as a placeholder to test your site. Leave Notepad open to continue with the next tutorial.

< N O T E >

You saved the first file used for your site's no-frames version using a prefix "n_". When you are working with your site files, this trick makes it simple to determine which pages are for the frames version and which are for the no-frames version. You can also use a suffix "_n" to achieve much the same outcome, except that the pages are then sequenced in pairs in your folder.

Tutorial
» Expanding the Navigation Page's Table

Now that you have added more pages to your site, it's time to go back to the navigation page. In this tutorial, you add several rows to the `nav_left.html` page's table and add more text for links. You also add text for a link to the no-frames version of the site.

1. **In Notepad, open the `nav_left.html` page.**
   You modify the table on the page in this tutorial.

2. **Go to line 13, and change the `rowspan` attribute value from 4 to 9.**
   You add five more rows for links and use the same background wave image in the left column of the table.

3. **Go to line 15, and select the text in lines 15 through 24.**
   Copy the text.

4. **Go to line 25. Type: `<tr>` and press Enter to go to the next line.**

5. **Paste the copied text into line 26.**
   The pasted text is added to the page from lines 26 to 37. The `</table>` tag moves to line 38 following all the text that you just added.

6. **Change the text for the second set of table rows as follows:**
   In line 26, type: BOOKING
   In line 29, type: AIRLINES
   In line 32, type: STORE
   In line 35, type: FINE PRINT
   The second set of table rows have text added. You have a total of eight rows in the table to this point.

7. **Go to line 37, and press Enter to add a blank line.**

8. **In lines 37 to 39, type:**
   ```
   <tr>
   <td> View without <br /> Frames</td>
   </tr>
   ```
   You add one more row to the table. The `<br />` tag wraps the text over two lines in the table cell. The `</table>` tag moves to line 40 after the text you just added.

<NOTE>
The text in the bottom row is used to link to the no-frames version of your site.

9. **Save the `nav_left.html` file.**
   You added more rows and text to your site's navigation table. Leave the file open for the next tutorial.

10. **Preview the page in your browser.**
   The additional row spans the width of the table. Close the browser.

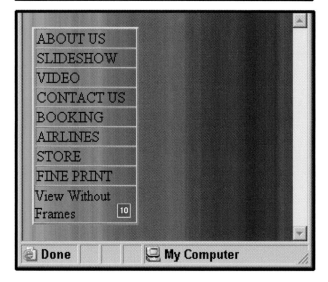

<TIP>
Open `index.html` in your browser to preview the file in your site's frameset.

Tutorial
» Linking Pages in Your Site's Frames

Your frameset is built, and your navigation table is expanded. You have added the pages for your site that link from the navigation frame. In this tutorial, you make the links from the text in the navigation table on the `nav_left.html` page to your site's pages.

```
13    <td rowspan="9"></td>
2  14    <td><a href="main.html" target="main">ABOUT US</a></td>
   15    </tr>
   16    <tr>
3  17    <td><a href="ss1.html" target="blank">SLIDESHOW</a></td>
   18    </tr>
   19    <tr>
4  20    <td><a href="video.html" target="main">VIDEO</a></td>
   21    </tr>
```

<NOTE>
As you click through the links, note that the URL shown at the top of the browser window doesn't change; your frameset is loaded at all times, and only the content of frames changes.

1. **In Notepad, open** `nav_left.html`.
   The page is open if continued from the previous tutorial.

2. **Go to line 14, and expand the tag to read:** `<td><a href="main.html" target="main">ABOUT US</a></td>`
   You add an anchor tag. The reference (`href` attribute) is the `main.html` page, the page that loads when the link is clicked. The `target` attribute defines the frame into which the page loads when the link is clicked. The value, `"main"`, is the name (and id) given to the main frame of your frameset.

<NOTE>
In the figures from this point on, the anchor tag and its attributes are shown in bright green.

3. **Go to line 17, and expand the tag to read:** `<td><a href="ss1.html" target="blank">SLIDESHOW</a></td>`
   The text has a link. The `target` attribute's value `"blank"` means that when the link is clicked, the first slideshow page opens in a new window.

4. **Go to line 20, and expand the tag to read:** `<td><a href="video.html" target="main">VIDEO</a></td>`
   The `video.html` page is linked from the text and displays in the main frame when clicked.

5. **Save the file.**

6. **Open your browser, and then open the** `index.html` **file. View and test the links through the frameset.**

7. **Click the VIDEO link in the Navigation frame.**
   The Video page's placeholder page loads in the main frame of the site. If you don't see the page in the main frame, check the anchor tag you added in Step 4.

8. **Click the ABOUT US link in the Navigation frame.**
   The introductory page for the site reloads in the main frame. If you don't see the page in the main frame, check the anchor tag you added in Step 2.

<NOTE>

As you click through the links, you notice that their colors change from blue to maroon. These are the global template colors that the browser assigns to hyperlinks by default. You build custom styles in Session 9.

9. Click the SLIDESHOW link.

A new browser window opens, and the first slideshow page displays. Leave the Slideshow window open.

<NOTE>

Unlike the other pages in your site, the Slideshow window displays an address in the address bar when its separate browser window opens.

10. Click another link on the Navigation frame to load another page in the frameset, and then click the SLIDESHOW link again.

You see the browser processing the link, but it doesn't open another copy of the slideshow as you assigned a blank window as the slideshow target, and it is already open in your browser.

11. Close the Slideshow window, and minimize the browser.

Your first three links are tested and functional.

12. In Notepad, add the anchor tags and hyperlinks for the next five link titles. Expand the content as shown in Table 7-2.

<CAUTION>

The table references line numbers. Your line numbering may differ slightly from that shown in the tutorials. Use the line numbers as references to different areas of a page, but read the content of the line carefully as you follow the steps to ensure you are modifying or adding code to the correct line.

13. Go to line 39. Add the anchor tag, and expand the content to read:

```
<td ><a href="n_main.html" target="blank">
View Without <br />Frames</a></td>
```

You create a link to the no-frames version of the site using the text in the table.

<NOTE>

The text is wrapped over lines 39 and 40 in the figure.

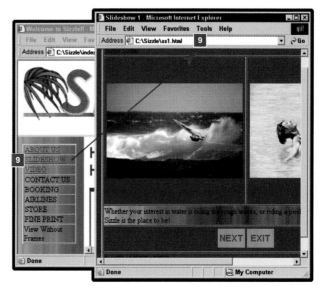

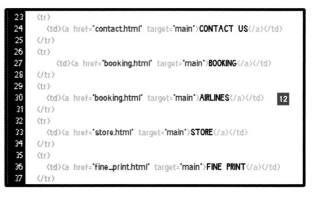

14. **In Notepad, save the** `nav_left.html` **page.**

    You added the main links from the navigation frame to your site's pages and defined a frame or window for the pages' display. Leave Notepad open for the next (and final) tutorial of this session.

15. **Open your browser, and then open the** `index.html` **page. Click the View Without Frames link.**

    The no-frames version link opens a new blank window, displaying the page's address in the browser's address bar.

< N O T E >

The BOOKING and AIRLINES links both link to the same page. In the next tutorial, you modify the page's code to allow different parts of the page to display.

Frame Targets

In addition to named frames, additional options to the `blank` and `top` targets that you used in the tutorial are available:

» `Parent` opens the linked document in the parent frameset of the frame in which the link appears, replacing the entire frameset.

» `Self` opens the link in the current frame, replacing the content in that frame.

You used the `top` and `blank` values for two of your links. If you link to sites and pages external to your site, use the `top` or `blank` values to remove your frameset from others' sites.

Table 7-2: Tags for Navigation Links

Line	Expand Text to Read...
24	`<td><a href="contact.html" target="main">CONTACT US</a></td>`
27	`<td><a href="booking.html" target="main">BOOKING</a></td>`
30	`<td><a href="booking.html" target="main">AIRLINES</a></td>`
33	`<td><a href="store.html" target="main">STORE</a></td>`
36	`<td><a href="fine_print.html" target="main">FINE PRINT</a></td>`

Tutorial
» Linking to a Page Location

You added links from the text in the navigation frame to pages in your site, and you either loaded the targeted page into the main frame of the page or into a new browser window. Two of the links load the same page into the browser frame. In the final tutorial of this session, you add a tag to the booking page and then reference it from the navigation page.

1. **In Notepad, open** booking.html.
   You define a page location in the file.

2. **Go to line 34, and press Enter to add a blank line.**
   You add the anchor tag to its own line for clarity.

3. **In line 34, type:** <a name="airlines" id="airlines"> </a>
   A named location is added to the page, with both name and id values of "airlines".

4. **Save the** booking.html **file.**
   The anchor is added to the page.

5. **Open the** nav_left.html **file.**
   You modify the AIRLINES link.

6. **Go to line 30, and modify the** href **attribute to read:**
   href="booking.html#airlines"
   The link is made to the location named "airlines" on the booking page.

7. **Open your browser, and then open the** index.html **page.**
   You test the link through the frameset.

8. **Click the AIRLINES link in the navigation frame.**
   The booking.html page loads at the location of the "Getting Here" title. If the page doesn't load at the correct location, review the tags added in Steps 3 and 6. Close the browser.

9. **Save the** index.html **file.**
   You added a named anchor to a page and used the location as a target value on your navigation page.

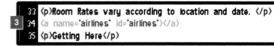

<NOTE>

Where you place the anchor makes a difference in the page display. If you use the location specified in the tutorial, the page loads with the "Getting Here" title displayed; if you add the anchor tag within the <p> tags of the title, the page loads below the title's paragraph.

» Session Review

This session covered the creation of your site's frameset, frames, and some of the main links in the site. You learned how to build a frameset and how to add the information that allows browsers to recognize the file as XHTML Frameset code. You learned how to divide the browser into frames and how to configure the frames to display pages. You assigned attributes to the frames depending on their function. You added <noframes> tags to identify content for readers using browsers or devices that don't support frames.

You created several more pages for your Web site and expanded the navigation table to include the additional pages. The initial image in this session shows the navigation table as it appeared at the start of this session. You set links from text in the navigation table to your site's pages. The final image in the session shows the completed frameset and the frame contents, including the expanded navigation options. You also added a link from your navigation frame to the first page of the frames-free version of your site. You learned how to set a named anchor in a page to specify a location that displays in your browser in response to clicking a link.

Answer the questions below to review the information in this session. Find the answers to the questions in the tutorial noted in parentheses.

1. What is one of the biggest differences between a frameset page and a regular Web page? (See Discussion: Using a Frameset.)
2. Can a frameset use both column and row specifications? (See Discussion: Using a Frameset.)
3. How do you assign a page to a frame? (See Discussion: Using a Frameset.)
4. How does the document type and DTD differ for a frameset? (See Tutorial: Creating the Frameset Page.)
5. Why are frameset pages commonly named index.html? (See Tutorial: Creating the Frameset Page.)
6. Can you use a <body> tag in a frameset? Why or why not? (See Tutorial: Splitting a Browser Window Display into Frames.)
7. What ways can you define the sizes of rows or columns in a frameset? (See Tutorial: Splitting a Browser Window Display into Frames.)
8. How are default frames displayed in a browser? (See Tutorial: Splitting a Browser Window Display into Frames.)
9. What attributes control movement or resizing of a frame? (See Tutorial: Setting Frame Attributes and Content.)
10. Is it necessary to display borders around the frames? How are the frames' borders controlled? (See Tutorial: Setting Frame Attributes and Content.)
11. Can you use both column and row spans in the same table? (See Tutorial: Expanding the Navigation Page's Table.)
12. Is it necessary to use the target attribute when making links in a site that uses frames? Why? (See Tutorial: Linking Pages in Your Site's Frames.)
13. When should you use a blank or top value for the target attribute for a page link? (See Tutorial: Linking Pages in Your Site's Frames.)
14. How do you reference an anchor location when making a link from another page? (See Tutorial: Linking to a Page Location.)

» Other Projects

Open the W3C XHTML Validator. Validate your frameset page. How does the evaluation differ from previous validation tests?

Add other anchor tags to pages and links to the navigation table. For example, add anchors to the Fine Print page and link the sections, such as Vaccinations, to separate links. Make copies of the files to use for experimentation.

ABOUT US
SLIDESHOW
VIDEO
CONTACT US
BOOKING
AIRLINES
STORE
FINE PRINT
View Without
Frames

Hot Beaches - Hot Times

We started Sizzle Resorts to meet our own
needs, and those of other like-minded young
vacationers.

Adding More Navigation Options to the Site

With that philosophy in mind, the first Sizzle opened on an experimental basis.

There are now 3 Sizzle locations in the Caribbean, with more in the planning stage.

The experiment is a success. Join us.

Session Introduction

A navigation menu shouldn't be the only means that a reader can use to get around your site. If a reader is scrolling through a page and decides he wants more information on a specific topic or wants to view an associated page, integrated links should be on the pages as well. It is simpler for a reader to click a link on a page to access the additional information than it is to look through the list on the navigation table and click an option to load a frame.

Your site has a frameset that displays a navigation frame with multiple links to other pages in your site, but you do not have any links between the pages. You add more links connecting your site's pages in this session.

You learn how to build a site map, which is a links page outside the frameset that your reader can use to move through your site's contents.

Links aren't restricted to pages within your own site. In this session, you add links to external sites. You also learn how to use images as navigational links.

TOOLS YOU'LL USE
Notepad, Internet Explorer

CD-ROM FILES NEEDED (Storage Folder)
sitemap.txt, main.html

FILES CREATED
sitemap.html

FILES MODIFIED
booking.html, fine_print.html, main.html,
nav_left.html, sizzle_east.html, sizzle_south.html,
sizzle_west.html

TIME REQUIRED
90 minutes

Discussion

Planning Your Site's Navigation

The best way to assure that your visitors experience what your site has to offer is to provide different ways to navigate through the pages. So far, you have added a navigation frame in your site, which is a popular way of providing navigation using text or image links. The navigation frame lists the major elements of your site, accessible by clicking a text link.

Links are also used extensively within a site's pages. As visitors read about your site, adding links that provide more information on specific topics is a good way to assist them in reading all that you have to offer with a minimum of effort on their part.

Another common navigation element is a site map. The site map is fundamentally a site outline, showing the structure and how the content branches from level to level. Your Sizzle site is simple in that it has only two levels or branches; sites can have many levels—at times it seems an infinite number of levels! Site maps

may have basic information about the pages, or they may be presented merely as a list of text links.

Sites can use menus that are controlled by JavaScript to open submenus and windows or frames. Other navigation aids include buttons and menus. In Session 13, you add buttons to the slideshow pages in your site that are controlled by JavaScript to open subsequent slides or to close the slideshow. Another navigation option is an image map, a specially-coded image that provides some of the same functionality as JavaScript without scripting. The figure shows a set of navigation buttons.

The buttons can be used individually with JavaScript for navigation; they can also be incorporated into a single image and used with mapping tags. To the user, they work in the same fashion. You create an image map for your site in the next session.

Tutorial
» Adding Links from the Main Page

When your site is loaded into Internet Explorer, it displays the `main.html` page in the main frame of the page, giving your readers an overview of the Sizzle resorts. Your readers may want to visit the individual resorts directly from the introductory page. In this tutorial, you add a table and text links to the `main.html` page so readers can do this.

1. **Open Notepad, and then open main.html.**

2. **Go to line 40, and press Enter to add a blank line.**
   You add the new code starting at line 40.

<CAUTION>

The tutorial steps reference line numbers. Your line numbering may differ slightly from that shown in the tutorial figures or listed in the steps. Use the line numbers as references to different areas of a page, but read the content of the line carefully as you follow the steps to ensure you are modifying or adding code to the correct line.

3. **In line 40, type:** `<br />`.
   A line break is added after the table on the page to provide visual separation between the tables.

4. **Starting in line 41 and continuing to line 48, type:**
   ```
   <table class="booking" width="85%" border="0"
   cellpadding="12">
   <tr>
   <td>Read about our Resorts:</td>
   <td>SIZZLE EAST</td>
   <td>SIZZLE WEST</td>
   <td>SIZZLE SOUTH</td>
   </tr>
   </table>
   ```
   A single-row, four-column table is added to the page. The table uses the same style class that you designed for the tables on the `booking.html` page, which displays a medium green border across the top of the table. The other attributes are the same as the first table on the `main.html` page.

5. **Save the file and preview the page in Internet Explorer.**
   Note the style applied to the table and how the color border is separated from the larger table. Minimize the browser.

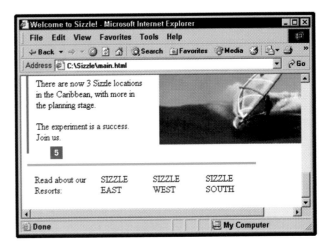

```
42    <tr>
43      <td>Read about our Resorts:</td>
44      <td><a href="sizzle_east.html" target="main">SIZZLE EAST</a></td>
45      <td><a href="sizzle_west.html" target="main">SIZZLE WEST</a></td>
46      <td><a href="sizzle_south.html" target="main">SIZZLE SOUTH</a></td>
47    </tr>
```

6. Modify the text in lines 44 to 46 to read:
```
<td><a href="sizzle_east.html"
target="main">SIZZLE EAST</a></td>
<td><a href="sizzle_west.html"
target="main">SIZZLE WEST</a></td>
<td><a href="sizzle_south.html"
target="main">SIZZLE SOUTH</a></td>
```

A link is added to each resort's name. Each link targets the main frame on the site's frameset.

7. Choose File→Save and save the file.

8. Open Internet Explorer, and then open index.html.
The frameset for your site loads.

9. At the bottom of the main frame, click one of the new links added in this tutorial.
The resort page loads.

10. Click About Us in the navigation frame to return to the main.html page.
Scroll down the page, and test another link.

<NOTE>
When you move the cursor over a link, the cursor turns to a hand with a pointing finger and the address for the page is shown in the status bar at the bottom of the Internet Explorer window.

11. Test the three links.
If the links are not working as described in the tutorial, check the code you added in Step 6 for errors. Close your browser. You added a small table and applied a table style. You added and tested internal links to the resorts' pages.

Tutorial
» Constructing Inter-Page Links

When you originally constructed the three resort pages, you added text and a horizontal rule at the bottom of the page. In this tutorial, you create the links for the three pages using this text. After an intial check of the first page's links, rather than testing pages one-by-one, you use a method closer to a real workflow where you attach the links to the pages and then test them.

1. **Open Notepad, and then open** `sizzle_east.html`.
   You add the links to the first resort page.

2. **Go to line 36, and expand the text to read:** `<p>`Watch our Sizzle`<a href="ss1.html" target="blank">` slideshow `</a></p>`
   You add a link to the word *slideshow*. When the reader clicks the word, the first slideshow page opens in a blank window, outside your main frameset.

3. **Go to line 38. After the first sentence, type:** `<a href= "booking.html" target="main">`Book HERE`</a>`
   You add a link to the phrase *Book HERE*. When the reader clicks the phrase, the booking page opens in the main frame window.

4. **Choose File→Save and save the file.**

5. **Open Internet Explorer, and then open the** `sizzle_east.html` **page.**

6. **Click the slideshow link at the bottom of the page.**
   The `ss1.html` page opens in a new window. Close the new window.

7. **Click the booking link at the bottom of the page.**
   The `booking.html` page opens in a new window. Close the new window. If either the slideshow or booking links are not working, check the code you added in Steps 2 and 3.

8. **Close Internet Explorer.**
   You tested the links on the page.

9. **In Notepad, copy lines 36 to 38 on the** `sizzle_east.html` **page, which includes the tags for both the slideshow and booking pages' links.**
   You paste the links to the other resort pages.

10. **Choose File→Open, and select the** `sizzle_west.html` **page.**
    When prompted to save the `sizzle_east.html` page, click Yes.

11. **Select the text in lines 35 to 37 on the** `sizzle_west.html` **page.**
    The lines contain the paragraph text as well as the horizontal rule tag.

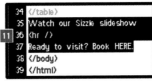

< N O T E >
In the `sizzle_east.html` page, you specified that the `booking.html` page should open in the main frame of the frameset. However, because the `sizzle_east.html` page isn't displayed in Internet Explorer through your frameset, the `booking.html` page isn't controlled by the frameset either, so it opens in a blank window as well. Later in the tutorial, you test the links through the frameset.

12. **Paste the copied text into the lines.**
    The content of the lines is replaced, and the tags are added to the page.

13. **Repeat Steps 9 through 11 using the `sizzle_south.html` page.**

14. **Save the `sizzle_south.html` page.**

15. **Open Internet Explorer, and then open `index.html`.**
    The frameset for your site opens, and the initial pages load into the frames.

16. **Scroll down the `main.html` page displayed in the main frame.**

17. **At the bottom of the page, click the link to Sizzle East.**
    The page loads in the main frame.

18. **Using the scrollbars, scroll down the page to the links at the bottom of the `sizzle_east.html` page.**
    You test the links from the frame.

19. **Click the slideshow link.**
    The `ss1.html` page opens in a blank window. Close the window.

20. **At the bottom of the page, click the Book HERE link.**
    The `booking.html` page opens in the main frame of the frameset.

<TIP>
The links should work as described if you copied and pasted the content. If not, check the code in lines 36 to 38.

21. **Click Internet Explorer's Back button twice to return to the `main.html` page.**
    The page's titles display in a text box under the Back button when you move your mouse over the buttons.

<NOTE>
A well-designed site does not rely on the use of a browser's navigation buttons, such as the Back button. Later in the course, you create an image map for the site that links to the three resort pages.

22. **Test the two other resort pages' links.**
    The slideshow opens in its own window; the booking information opens in the main frame of the frameset.

23. **Close Internet Explorer.**
    You added two internal links to each of the three resort pages.

Tutorial

» Building a Site Map

One way to help users understand where they can go on your site is to provide a visual structure of its contents. Site maps are one of the oldest types of Web site usability devices. Site maps are commonly used with large, extensive sites. Although the Sizzle site isn't complex, a site map is still a useful element. In this tutorial, you create the site map's page and add text copied from a supplied text file. You add anchor tags to two other site pages to use as site map links.

1. **In Notepad, open the** `sitemap.txt` **file.**
   The file is located in the Storage folder of your Sizzle site folder.

2. **Select the text, and copy it.**
   You use the text for the site map page.

< N O T E >

Blank lines are added to the text file to separate groups of paragraphs. Blank lines make the sections of the page easier to identify.

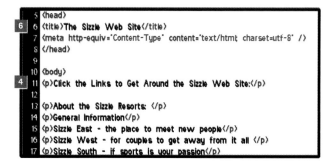

3. **Choose File→Open, and select the** `basic.html` **file.**
   The file is also located in the Storage folder of your Sizzle site folder.

4. **Go to line 11, and select the placeholder body text, "Add the page content here." Press Delete.**
   You replace the text with the `sitemap.txt` file's content.

5. **Choose Edit→Paste.**
   The text copied from the `sitemap.txt` file is pasted to the page. Make sure that the closing <body> tag follows the pasted text.

6. **Go to line 6, and change the default <title> tag text.**
   Type: `The Sizzle Web Site`
   The page now has a title.

7. **Save the file as** `sitemap.html` **in your Sizzle site folder.**
   You created another page for your site.

8. **Open the** `fine_print.html` **page located in your Sizzle site folder.**
   You add two anchors to the page.

< N O T E >

Notice that lines of text are used for links that are not yet identified. Later in this tutorial, you add the anchors to your site's page.

< N O T E >

If you read through the text for links in the `sitemap.html` page, you find three references to content on the `fine_print.html` page. The first reference, to insurance, starts at the top of the page and doesn't need a named anchor.

9 41
10 42 `<a name="vaccinations" id="vaccinations"></a>`
43 `<p>Vaccinations</p>`
44
45 `<p><img src="Images/shell3.jpg" class="shells" alt="seashell image" />`

11 50
51 `<a name="visas" id="visas"></a>` **12**
52 `<p>Visas</p>`
53
54 `<p>Visas or tourist cards are required. The cards are available at the airports`

9. **Go to line 41, and press Enter to add another blank line.**
   The paragraph title for the page's vaccination information starts on a blank line; adding another line simply maintains the visual separation on the page.

10. **In line 42, type:** `<a name="vaccinations" id="vaccinations"></a>`
    You add a named anchor at the start location for the information on vaccinations, used as a link from the `sitemap.html` page.

11. **Go to line 50, and press Enter to add another blank line.**
    The title for the page's visa information starts on a blank line; adding another line simply maintains the visual separation on the Notepad page.

12. **In line 51, type:** `<a name="visas" id="visas"></a>`
    You add another named anchor at the start location for the visa information, used as a link from the `sitemap.html` page.

13. **Save the** `fine_print.html` **page.**
    You added two named anchors to the page. The anchors are referenced in the `sitemap.html` page that you created in this tutorial.

Tutorial
» Attaching Links from the Site Map

In the previous tutorial, you created the site map page and added anchor tags to other pages in your site. Now, all the links are available. In this tutorial, you create the set of links from the `sitemap.html` page. For many of the items, links are made from the important text in a sentence or phrase; add the tags carefully. All the tags include a target attribute as well. If you add the link without defining a target, the linked page loads into the `sitemap.html` page. The text in the site map is broken into two sections; the steps in the tutorial are broken into two segments as well.

1. **In Notepad, open the** `sitemap.html` **file.**
   The file is located in your Sizzle site folder.

2. **Go to line 14.**
   Lines 14 through 24 contain link text for the first segment of the site map—information about the resorts.

3. **Modify the content of the first segment of text according to the listing in Table 8-1.**
   Each line of text requires opening and closing <a> tags, as well as attributes.

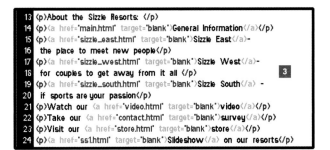

<NOTE>
The line numbers, original content, and amended content of each line are listed in the table. The text for the three resorts' pages are wrapped over two lines for increased visibility.

Table 8-1: Link Tags for the First Segment of the Site Map Page

Line	Original Text	Modify to Read...
14	<p>General Information</p>	<p><a href="main.html" target="blank">General Information</a></p>
15-16	<p>Sizzle East - the place to meet new people</p>	<p><a href="sizzle_east.html" target="blank">Sizzle East</a>- the place to meet new people</p>
17-18	<p>Sizzle West - for couples to get away from it all </p>	<p><a href="sizzle_west.html" target="blank">Sizzle West</a>- for couples to get away from it all </p>
19-20	<p>Sizzle South - if sports are your passion</p>	<p><a href="sizzle_south.html" target="blank">Sizzle South</a> - if sports are your passion</p>
21	<p>Watch our video </p>	<p>Watch our <a href="video.html" target="blank">video</a></p>
22	<p>Take our survey</p>	<p>Take our <a href="contact.html" target="blank">survey</a></p>
23	<p>Visit our store </p>	<p>Visit our <a href="store.html" target="blank">store</a></p>
24	<p>Slideshow on our resorts </p>	<p><a href="ss1.html" target="blank">Slideshow</a> on our resorts</p>

```
26 <p>Arranging a Visit:</p>
27 <p><a href="booking.html" target="blank">Booking information</a></p>
28 <p><a href="booking.html#airlines" target="blank">Airlines </a></p>     5
29 <p><a href="fine_print.html" target="blank">Insurance </a></p>
30 <p><a href="fine_print.html#vaccinations" target="blank">Vaccinations </a></p>
31 <p><a href="fine_print.html#visas" target="blank">Visas </a></p>
```

4. **Go to line 26.**
   Lines 26 through 32 contain link text for the second segment of the site map, which links to information about trip arrangements.

5. **Modify the content of the second segment of text according to the listing in Table 8-2.**
   Each line of text requires opening and closing <a> tags, as well as hypertext reference and target attributes.

6. **In Notepad, save the `sitemap.html` page.**
   You added links from the site map to pages and named page locations in your site's pages. Leave Notepad open for the next tutorial.

7. **Open Internet Explorer.**
   Open the `sitemap.html` page.

8. **Test the links.**
   Click the links in sequence. The first link clicked opens a new browser window; all subsequent links open in the same window.

<TIP>
Make sure to test all the links. Check that the correct page loads and that each page loads into the second browser window. Check the named anchor links open at the correct page locations. If you find any links that don't work, or don't work correctly, check the code added in Steps 3 and 5.

9. **Close your browser windows.**
   You have two open browser windows.

Table 8-2: Link Tags for the Second Segment of the Site Map Page

Line	Original Text	Modify to Read:
27	<p>Booking information </p>	<p><a href="booking.html" target="blank">Booking information</a></p>
28	<p>Airlines </p>	<p><a href="booking.html#airlines" target="blank">Airlines </a></p>
29	<p>Insurance </p>	<p><a href="fine_print.html" target="blank">Insurance </a></p>
30	<p>Vaccinations </p>	<p><a href="fine_print.html#vaccinations" target="blank">Vaccinations </a></p>
31	<p>Visas </p>	<p><a href="fine_print.html#visas" target="blank">Visas </a></p>

Tutorial
» Accessing the Site Map from the Site's Frameset

You have created a site map and established links between the site map and your site's pages. You need a way to access the site map from your frameset. In this tutorial, you add another link to the navigation page's table.

1. **In Notepad, open the** `nav_left.html` **page.**
   You add a link to the site map from the navigation frame.

2. **Go to line 14, and change the rowspan attribute's value from 9 to 10.**
   You add one more row to the table and extend the first column the full height of the table.

3. **Go to line 42, and press Enter to add a blank line.**
   You add code for an additional table row.

4. **In lines 42 through 44, type:**
   ```
   <tr>
   <td> <a href="sitemap.html" target="blank">
   Site Map</a></td>
   </tr>
   ```
   A row is added to the table. The text *Site Map* is linked to the `sitemap.html` page.

5. **Save the** `nav_left.html` **page. Leave Notepad open for the next tutorial.**
   You created a link from your site's frameset to the site map page.

6. **Open Internet Explorer, and then open the** `index.html` **page.**
   Your site's frameset loads.

7. **Click the Site Map link at the bottom of the navigation table.**
   The Site Map page opens in a blank window. Close the browser.

The Difference between a Site Map and an Accessible Site

You constructed and attached a site map to your site in this session. Although the site map breaks your reader out of your frameset, it is not the same as a no-frames site. With the site map, your reader can view any page in your site, but must use two browser windows and must return to the `sitemap.html` page to select another link. In a no-frames site, the navigation controls are included on all pages and allow the reader to move throughout the site in one window. You use the `sitemap.html` page as the basis for some of the work you do in Session 14 to complete the no-frames and accessible site portions of the project.

< N O T E >
Code external links from your site to open in their own windows. That prevents the appearance of another site belonging to your site. If you don't define a target, the browser loads the linked page into your Sizzle frameset's page.

Tutorial
» Using Images as Links

The site map for your site is complete and available from your navigation frame. You have added numerous text-based links in your site. The `booking.html` page contains images of logos from a number of airlines. In this tutorial, you attach a link from one of the airline logo images to the airline's Web site. The airlines in the Sizzle site are fictitious, as are their logos and Web addresses.

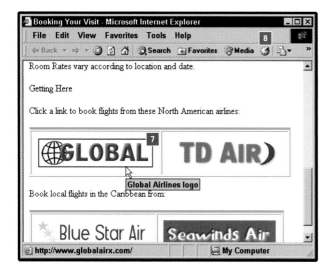

Document Paths

Up to this point, you have linked to documents in your site, using a document-relative path. The linked item is identified by its name and file type, as well as a folder name if the file resides in another folder in the site, such as your Image folder contents. To link to a document outside of your site, use an absolute path. An absolute path contains the complete URL of the linked document, including the protocol to use, which is usually `http://` for Web pages. The addresses for the airline links are absolute paths.

<NOTE>
You can test the links from the page rather than opening your site's frameset and then clicking through pages to the links. The linked Web site is not associated with the tutorial, but is used as an example.

1. **In Notepad, open** `booking.html`.
   You add the links to the page.

2. **Go to line 39.**
   Lines 39 and 40 contain the image tag for the Global Airlines' logo, placed in a table row.

3. **After the <td> tag on line 39, type:** `<a href="http://www.globalairx.com" target="blank">`
   You add the opening anchor tag and its hyperlink reference, and you assign a blank window as the target frame. You must include the entire, or absolute, path to link the image to a Web site.

4. **Go to the end of the airline's tag. Before the closing </td> tag, now on line 41, type:** `</a>`
   The anchor tag is closed.

5. **Save the** `booking.html` **page.**
   You added the first image link.

6. **Open Internet Explorer, and then open the** `booking.html` **page.**

7. **Click the Global Airlines logo.**
   A colored border displays around the logo image. The link opens another browser window, displaying a message the Web page cannot be found—don't worry, the Web address is not linked to an actual Web site.

<TIP>
As you move the mouse cursor over the image, the cursor turns to a pointing hand, the alternate text is displayed, and the link displays in the status bar at the bottom of the browser window.

8. **Minimize the browser.**

<NOTE>
You have seen blue underlined text when you add a text link, which turns to maroon when you click the link. These are the browser's default link colors. Another browser default is to add a border around your image links.

9. **In Notepad, type** `border="0"` **at the end of the image tag on line 39.**

   Make sure that the attribute is added before the closing bracket of the <image> tag.

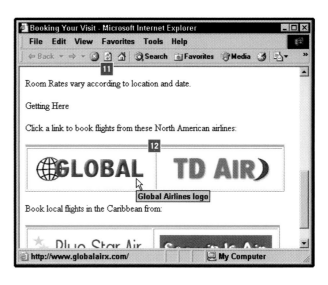

10. **Save the** `booking.html` **file.**

    You added another attribute to the <image> tag.

11. **Reopen your browser, and click Refresh to reload the page.**

    The new version of the page is loaded into the browser.

12. **Click the logo image to test it again.**

    The airline's Web site opens in a new window; the image is now borderless.

13. **Close the browser.**

    Close both browser windows. You added and tested an image link, and modified the <image> tag to remove the default border. Leave the copies of Notepad open to continue with the next tutorial.

Saving Time Loading Your Site

Rather than using the File→Open process to load your frameset whenever you open Internet Explorer, set the page as a favorite. Open the browser, load the `index.html` page, and then choose Favorites→Add to Favorites. The dialog box shown here opens, displaying your frameset page's title.

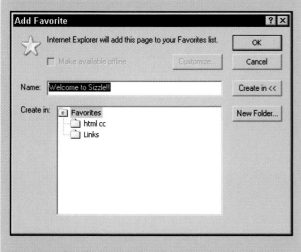

When you click OK, the page is added to your Favorites. Now you can select it from the Favorites list.

Computer Addresses

A set of protocols, or rules, called TCP/IP (Transmission Control Protocol/Internet Protocol) define how messages are transmitted from one computer to another. *TCP* refers to the process of moving data from computer to computer; *IP* refers to pieces of information, divided into small segments called packets.

Every computer has a unique IP address. Look at the bottom left of the browser window when you are online. You often see a string of numbers, like the image here shows, that display before the page is loaded. This is the page's IP address.

> 20.40.60.80

Every Web site that you visit has an address in this format, although generally it is simpler to remember an alias for an IP address (such as google.com) rather than the string of numbers.

Tutorial
» Linking the Airline Logos

In the previous tutorial, you added link information to create an image link from the fictitious Global Airlines logo to its Web site. In this tutorial, you create links from the other images on the `booking.html` page to the respective airlines' Web sites.

```
2  42  <td> <a href="http://www.tdairx.com" target="blank">
   43  <img src="Images/air_td.gif" width="200" height="45"
   44  alt="TD International Airlines logo" border="0"/></a></td>
   45  </tr>                               3        4
```

```
   50  <tr>
   51  <td><a href="http://www.bluestarairx.com" target="blank">
7  52  <img src="Images/air_bluestar.gif" width="200" height="45"
   53  alt="BlueStar Airways logo" border="0"/></a></td>
   54  <td><a href="http://www.seawindsairx.com" target="blank">
9  55  <img src="Images/air_seawinds.gif" width="200" height="45"
   56  alt="Seawinds Airline logo" border="0"/></a></td>
   57  </tr>
```

<TIP>
Make sure that the border attribute is within the closing /> of the image tag.

<NOTE>
The tags for each image are arranged over two lines in the session's `booking.html` page.

1. **Go to line 42 on the** `booking.html` **page.**
   Find the table cell containing the image for the TD Air logo.

2. **After the opening <td> tag, type:** `<a href="http://www.tdairx.com" target="blank" >`
   You add the opening anchor tag and its hyperlink reference, and you assign a blank window as the target frame.

3. **Go to the end of the image's tag. After the** `alt` **attribute, type:** `border="0"` **to set the image's border to invisible.**

4. **Go to the end of the airline's tag. Before the closing </td> tag, now on line 44, type:** `</a>` **to close the anchor tag.**

5. **Save the** `booking.html` **file.**
   You added another image link.

6. **Go to line 51.**
   The line contains the opening tags for the BlueStar Air image.

7. **Repeat Steps 2 through 4. Use the URL:** `http://www.bluestarairx.com`
   You add a link and target frame, and you remove the link border.

8. **Go to line 54.**
   The line contains the opening tags for the Seawinds Air image.

9. **Repeat Steps 2 through 4. Use the URL:** `http://www.seawindsairx.com"`
   You add a link and target frame, and you remove the link border.

10. **Test the links in your browser, and then minimize the browser.**

11. **Save the file, and close Notepad.**
    You added image links to the airline logo images on the `booking.html` page.

12. **Open your browser, and then open the** `index.html` **page.**

13. **Click Airlines in the navigation frame.**
    The `booking.html` page loads in the main frame at the Airlines anchor's location.

14. **Test the remaining links.**
    Each Web site loads into the same browser window.

15. **Close the browser.**
    You added links to the logo images on the `booking.html` page; you tested the links from the page and also from within your site's frameset.

» Session Review

In this session, you added numerous links to your site. You added internal links on the pages that allow the reader to browse through your site's pages and get more information on topics of interest without using the navigation menu. The opening image in this session shows the bottom of the main page of your site; the final image in this session shows the same page with the new internal links attached.

You learned how to create a site map and linked it to pages in your site. You also linked images to pages in this session using absolute links for the first time. The links were attached to airline logos, and they open the airlines' Web sites when clicked. You set the links to open in their own window separate from your site.

Here are some questions to help you review the information in this session. The answer to each question is located in the tutorial noted in parentheses.

1. Should you use more than one method of navigation in your site? Why or why not? (See Discussion: Planning Your Site's Navigation.)

2. Why is it useful to provide a site map? (See Discussion: Planning Your Site's Navigation.)

3. Where can you see the address for a linked item in a browser window? (See Tutorial: Adding Links from the Main Page.)

4. Can you view a page outside of a site's frameset? How? When would you do this? (See Tutorial: Constructing Inter-Page Links.)

5. Should you rely on a browser's BACK button to control navigation in your site? (See Tutorial: Constructing Inter-Page Links.)

6. What does a site map do? Why can it be valuable to the reader? (See Tutorial: Building a Site Map.)

7. If you link to information on a page, is it necessary to add an anchor if the location is the top of the page? (See Tutorial: Building a Site Map.)

8. When is it necessary to include a target attribute when you are using an anchor tag? (See Tutorial: Attaching Links from the Site Map.)

9. How do you write a named anchor when writing a `href` attribute? (See Tutorial: Attaching Links from the Site Map.)

10. Do you have to modify a table's rowspan attribute when adding lines to a table? (See Tutorial: Accessing the Site Map from the Site's Frameset.)

11. Does Internet Explorer use default styles for links? (See Tutorial: Using Images as Links.)

12. How can you remove the default border from an image link? (See Tutorial: Using Images as Links.)

13. What is an absolute path? When do you use it? (See Tutorial: Using Images as Links.)

14. What items are displayed in your browser when you move the mouse over a linked image? (See Tutorial: Linking the Airline Logos.)

» Other Projects

Use the W3C Validator to test the `booking.html` page; use the Validator to test the `sitemap.html` page.

Embellish the content on the `sitemap.html` page using the styles that you created in earlier sessions. Here are some suggestions: Use the seashell images, and place them in the text using styles; add a table to the page, and format the table using styles. Don't amend the background, because you create a style for the page's background in the next session.

With that philosophy in mind, the first Sizzle opened on an experimental basis.

There are now 3 Sizzle locations in the Caribbean, with more in the planning stage.

The experiment is a success. Join us.

Read about our Resorts:

 SIZZLE EAST

 SIZZLE WEST

 SIZZLE SOUTH

Part VI
Visually Enhancing
Your Site

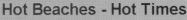

Hot Beaches - Hot Times

We started Sizzle Resorts to meet our own needs, and those of other like-minded young vacationers.

Using Styles for Text and Positioning

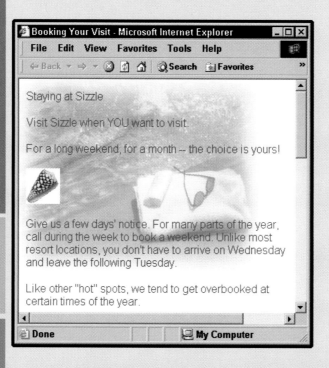

Session Introduction

You built a number of styles for your Sizzle site, most of which are used for tables on different pages. You created one style for a page background and used a style to set the size of the small seashell images used on your site. You have seen how styles are configured and applied to different page elements.

In this session, you work with the site's text, as well as some page background styles. You continue building styles for your Web site. You build some text styles for headings and paragraphs, and you create a list style.

Although all the pages in your site require styles, the four pages you work with in this tutorial use a variety of heading styles and also some custom paragraph and list styles. You add new styles to your style sheet file and then apply the style to the pages.

You also work with different positioning properties in this session. In Session 6, you aligned the small seashell images with the text using a positioning style. In this session, you use positioning for background images and text. You position the image added to the `booking.html` page's background using the custom `.bookingbkgd` style. You also position another image on a page background using the layer stacking order, or z-index property.

TOOLS YOU'LL USE
Notepad, Internet Explorer

CD-ROM FILES NEEDED (Image Sources Folder)
`palm_bkgd.jpg`

FILES MODIFIED
`booking.html`, `fine_print.html`, `sitemap.html`, `sizzle.css`

TIME REQUIRED
90 minutes

Tutorial

» Writing Heading and Text Styles

On your site's pages, you have seen how text and links are configured by default. You see black text in varying sizes for different heading tags, as well as plain black Times text for the bulk of the pages' text. The default styles coexist with the custom styles that you create for your site. In this tutorial, you create several styles for the site's heading tags. You start with a style that sets several properties for all the tags, and then you write additional custom styles for some tags.

< N O T E >

The tutorial steps reference line numbers. Your line numbering may differ slightly from that shown in the tutorial figures or listed in the steps. Use the line numbers as references to different areas of a page, but read the content of the line carefully as you follow the steps to ensure you are modifying or adding code to the correct line.

< N O T E >

You can assign a color to text, and not assign a color to the background. However, if you test the CSS page in the W3C CSS Validator, you receive a warning. It is a good practice to consider potential areas of conflict in your styles; foreground and background color is one of them.

< N O T E >

If you validate the page using CSS2, you can combine the h2 selector with the selectors listed in Step 4, the file is valid, and the text appears correctly when viewed in a browser. However, if you validate the page using CSS3, a warning states that two colors are defined for the same selector.

< N O T E >

No further customizations are required for the <h3> tag. The tag uses the browser's default size, and the font and color were set in the general heading tag that you wrote in Step 4.

1. **Open Notepad. Open** `sizzle.css`.

2. **Go to the last line of the page, and press Enter twice.**
   The last style written on the page is the `div.center` style created for the <div> tag added to the buttons on the slideshow page.

3. **On line 74, type:** `/* headings */`
   You add several text styles; add a comment to define the group of styles that follows.

4. **Press Enter to add one more blank line. On lines 76 to 80, type:**
   ```
   h1,h3,h4 {
   color: #333366;
   background-color: transparent;
   font-family: Arial, sans-serif;
   }
   ```
   You add a basic style for three headings on the site. The text is one of the custom colors, and it uses Arial font. The background color with a transparent value fulfills the CSS requirement for a text selector.

5. **Press Enter to add a blank line. On lines 82 to 88, type:**
   ```
   h2 {
   color: #FF0033;
   background-color: transparent;
   font-family: Arial, sans-serif;
   font-style: italic;
   letter-spacing: 1px;
   }
   ```
   You add a style for the second-largest heading selector. The color is your site's custom red color. The letter-spacing property sets the letters further apart from one another on the line.

6. **Press Enter to add a blank line. On lines 90 to 92, type:**
   ```
   h4 {
   font-variant: small-caps;
   }
   ```
   You add a custom style for the level-4 heading selector. The text assigned to this selector uses a small cap style, rather than uppercase and lowercase letters.

7. **Press Enter to add another blank line. On line 94, type:**

   ```
   /* paragraph and list tags*/
   ```

   You add the first of the paragraph tags.

8. **On lines 96 to 100, type:**

   ```
   p {
   color: #003366;
   font-family: Arial, sans-serif;
   background-color: transparent;
   }
   ```

   You add a generic style for the paragraph tags.

9. **Choose File→Save.**

   You added four additional styles to your style sheet.

< T I P >

You add the list tags to two of your site's pages and create list styles later in the session.

< N O T E >

You can add the paragraph selector to the earlier list of selectors (the headings). To make it simpler for you to understand how the styles are created, the paragraph styles are separated from the headings and the general paragraph style is written in full.

Style Properties

You created a generic style for the headings, and then added other properties and values specific to a heading selector. Default style properties for paragraphs, headings, lists, and so on are taken from their default parent, the body selector. If you change a parent property, such as color, all content that is a child element to the body element (which is basically everything on a Web page) is given that color.

Changes are specific to the style selector that you modify. For example, changing a font-family does not change a font's color.

The styles created in the first tutorial maintain default style characteristics unless they are assigned properties and values. Otherwise, style characteristics such as size retain the default style, as you can see in the image.

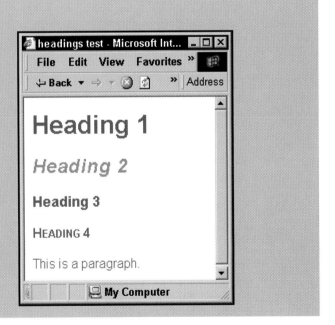

Tutorial
» Applying Heading Styles

You created several styles for the headings and paragraphs in your site. In this tutorial, you apply the styles to two of your site's pages. If you recall from early sessions, you built some pages using <p> tags to visually separate content. Some of those <p> tags are changed to heading tags in this tutorial.

```
11  <body class="bookingbkgd">
12  <h1> Staying at Sizzle</h1>  2
13
14  <p> Visit Sizzle when YOU want to visit. <br />    3
15  For a long weekend, for a month -- the choice is yours!</p>
```

1. **Choose File→Open, browse to your Sizzle site folder, select** `booking.html`, **and click Open.**
   The file opens in Notepad.

2. **Go to line 12. On line 12, replace the <p> tags. Type** <h1> **before the welcome message and** </h1> **after the message.**
   You add the main heading for the page.

3. **Combine the two paragraphs on lines 14 and 15, and then break the line. Type:** <p> Visit Sizzle when YOU want to visit.
 For a long weekend, for a month — the choice is yours!</p>
   The two paragraphs are combined using the <br /> tag.

< N O T E >
Later in this session, you apply a custom paragraph style.

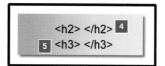

4. **Go to line 37, and revise the tags to read:** <h2>Getting Here</h2>
   You change the content to a heading tag from a paragraph tag.

5. **Go to line 38, and replace the <p> tags with <h3> </h3> tags; the line reads:** <h3>Click a link to book flights from these North American airlines:</h3>
   The text is changed from a paragraph to a heading.

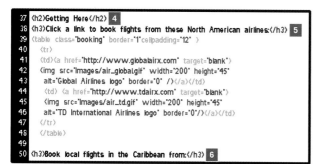

```
37  <h2>Getting Here</h2>  4
38  <h3>Click a link to book flights from these North American airlines:</h3>  5
39  <table class="booking" border="1" cellpadding="12"  >
40    <tr>
41    <td><a href="http://www.globalairx.com" target="blank">
42    <img src="Images/air_global.gif" width="200" height="45"
43    alt="Global Airlines logo" border="0" /></a></td>
44    <td> <a href="http://www.tdairx.com" target="blank">
45    <img src="Images/air_td.gif" width="200" height="45"
46    alt="TD International Airlines logo" border="0"/></a></td>
47    </tr>
48    </table>
49
50  <h3>Book local flights in the Caribbean from:</h3>  6
```

6. **Go to line 50, and change the <p> tags to <h3> </h3> tags; the line reads:** <h3>Book local flights in the Caribbean from:</h3>
   You added the final heading tags for the page.

7. **In Notepad, choose File→Save.**
   The `booking.html` page is saved with its altered heading tags.

8. **Open Internet Explorer, and then open** `booking.html`.
   The page opens in your browser.

9. **Scroll down the page.**

   Note the headings on the page and the general paragraph text on the page. Minimize the browser.

10. **Choose File→Open, select** `fine_print.html`, **and click Open.**

    The file opens in Notepad.

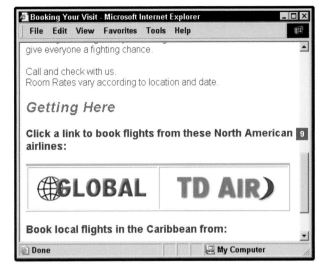

11. **Go to line 13, and change the <p> tags to create the first heading on the page. Type:** `<h2>Travel Insurance</h2>`

    You add the first heading for the page.

12. **Go to line 43, and repeat Step 12.**

    You create a heading titled "Vaccinations".

13. **Go to line 52, and repeat Step 12.**

    You create another heading, titled "Visas".

14. **In Notepad, choose File→Save.**

    The `fine_print.html` page is saved with its new heading tags. You converted paragraph tags to heading tags in two of your site's pages, their appearance defined by the styles that you created in an earlier tutorial. Leave Notepad open for the next tutorial.

15. **Preview the page in Internet Explorer.**

    Note the red headings, defined by the styles that you created for the h2 selector. Minimize the browser.

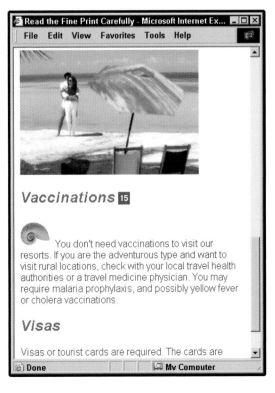

Tutorial
» Finishing the Heading Styles

In the previous tutorial, you applied heading styles to two of your site's pages. In this tutorial, you add styles to two more pages. You also see how much simpler it is to use a style on a page instead of typing attributes.

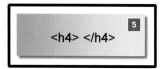

1. **In Notepad, choose File→Open, browse to your Sizzle site folder, select** main.html, **and click Open.**
   The file opens in Notepad.

2. **Go to line 12. Lines 12 and 13 read:**
   ```
   <h1><font color="#003366" face="Arial,
   Helvetica, sans-serif"><strong>
    Hot Beaches - Hot Times
   </strong></font></h1>
   ```
   You added inline attributes for the text when you originally constructed the page.

3. **Delete the attribute tags attached to the text, leaving the welcome message and the <h1> tags. Line 12 now reads:** `<h1> Hot Beaches - Hot Times </h1>`
   You delete the written attributes.

4. **Go to line 42, the code for the first cell in the navigation table at the bottom of the page.**
   You add a heading style.

5. **Add <h4> tags to the line within the <td> tags. The line reads:** `<td><h4> Read about our Resorts: </h4></td>`
   You added a heading style.

6. **In Notepad, choose File→Save.**
   Save the main.html page. You replaced in-line text attributes with a heading style and applied another heading.

7. **Open Internet Explorer, and then open** main.html.
   You see that the main heading on the page now has the style applied. Scroll down the page to the table at the bottom to see the heading applied to the table text. Minimize the browser.

8. **Choose File→Open, select** sitemap.html, **and click Open.**
   The file opens in Notepad.

9. **Go to line 8, and press Enter.**
   You add a blank line.

10. **On line 8, type:** `<link href="sizzle.css"`
    `rel="stylesheet" type="text/css" />`
    You attach the style sheet to the page.

11. **Go to line 12.**
    Lines 12 and 14 contain the text for the two levels of head-ings for the page. Both lines currently use <p> tags.

12. **Replace the <p> tags with <h3> and <h4> tags. The lines read:**
    `<h3>Click the Links to Get Around the Sizzle`
    `Web Site:</h3>`
    `<h4>About the Sizzle Resorts: </h4>`
    You add heading tags to the page.

13. **Go to line 28, which reads:** `<p>Arranging a Visit:</p>`
    You change the tags.

14. **Replace the <p> tags with <h4> tags. The line reads:**
    `<h4>Arranging a Visit:</h4>`
    You replaced the paragraph tags with heading tags.

15. **Choose File➡Save.**
    Save the `sitemap.html` page. You added heading styles to two more pages of your site.

16. **Preview the page in Internet Explorer.**
    Note the two levels of headings at the top of the page. You see that the <p> style is applied to the text on the page. Scroll down the page to see the third heading. Close the browser.

```
 7  <meta http-equiv="Content-Type" content="text/html; charset=utf-8" />
 8  <link href="sizzle.css" rel="stylesheet" type="text/css" /> 10
 9  </head>
10
11  <body>
12  <h3>Click the Links to Get Around the Sizzle Web Site:</h3> 12
13
14  <h4>About the Sizzle Resorts: </h4>
```

```
28  <h4>Arranging a Visit:</h4> 14
29  <p><a href="booking.html" target="blank">Booking information</a></p>
30  <p><a href="booking.html#airlines" target="blank">Airlines </a></p>
```

The Sizzle Web Site - Microsoft Internet Explorer

File   Edit   View   Favorites   Tools   Help

Click the Links to Get Around the Sizzle Web Site:

ABOUT THE SIZZLE RESORTS:

General Information

Sizzle East- the place to meet new people

Sizzle West- for couples to get away from it all

Sizzle South - if sports are your passion

Watch our video

Done   My Computer

Tutorial
» Using Lists on the Web Pages

You added heading styles to several pages in your site. You also attach <p> styles to all the text identified with the <p> tags in the pages. Two pages on your site contain text that must be arranged in a list. In this tutorial, you add another style to use for the lists. Then you add the tags to the pages and apply the style.

```
101
102  ul.square {
103  list-style-type:  square;
104  color:  #003366;                        3
105  background-color:  transparent;
106  font-family:  Arial,sans-serif;
107  font-size:  10pt;
108  font-style:  oblique;
109  }
```

1. **In Notepad, choose File→Open, select the** `sizzle.css` **file, and click Open.**
The style sheet opens in Notepad.

2. **Go to the last line on the page, and press Enter to add a blank line.**
You add a new style; leave spaces to separate the styles visually on the page.

3. **On lines 102 to 109, type:**
```
ul.square {
list-style-type: square;
color: #003366;
background-color: transparent;
font-family: Arial, sans-serif;
font-size: 10pt;
font-style: oblique;
}
```
The style is a class of style used for the unordered list <ul> tags. The property type is given a square value, which means the bullet is a small square. The text properties are those used for paragraphs, but the font is smaller and oblique.

<TIP>
Other list-style-type values include disc, circle, and none. The disc and circle are two other bullet shapes; none displays no bullet. You can also use an image for a bullet.

4. **Choose File→Save, and save the** `sizzle.css` **file. Open the** `booking.html` **file.**
You add list tags and the style to the page.

```
22  <p>You have to prebook during these times: </p>  5
23  <ul> <li>last week of December</li>
24  <li>first week of January</li>
25  <li>Spring Break week </li></ul>  6
26  <p>Rooms are reserved during these times, and tend to fill up quickly. We
```

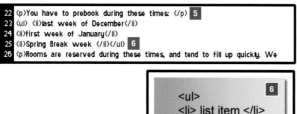

```
                                             6
        <ul>
        <li> list item </li>
        </ul>
```

5. **Go to line 22, and add a </p> tag to the line. The line now reads:**
```
<p>You have to prebook during these times:
</p>
```
You close the paragraph.

6. **Add tags to the text in lines 23 to 25. Type:**
```
<ul> <li>last week of December</li>
<li>first week of January</li>
<li>Spring Break week </li></ul>
```
The three lines create a bulleted list, called an unordered list (an ordered list is numbered or alphabetized). The <ul> tags define the content for the entire list. The <li> tags define the content for each list item, or line of the list.

7. **Choose File→Save to save the** `booking.html` **file.**

8. **Open Internet Explorer, and then open** `booking.html`.

9. **Scroll down the browser page. Note that the list is added to the page, but it uses default values.**
   The text is black Times, and the bullets are circles. Minimize the browser.

10. **In Notepad, go to line 23. Expand the opening <ul> tag, and type:**
    `<ul class="square">`
    The unordered list style, "square," is attached to the tag page.

11. **Choose File→Save to save the save the** `booking.html` **page.**

12. **Preview the page in Internet Explorer again.**
    You see that the text and bullets defined in the style are attached to the list. Minimize the browser.

13. **In Notepad, choose File→Open and open the** `fine_print.html` **file.**

14. **Add tags to the text in lines 30 to 33. Type:**
    ```
    <ul class="square"> <li>a personal medical
    emergency</li>
    <li>medical emergency involving an immediate
    family member</li>
    <li>medical emergency involving your
    travelling companion </li>
    <li>missed connections because of mechanical
    problems or weather conditions.</li></ul>
    ```
    You create a four-item list and apply the style.

15. **Choose File→Save to save the save the** `fine_print.html` **page.**

16. **Preview the page in Internet Explorer.**
    The text and bullets defined in the style are attached to the list. Close the browser. You created a style for bulleted lists and added list tags and applied the style to two pages.

Tutorial
» Creating a Special Paragraph Style

You worked with several types of styles and tags in this session. In this tutorial, you create a paragraph class style. The style is used to emphasize text on some of your site's page. The style is complex and has numerous components. Fortunately, you can write and test the style once, and then quickly apply it to other pages as required.

```
110
111 p.caption {
112 text-align: center;          2
113 color: #333366;
114 font-family: arial,sans-serif;
115 font-size: 11pt;
116 font-style: oblique;
117 line-height: 150%;
118 background-color: #E1FFFF;
119 border-color: #009966;
120 border-width: 2px;
121 border-style: groove double;
122 }
```

1. **In Notepad, open** `sizzle.css.` Go to the last line on the page, and press Enter to add a blank line to separate the styles.

2. **On lines 111 to 122, type:**
   ```
   p.caption {
   text-align: center;
   color: #333366;
   font-family: arial, sans-serif;
   font-size: 11pt;
   font-style: oblique;
   line-height: 150%;
   background-color: #E1FFFF;
   border-color: #009966;
   border-width: 2px;
   border-style: groove double;
   }
   ```

   The style is added to the style sheet. The properties and their meanings are described in Table 9-1.

3. **Choose File→Save.**
   The `sizzle.css` style sheet is saved with the new paragraph style.

4. **Choose File→Open, select** `fine_print.html`, **and click Open.**
   You add the style class to the page.

```
19
20 <p class="caption">Travel insurance costs only a few dollars -- and is worth
21                                                          5
```

5. **Go to line 20, and expand the opening <p> tag. Type:** `<p class="caption">`
   The style class is attached to the <p> tag. The line reads `<p class="caption">Travel insurance costs only a few dollars — and is worth every cent.</p>`.

6. **Open Internet Explorer, and then open** `fine_print.html` **to preview the page.**

7. **In Notepad, choose File→Save to save the fine_print.html page.**
   You added another style to the page.

8. **Scroll down the page to the stylized text. Drag the lower right sizing handle to increase and decrease the width of the page.** You see the content of the stylized paragraph resizes in the same way as the rest of the text on the page. Minimize the browser.

9. **Choose File→Open, select** booking.html, **and click Open.** You add the custom paragraph style to the page.

<NOTE>

Remember, the tutorial steps reference line numbers. Your line numbering may differ slightly from that shown in the tutorial figures or listed in the steps. Use the line numbers as references to different areas of a page, but read the content of the line carefully as you follow the steps to ensure you are modifying or adding code to the correct line.

Table 9-1: Understanding the p.caption Style

Style Property and Value	Means...
p.caption {	This is the style class; "caption" is a style specific to the p selector, applied to the <p> tag. The opening curly bracket must be used to open the style's description.
text-align: center;	This is the horizontal alignment for text; the default is left aligned.
color: #333366;	This is the text color, one of the custom colors used in the site.
font-family: arial, sans-serif;	This provides choices of fonts to use for the text. Preference is given to Arial; if Arial is unavailable, the system sans-serif font is used.
font-size: 11pt;	This specifies a slightly smaller font. The same size is used for the bulleted lists.
font-style: oblique;	The same font style is used for the bulleted list; letters are slanted less than italic style.
line-height: 150%;	The distance between lines of text in the paragraphs is increased to 150%.
background-color: #E1FFFF;	The background behind the lines of text is colored using the pale blue custom site color.
border-color: #009966;	The paragraph is bordered using the grass green custom color for the site.
border-width: 2px;	The border width is specified as 2 pixels.
border-style: groove double;	The borders are grooved, which adds a dark line within the border at the top and bottom margins. The double border's total width is based on the border-width property value.
}	The closing curly bracket must be used to end the style.

```
14 <p class="caption"> Visit Sizzle when YOU want to visit. <br /> [10]
15 For a long weekend, for a month -- the choice is yours!</p>
```

10. **Go to line 14, and expand the opening <p> tag. Type:**
    ```
    <p class="caption">
    ```
    The style is added to the tag.

11. **Go to line 34, and repeat Step 10.**
    The style is added to another paragraph tag.

<NOTE>
For both of the paragraphs on the booking.html page, the paragraphs are broken over two lines using the <br /> tag.

12. **Open booking.html in Internet Explorer.**
    You preview the page.

13. **In Notepad, choose File→Save to save the booking.html page.**
    You created a complex paragraph class style and applied it to two pages on your site.

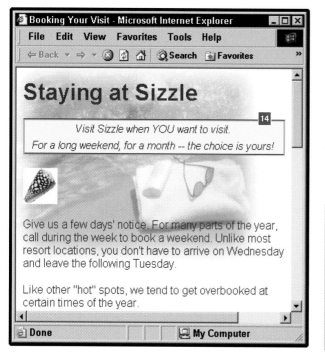

14. **Drag the lower right sizing handle to increase and decrease the width of the page.**
    You see that the content of the stylized paragraph resizes with the window size, but it remains on two lines, broken where you added the <br /> tag. Close the browser.

<NOTE>
The configuration of elements on the booking.html page is incomplete. You see the background image on the page, the small seashell overlay (with its white background visible), and now the paragraph overlay as well. In the next tutorial, you take care of the page's layout using styles.

CSS Positioning Properties

You use positioning properties in this session to specify placement of text and image elements. You used the properties earlier to place the seashell images on the pages as well. In addition to specifying left, right, top, and bottom positions of an element, you can also set the shape, stack elements in layers, and specify what happens if an element's content is too large to fit into a specified area.

Tutorial
» Placing Content on a Page Using Styles

In the previous tutorial, you added a paragraph class to the style sheet and applied it to three blocks of text on your Web site's pages. You saw how unwieldy the content appears on the `booking.html` page due to the background content on the page. In this tutorial, you revise the style adding positioning properties. You also position two paragraphs of text on the `fine_print.html` page using new styles and positioning properties.

1. **In Notepad, open** `sizzle.css`.

2. **Go to line 37, the starting location for the** `body.bookingbkgd` **style.**
   The style contains background image and repeating properties.

3. **Go to line 40, and press Enter to add a blank line. Type:**
   `background-position: 100px 150px;` **Save the file again.**
   You add positioning information for the image. The closing curly bracket moves to line 41.

4. **Open Internet Explorer, and then open** `booking.html` **to preview the page.**
   The image is now located below the text and the opening paragraphs and to the right of the seashell image. Minimize the browser.

5. **In Notepad, scroll down to the end of the** `sizzle.css` **file, and press Enter to add a blank line after the last paragraph style.**

6. **On lines 125 to 128, type:**
   ```
   p.block {
   position: absolute;
   left: 220px;
   }
   ```
   You add a paragraph style. The position property is assigned a value of absolute — the value is constant and doesn't fluctuate. The left position has a value of 220px, so the paragraph aligns 220 pixels from the left side of the page when applied.

< N O T E >
The style places a paragraph to the right of the image on the page. For an image that is 200 pixels wide, setting the left position at 220 pixels provides white space between the image and the text.

7. **Leave a blank line. On lines 130 to 133, type:**
   ```
   p.block2 {
   position: absolute;
   left: 320px;
   }
   ```
   You add another paragraph style. The position is absolute, and the paragraph aligns 320 pixels from the left.

```
36
37  body.bookingbkgd {
38  background-image: url(Images/pooLbkgd.jpg);
39  background-repeat: no-repeat;
40  background-position: 100px  150px; 3
41  }
```

< N O T E >
Content is positioned from the top left of the page. The upper-left corner has a value of 0 both horizontally and vertically.

< N O T E >
The style, `body.bookingbkgd` was attached to the page's <body> tag in Session 5, so you don't have anything to modify in the HTML file.

```
124
125  p.block {           6
126  position: absolute;
127  left: 220px;
128  }
129
130  p.block2 {
131  position: absolute;
132  left: 320px;
133  }          7
134
```

```
16 <p class="block"> 10  highly recommend travel insurance for all our visitors.
17 inherent risks. The range of sports and activities many people indulge in
18 at our resorts can be a little extreme.</p>
19
```

```
34
35 <p class="block2"> By the way – if your trip is cancelled for any of these  11
36 issues you a voucher for one free day at any of our resorts for each
37 week or part of a week you had to cancel. This is in addition to any
38 kind of reimbursements you may receive from your insurer.</p>
```

8. **Choose File→Save.**
   The style sheet is saved with two more paragraph styles.

9. **Choose File→Open to open** `fine_print.html`.
   You add the new styles to the page.

10. **Go to line 16, and expand the <p> tag. Type:**
    `<p class="block">`
    The first new paragraph style is added to the tag.

11. **Go to line 35, and expand the <p> tag. Type:**
    `<p class="block2">`
    The second new paragraph style is added to the paragraph's tag.

12. **Choose File→Save to save the** `fine_print.html` **page.**
    You added new styles to the page.

13. **Open Internet Explorer, and then open** `fine_print.html`.
    You preview the page.

14. **Resize the browser window.**
    The text decreases in width and wraps to the next line. When the text space is narrow, the text continues over the paragraphs below it on the page.

<NOTE>
The text overlapping is a result of the positioning property. In regular page viewing, the overlap is not likely to appear.

15. **In Internet Explorer, choose File→Open and select** `index.html`.
    Your site's frameset loads in the browser window.

16. **Click Fine Print.**
    The `fine_print.html` page loads in the main frame.

17. **Resize the browser window, and watch the effect on the styled text.**
    The text resizes itself according to the browser window's size. Close the browser.

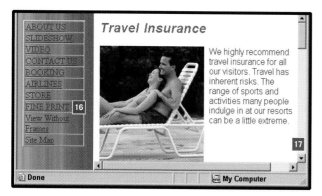

Tutorial
» Positioning an Image on a Page

In this final tutorial you use one more positioning property to set a page background. Instead of attaching a style to the <body> tag, you add a style to an image tag, and set its z-index value. Before you start the tutorial, open the Sizzle Site folder or the CD Tutorial Files and copy the `palm_bkgd.jpg` image from the Image Sources folder to your site's Images folder. You don't see the image placed in this tutorial if you view the page using a Netscape browser.

1. **In Notepad, open `sizzle.css`, and go to the last line on the page.**
   You add another category of styles and a new style.

2. **Press Enter to add a blank line. On line 135, type:**
   `/* miscellaneous */`
   You start another category of style. Some styles don't belong to specific content areas or types on the site; include these under the same comment heading.

3. **Press Enter to add another blank line. On lines 137 to 142, type:**
   ```
   img.z {
   position:absolute;
   left:150px;
   top:30px;
   z-index:-1;
   }
   ```
   You add another style. The z-index property value describes the image's position in the stacking order of the page. The value -1 means that the image is placed behind the rest of the page's content. The style also includes positioning locations on the page.

```
134
135  /* miscellaneous */  2
136
137  img.z
138  {
139  position:absolute;
140  left:150px;
141  top:30px;   3
142  z-index:-1
143  }
```

< N O T E >
The default z-index value is 0. A negative value places the content behind the rest of the page. Unless a style is established, the page's elements use the default z-index value.

4. **Choose File→Save.**
   You added one last style to the `sizzle.css` style sheet.

5. **Choose File→Open.**
   Select the `sitemap.html` page, and click Open. The page opens in Notepad.

6. **Go to line 13.**
   The line is currently a blank line between the two heading tags.

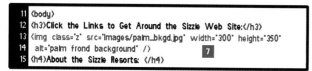

```
11  <body>
12  <h3>Click the Links to Get Around the Sizzle Web Site:</h3>
13  <img class="z" src="Images/palm_bkgd.jpg" width="300" height="350"
14    alt="palm frond background" />
15  <h4>About the Sizzle Resorts: </h4>
```
7

7. On line 13, and wrapping to line 14, type: `<img class="z" src="Images/palm_bkgd.jpg" width="300" height="350" alt="palm frond background" />`
The image is added to the page. The image source and `width`, `height`, and `alt` attributes are specified. The new style, `img.z`, is applied to the image.

<NOTE>
The exact location on the page isn't important. The style is applied to a stacking order, not a vertical or horizontal location on a page.

8. Choose File→Save.
The `sitemap.html` page is saved with its new style.

9. Open Internet Explorer, and then open `sitemap.html` to preview the page.
You see the palm frond placed on the background of the page behind the text. Close the browser. You added an image to a page background using positioning.

The Sizzle Web Site - Microsoft Internet Explorer

File Edit View Favorites Tools Help

Back · Search Favorites Media

Click the Links to Get Around the Sizzle Web Site:

ABOUT THE SIZZLE RESORTS:
9

General Information

Sizzle East- the place to meet new people

Sizzle West- for couples to get away from it all

Sizzle South-if sports are your passion

Watch our video

Take our survey

Visit our store

Slideshow on our resorts

Done   My Computer

» Session Review

This session looked at different types of styles. You learned to create and apply styles to different levels of headings on your pages. You learned how to set common properties and how to configure individual style properties as well. You learned how to build and apply some custom paragraph styles, and you worked with a bulleted, or unordered, list.

You worked with positioning properties in the session. The opening image in this session shows the `booking.html` page with the text and seashell image overlying the background image. After positioning the background image and applying several text styles, the result is the final image in this session. You positioned paragraphs of text using positioning styles. Finally, you added a background image to a page using an image class style that placed the image behind the other content on the page.

Here are some questions to help you review the information in this session. You can find the answer to each question in the tutorial noted in parentheses.

1. Can you write one style for more than one selector simultaneously? (See Tutorial: Writing Heading and Text Styles.)

2. What types of properties can you set for a font? (See Tutorial: Writing Heading and Text Styles.)

3. Do you need to use a paragraph tag in conjunction with a heading tag to separate the content visually in a browser? Why or why not? (See Tutorial: Applying Heading Styles.)

4. Do you use both HTML attributes and styles tags? Why or why not? (See Tutorial: Finishing the Heading Styles.)

5. What types of list styles are available? (See Tutorial: Using Lists on the Web Pages.)

6. What is an ordered list? How is it different from an unordered list? (See Tutorial: Using Lists on the Web Pages.)

7. What tags are used to identify items for a list? (See Tutorial: Using Lists on the Web Pages.)

8. How can you specify the height of a line in a paragraph? (See Tutorial: Creating a Special Paragraph Style.)

9. Can you apply a background to a paragraph? How? (See Tutorial: Creating a Special Paragraph Style.)

10. How do you specify a value for a background-position property? Can you express the value in more than one way? (See Tutorial: Placing Content on a Page Using Styles.)

11. How is the layout of a page determined? What is the value of the upper-left corner of the browser window? (See Tutorial: Placing Content on a Page Using Styles.)

12. What is an absolute value? (See Tutorial: Placing Content on a Page Using Styles.)

13. What happens to text using a positioning style when it is resized on a page? (See Tutorial: Placing Content on a Page Using Styles.)

14. What is a z-index property value? (See Tutorial: Positioning an Image on a Page.)

» Other Projects

Working with the text and font properties, experiment with other property values. Experiment with borders, font styles, and so on.

Experiment with positioning properties. Change the values from absolute values to percentages to see how the page appearance changes. Try constructing a table using positioning styles rather than table tags.

Create a style for the `sitemap.html` page's body selector. Position the style as part of the background.

Staying at Sizzle

Visit Sizzle when YOU want to visit.
For a long weekend, for a month -- the choice is yours!

Give us a few days' notice. For many parts of the year, call during the week to book a weekend. Unlike most resort locations, you don't have to arrive on Wednesday and leave the following Tuesday.

Like other "hot" spots, we tend to get overbooked at certain times of the year.

You have to prebook during these times:

- *last week of December*
- *first week of January*
- *Spring Break week*

Attaching Navigation Styles and Elements

ABOUT US
SLIDESHOW
VIDEO
CONTACT US
BOOKING
AIRLINES
STORE
FINE PRINT
View Without
Frames
Site Map

Discussion: **Understanding Pseudo-Classes and Pseudo-Elements**

Tutorial: **Writing Link Styles for the Sizzle Site**

Tutorial: **Applying a Tiled Image to the Navigation Page's Table**

Tutorial: **Writing Styles for the Navigation Table's Cells**

Tutorial: **Coloring and Positioning Cells in the Navigation Table**

Tutorial: **Creating Link Styles for the Navigation Frame**

Tutorial: **Working with a Drop-Cap Style**

Session Introduction

Your site is starting to take shape visually. One area you may have noticed looking less than attractive are the links. At this point, the links on your site use the default text and colors. In this session, you change the looks of the links using styles.

The navigation frame of your site needs some work as well. You configure the table using styles and add the striped background tiled image created in Session 4. You position the table on the page using a style and create styles for the navigation table's text links. You also add drop-caps to text on two pages using a special CSS category called a pseudo-element.

You complete the basic navigation for much of the site (with the exception of two elements) at the end of the session. You add an image map to the logo page in Session 12 to visually link to the resorts' pages. The slideshow's navigation isn't finished either; the coding and styles required to finish the slideshow are combined into one separate session. That's ahead in Session 13.

TOOLS YOU'LL USE
Notepad, Internet Explorer

CD-ROM FILES NEEDED
booking.html, fine_print.html, index.html, nav_left.html, sizzle.css

TIME REQUIRED
90 minutes

Discussion

Understanding Pseudo-Classes and Pseudo-Elements

Just when you thought you understood how CSS and styles work, along come categories that aren't really classes or elements at all; rather, they are pseudo-classes and pseudo-elements. You can write a style for a link; you can use a pseudo-class to distinguish between the link states. You can write a style for a paragraph; you write a pseudo-element style for the first letter or the first line of a paragraph.

Pseudo-Classes

You are familiar with one type of pseudo-class: the anchor tag used for links. Your browser has four built-in anchor tag styles. The <a> tag is the tag that you write in your page of code. The browser interprets the tag according to activity. A new <a> tag is underlined in blue. When you move the mouse over the tag, it turns red. After the tag content has been clicked once, the tag content turns maroon.

The four main anchor pseudo-class tags are:

>> **a:link**—not selected and not visited recently

>> **a:visited**—already visited

>> **a:hover**—mouseover

>> **a:active**—selected and in process

An additional pseudo-class, called a:focus, applies to form fields.

When you write styles for anchor pseudo-classes, you must write the style in a particular sequence. The a:link and a:visited definitions are first, followed by the a:hover style, and finally the a:active style. In your Sizzle site, you use the a:link, a:visited, and a:hover styles. Writing anchor pseudo-classes affects only the style sheet; the HTML markup of the page does not change.

Pseudo-Elements

Paragraphs are identified on your pages using the <p> tag. You can add styles galore to the paragraphs, but without using pseudo-elements, you can't add a special style to the first letter or the first line of the paragraph. Pseudo-elements can be used with any block-level element, such as paragraphs and headings. A style written for the first letter of a paragraph such as this:

```
p:first-letter {
font-size: 250%;
color:#996600;
background-color: transparent;
float: left;
}
```

produces a paragraph that looks like this:

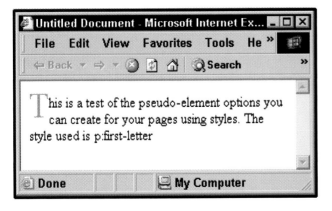

The first-line pseudo-element is used to modify the appearance of the first line of a paragraph or other block element. A style written for the first line of a paragraph such as this:

```
p:first-line {
font-size: 120%;
color:#996600;
background-color: transparent;
font-weight: bold;
}
```

produces a paragraph that looks like this:

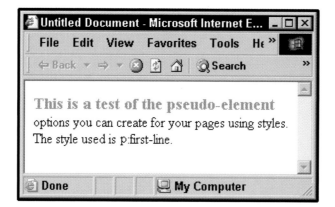

Rules for Using Pseudo-Classes and Pseudo-Elements

Write pseudo-class and pseudo-elements using this format:

```
selector:pseudo-class { property: value }
```

or

```
selector:pseudo-element { property: value }
```

You can attach a pseudo-class or pseudo-element to a style class as well. For example, if you are working with a drop-cap, you won't likely want the entire page or site to use drop-caps for each and every paragraph. In that case, define a class first. Write this:

```
selector.class:pseudo-element { property: value }
```

The pseudo-element styles previously written could be called `p.dropcap:first-line` or `p.dropcap:first-letter`. Attaching the class to the specific paragraph tags on the page adds the style only to the applicable character or words.

Tutorial
» Writing Link Styles for the Sizzle Site

In this tutorial, you create styles for the links in your site, and then you add the link styles to the miscellaneous group of styles on your style sheet. You don't have to attach the style to any content on your pages. Just as you added heading tags on the pages and the appropriate styles were attached, the same applies to links.

1. **Open Notepad. Choose File→Open, and browse to your Sizzle site folder. Choose** `sizzle.css`, **and click Open.**

2. **Go to line 144, and press Enter.**
   You add a blank line following the `img.z` style created in the last session.

3. **On lines 145 to 153, type:**
   ```
   a:link,a:visited {
   color: #336633;
   background-color: transparent;
   font-family: Arial,sans-serif;
   font-size:12px;
   font-weight: bolder;
   letter-spacing: 1px;
   text-decoration: none;
   }
   ```
   You create a style for the two anchor pseudo-classes a:link and a:visited.

4. **Press Enter to leave another blank line.**
   You need one more pseudo-class style.

5. **On lines 155 to 158, type:**
   ```
   a:hover {
   color: #009966;
   background-color:rgb(230,230,179);
   }
   ```
   You create a style for the hover state of the anchor tag. The hover state is when the mouse is over the text link.

<NOTE>
You have not used the RGB values for a style's color properties. Declare the `rgb` in lowercase, and separate the values with a comma. Surround the three values with parentheses. The color in the style is a pale gray-yellow and is about half the saturation value of the darker yellow custom color used on the site.

6. **Choose File→Save.**
   You save the style sheet with new link styles.

7. **Open Internet Explorer, and then open** `index.html`.
   You view the links in your site's pages.

8. **Scroll down the page.**
   You see the links at the bottom of the page that use the custom styles.

<NOTE>
The style in step 3 has several properties that you haven't worked with before. The `bolder` value for the `font-weight` property makes the text extra-bold. The `text-decoration` property refers to underline, overline, or strikethrough. The default styles use an underline; in order to remove the underline from the links, you must include the property and specify the value of `none`.

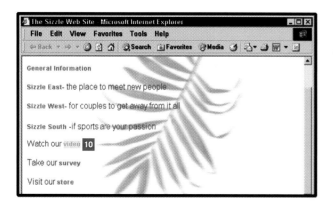

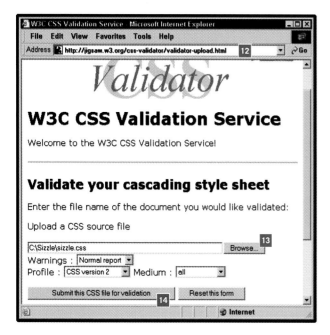

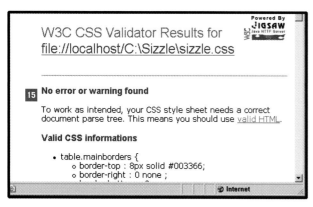

9. **Click Site Map in the Navigation frame.**
   The `sitemap.html` page opens in a blank window.

10. **Move the cursor over a link.**
   You see the background display.

11. **Close the `sitemap.html` window.**
   You added a set of link styles to your site and tested the styles.

12. **In the Internet Explorer Address bar, type:**
   `http://jigsaw.w3.org/css-validator/`
   `validator-upload.html`
   You need to test the style sheet against the W3C CSS guidelines.

13. **Click Browse to open an Explorer window. Select the**
   `sizzle.css` **file in your Sizzle site folder, and click OK.**
   The file's location loads in the W3C CSS Validator. Leave the default selections for the Warnings, Profile, and Media.

14. **Click Submit this CSS file for validation.**
   The page is processed.

15. **The results page displays. View the results.**
   If error or warning messages are appropriate, they display on the page.

16. **Close the browser.**
   You validated the content of your style sheet.

< N O T E >

Make a habit of testing your style sheet and site pages regularly. The process is included in this tutorial as a reminder.

Tutorial

» Applying a Tiled Image to the Navigation Page's Table

You constructed the navigation table and its page in Session 2. As you developed the pages for your site, you added rows to the table and it now contains two columns and ten rows. In this tutorial, you create the style for the tiled image and apply it to the page.

1. **Open Notepad. Choose File→Open, and browse to your Sizzle site folder. Choose** `sizzle.css`, **and click Open.**

2. **Go to the last line of the page, and press Enter.**
   You add a blank line following the previous styles.

3. **On line 160, type:** `/* navigation table*/`
   You start a new group of styles used for the navigation table. Press Enter to add another blank line.

4. **On lines 162 to 165, type:**
   ```
   td.nav {
   background-image: url(Images/stripe.jpg);
   background-repeat: repeat-y;
   }
   ```
   You create a style for the tiled image. The properties and their values are explained in Table 10-1.

5. **Choose File→Save. Choose File→Open, select** `nav_left.html`, **and click Open.**
   The new style is saved in your `sizzle.css` file.

6. **Go to line 8, and press Enter to add a blank line.**
   You link the stylesheet to the page in the <head> tags following the <meta> tag's line.

7. **On line 8, type:** `<link href="sizzle.css" rel="stylesheet" type="text/css" />`
   The style sheet is attached to the page.

8. **Go to line 15, and expand the <td> tag. The line should now read:**
   `<td class="nav" rowspan="10"></td>`
   The style is attached to the table.

9. **In Notepad, choose File→Save.**
   The `nav_left.html` file is saved. You wrote a style for the navigation table's tiled image and applied the style to the page.

10. **Open Internet Explorer, and then open the** `nav_left.html` **file.**
    Preview the file. The tiled stripe image is applied to the left column of the table.

11. **Minimize the browser.**
    You attached a style to the navigation table.

Table 10-1: Description of the `td.nav` Style Properties

Property and Value	Means...
background-image: url (Images/stripe.jpg);	The background image created in Session 3 is referenced.
background-repeat: repeat-y;	The repeat is specified on the y-axis (vertical). Other options are x-axis (horizontal) or a specified number of repeats.

Tutorial

» Writing Styles for the Navigation Table's Cells

The navigation frame's table has a striped tile image in the left column. The links are listed in the cells in the right column of the table. In this tutorial, you create styles for the cells in the right column of the table using four of the custom colors from your site's color palette.

```
166
167 td.nav1 {                    3
168 background-color: #336633;
169 color: inherit;
170 }
171
172 td.nav1 {                    5
173 background-color: #336633;
174 color: inherit;
175 }
```

```
171
172 td.nav2 {
173 background-color: #006666;   7
174 color: inherit;
175 }
176
177 td.nav3 {
178 background-color: #333366;   7
179 color: inherit;
180 }
181
182 td.nav4 {
183 background-color: #009966;   7
184 color: inherit;
185 }
```

1. **In Notepad, choose File→Open. Select** `sizzle.css`, **and click Open.**
   You add more styles for the table.

2. **Go to the last line of the page, and press Enter to add a blank line.**

3. **Go to line 167. On lines 167 to 170, type:**
   ```
   td.nav1 {
   background-color: #336633;
   color: inherit;
   }
   ```
   You add a style for one of the table's rows. The row styles include a background color and color properties.

   < N O T E >
   The color property has the value `inherit`, which means that it assumes the browser's default color for text. Later in the session, you add in-line styles to set color for the links' text on the table cells.

4. **Select the text in the rows added in Step 3, and copy the text.**
   You add several more copies of the style to the style sheet.

5. **Leave a blank line. Paste a copy of the** `td.nav1` **style on lines 172 to 175.**
   You have two copies of the style on the page.

6. **Repeat Step 5 two more times.**
   You have a total of four copies of the `td.nav1` style.

7. **Modify the content of the three pasted copies of the style.**
   Name the first copy `td.nav2`, **and change the color to** #006666
   Name the second copy `td.nav3`, **and change the color to** #333366
   Name the third copy `td.nav4`, **and change the color to** #009966
   You have four different styles.

8. **Save the** `sizzle.css` **file.**
   You added several new styles to the style sheet. You applied the first style to the table that displays the tiled image in the left column of the table. In the next tutorial, you add the new styles to the `nav_left.html` page. Leave Notepad open for the next tutorial.

Tutorial
» Coloring and Positioning Cells in the Navigation Table

When you constructed the navigation table and its page in Session 2, you added border and size attributes to the table to give them some visibility on your Web page for testing and development. In this tutorial, you remove the attributes from the HTML page. You attach the styles you created in the previous tutorial. You also write a style to position the table on the page.

1. **In Notepad, open** nav_left.html.
   You attach the table row styles to the page.

2. **Go to line 16, and expand the <td> tag to read:** <td class=
   "nav1">
   You attach the first row style to the table holding the "About Us" link.

<NOTE>
The tutorial steps reference line numbers. Your line numbering may differ slightly from that shown in the tutorial figures or listed in the steps. Use the line numbers as references to different areas of a page, but read the content of the line carefully as you follow the steps to ensure you modify or add code to the correct line.

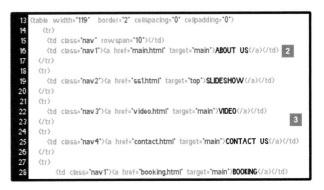

3. **Add the styles to the <td> tags as listed in Table 10-2.**
   In the table, the row is listed in the first column, and the <td> tag and style are listed in the second column. For reference, the text for each table cell is listed in the third column.

4. **Save the** nav_left.html **file.**
   You added class styles to numerous tags on the page.

Table 10-2: Class Styles Added to Table Cells

Line	Expand Tag to Read:	Link Text
19	<td class="nav2">	SLIDESHOW
22	<td class="nav3">	VIDEO
25	<td class="nav4">	CONTACT US
28	<td class="nav1">	BOOKING
31	<td class="nav2">	AIRLINES
34	<td class="nav3">	STORE
37	<td class="nav4">	FINE PRINT
40	<td class="nav1">	View Without Frames
43	<td class="nav2">	SITE MAP

5. Open your browser, and then open nav_left.html.
Preview the page. You see that the rows are colored using a sequence of colors as defined in the styles. Minimize the browser.

<NOTE>
It appears as though two links are missing. They are still there—the text and background colors are the same, so you can't see them. You add styles for the text later in the session.

```
11  <body background="Images/dk_bkgd.gif">
12
13  <table cellpadding="10"> 6
14      <tr>
```

6. In Notepad, go to line 13, the opening tags for the table. Rewrite the content of the line to read: <table cellpadding="10">
The attributes you added for visibility when you created the table, border and cellspacing, are removed. The dimensions of the table are controlled by the size of the contents. The cell-padding attribute adds space around the text content in the cells.

7. Choose File→Save to save the nav_left.html **page with the new table styles.**

8. Open Internet Explorer. Open index.html, **and check the navigation table in its frame.**
Note the gaps between the upper and left edges of the table and the frame. Minimize the browser.

9. In Notepad, open sizzle.css.
You write another style to position the table in the frame.

10. Go to the last line on the style sheet page, and press Enter to add a blank line.

11. **On lines 187 to 191, type:**
```
table.nav {
position: absolute;
left: 0px;
top: 0px;
}
```
You create a style for positioning the table on the frame.

< N O T E >

Use the absolute value for the position property to define where the table is placed using pixel locations. Other options are static (the element moves with the rest of the page content) and relative (the element moves relative to its static position).

12. **Choose File→Save to save the** `sizzle.css` **file. Open the** `nav_left.html` **page again.**
You add the style to the table.

13. **Go to line 13, and expand the <table> tag to read:**
```
<table class="nav" cellpadding="10">
```
You add the `class` style to the <table> tag.

< N O T E >

Your style sheet contains both a `td.nav` and a `table.nav` style. Because each class style pertains to a different selector, there is no conflict or error.

14. **Choose File→Save to save the** `nav_left.html`**-page.**
You added one more table style to the page. Leave Notepad open for the next tutorial.

15. **Open Internet Explorer, and open** `index.html`. **Check the navigation table in its frame.**
The table is aligned with the upper left of the frame. Close the browser. You applied several styles to the navigation table.

Inserting Style Sheets

You have worked with external style sheets. You can also define styles in other ways. An internal style sheet is inserted into a single document with unique styles, such as the navigation frame in the Sizzle site. A <style> tag is added to the head of the document and contains the style properties and values. When the browser reads the page, it formats the page according to the attached styles, as well as the styles in the internal style sheet. An in-line style is a style attached to a specific tag. Use the style attribute in the tag on the page. For example, <h1 style="color: red"> Red Rooster </h1> produces a red-colored heading when viewed in a browser.

Tutorial

» Creating Link Styles for the Navigation Frame

The navigation frame of the site is coming along. You have added styles to color and size the table's components. The links use the default link styles. The defaults aren't very attractive, and they're hard to read with the site's color scheme. In this tutorial, you build the styles for the links. Instead of adding the styles to the style sheet as you have done up to now, you add the styles at the top of the nav_left.html page.

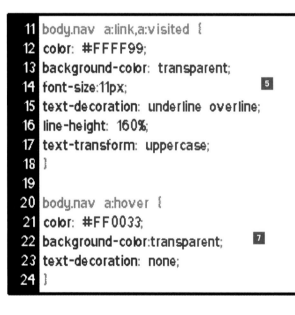

1. **In Notepad, open** nav_left.html.
   You add an internal style sheet for the navigation frame's links.

2. **Go to line 9, and press Enter to add a blank line.**
   You add the styles within the <head> tags on the page.

3. **On line 9, type:** <style type="text/css">
   You define the style type for an internal style sheet just as you do for an external style sheet.

4. **On line 10, type:** <!--
   You add the opening comment tag.

5. **On lines 11 to 18, type:**
   ```
   body.nav a:link,a:visited {
   color: #FFFF99;
   background-color: transparent;
   font-size:11px;
   text-decoration: underline overline;
   line-height: 160%;
   text-transform: uppercase;
   }
   ```
   You add the style for the first two link states. The style is a class named "nav" for the selector "body". The declaration applies to the a:link and a:visited states of the link.

6. **Press Enter to add a blank line.**
   You add a style for the hover link state.

7. **On lines 20 to 24, type:**
   ```
   body.nav a:hover {
   color: #FF0033;
   background-color: transparent;
   text-decoration: none;
   }
   ```
   You add a style for the hover link state. The style uses the characteristics of the style that you wrote in Step 5 except for the color and the text decoration.

<NOTE>
Older browsers may not be able to read internal style sheets, but they display the text written for the styles. Enclosing the internal styles in comment tags prevents the content from being displayed as text regardless of the browser used.

8. **On lines 26 and 27, type:**
   ```
   -->
   </style>
   ```
   You close the comment, and you close the <style> tag.

9. **Expand the <body> tag on line 29 to include the class attribute. Type:** `class="nav"` **within the opening <body> tag.**
   The line reads: `<body class="nav" background="Images/dk_bkgd.gif">`

10. **In Notepad, choose File→Save to save the** `nav_left.html` **page.**
    You added styles to the navigation links. Leave Notepad open for the next tutorial.

11. **Open Internet Explorer, and then open** `index.html`.
    The Sizzle frameset loads in the browser.

12. **Test the links. Move the mouse over the link to see the red hover state.** Close the browser.

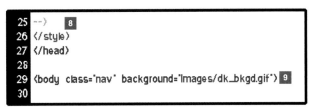

```
25  -->    [8]
26  </style>
27  </head>
28
29  <body class="nav" background="Images/dk_bkgd.gif">   [9]
30
```

Multiple Style Sheets

You use both external and internal style sheets with the navigation frame. A property value described in an internal style sheet is used for a selector. If no property description is provided, the external style sheet's value is used, or inherited. In your site, the font-family, font-weight, and letter-spacing are inherited from the external style sheet, and the text sizes and colors are replaced by the internal style sheet.

Using Text Decoration Styles

Text-decoration applies line effects such as overline, underline, and strikethrough. The default text decoration for a link is underline, and the external style uses no text decoration. Text-transform is an interesting property used to control lettercase.

If you refer to work you completed on the navigation table earlier, some of the headings are all caps, while others have only initial capitalization. The property automatically changes all text affected by the style to uppercase.

Tutorial
» Working with a Drop-Cap Style

At the start of the session, you learned how pseudo-classes and pseudo-elements work on a style sheet. You used the pseudo-classes when you built the links for the site and the navigation page. In the final tutorial for this session, you work with pseudo-elements. You create a drop-cap style and apply it to two pages on your site.

1. **In Notepad, open** `sizzle.css`.
   You add the pseudo-element to the style sheet.

2. **Go to line 134, following the bracket closing the** `p.block2` **style, and press Enter to add a blank line.**
   You add a new style.

3. **On line 135 to 139, type:**
   ```
   p.dropcap:first-letter {
   font-size:x-large;
   color:#333366;
   background-color: transparent;
   }
   ```
   The style uses the deep blue custom color for your site.

4. **Choose File→Save.**
   You save the style sheet with the added pseudo-element style.

5. **Choose File→Open, select** `fine_print.html`, **and click Open.**
   You add the style to the page.

6. **Go to line 28, and expand the <p> tag to read:** `<p class="dropcap">`
   You attach the style to the paragraph.

```
27
28 <p class="dropcap">Trip interruption insurance kicks in for emergencies such   6
29
30 <ul class="square"> <li>a personal medical emergency</li>
```

< N O T E >

The `font-size` uses a value that you haven't used before. Fonts can be sized as x-large, xx-large, x-small, xx-small, and so on, rather than using a percentage or an actual font size in pixels. The size is relative, and based on your browser's global or default template.

< N O T E >

The style is written as a class style for the p selector. If you don't use a class style, all paragraphs in your site use the drop-cap.

7. **In Notepad, choose File→Save to save the** `fine_print.html` **page.**
   You saved the file with the added style.

8. **Open Internet Explorer, and then open** `fine_print.html`.
   Scroll down the page to see the drop-cap added to the paragraph. Minimize the browser.

9. **In Notepad, choose File→Open, select** `booking.html`, **and click Open.**
   You add the style to the page.

10. **Go to line 22, the paragraph before the lines containing the list items. Expand the <p> tag to read:** `<p class="dropcap">`
    You add the style to the paragraph.

11. **Go to line 26, repeat Step 10, and then save the file.**
    You add the style to another paragraph.

12. **Open Internet Explorer, and then open** `booking.html`.
    Scroll down the page to see the drop-caps added to the paragraph. Close the browser. You added one more style to your style sheet and applied the style to paragraphs on two pages.

» Session Review

This session covered lots of work with links. The opening image in the session shows the navigation page of your site with the table and links using the default browser styles. You learned to use pseudo-classes to construct custom link appearances for the site. You also built specific link styles for the navigation table page. You wrote styles for the navigation table's image as well as the position of the table on the page. You learned to use a pseudo-element and constructed a style for drop-caps on your site.

The final image in the session shows the result of your hard work. The table is more decorative, and its color scheme is in keeping with the rest of your site.

Answer these questions to help you review the information in this session. You'll find the answer to each question in the tutorial noted in parentheses.

1. Can all browsers understand pseudo-classes and pseudo-elements? (See Discussion: Understanding Pseudo-Classes and Pseudo-Elements.)

2. What is a common type of pseudo-class? (See Discussion: Understanding Pseudo-Classes and Pseudo-Elements.)

3. If you create a generic style for a page element, must you attach the style to the tags on the HTML page? Why or why not? (See Tutorial: Writing Link Styles for the Sizzle Site.)

4. How do you remove the default underline from links on your pages? (See Tutorial: Writing Link Styles for the Sizzle Site.)

5. How do you control the number of times that an image is repeated in a tiled image? (See Tutorial: Applying a Tiled Image to the Navigation Page's Table.)

6. Can you specify the number of times that an image is used horizontally and vertically? How? (See Tutorial: Applying a Tiled Image to the Navigation Page's Table.)

7. What does the property value "inherit" refer to? (See Tutorial: Writing Styles for the Navigation Table's Cells.)

8. How do you position an object on a page precisely? (See Tutorial: Coloring and Positioning Cells in the Navigation Table.)

9. What other properties are used for positioning an element on a page? (See Tutorial: Coloring and Positioning Cells in the Navigation Table.)

10. What tag identifies an internal style sheet? (See Tutorial: Creating Link Styles for the Navigation Frame.)

11. What should you add to the page's code to prevent viewing content in older browsers? (See Tutorial: Creating Link Styles for the Navigation Frame.)

12. How does the text-transform property work? (See Tutorial: Creating Link Styles for the Navigation Frame.)

13. Do you have to specify font size in numbers? What other values can you use? (See Tutorial: Working with a Drop-Cap Style.)

14. How do you write the style to apply it to specific paragraphs only? (See Tutorial: Working with a Drop-Cap Style.)

» Other Projects

Experiment with the text and font attributes for the links. Try different combinations of properties in the tags.

Create a `p:first-line` pseudo-element for your site. Experiment with its configuration and use on your site's pages. Add the `p:first-letter` pseudo-element created in the final tutorial to other pages in your site.

ABOUT US

SLIDESHOW

VIDEO

CONTACT
US

BOOKING

AIRLINES

STORE

FINE PRINT

**VIEW
WITHOUT
FRAMES**

SITE MAP

My Computer

Part VII

Using Advanced Features in Your Site

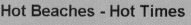

Hot Beaches - Hot Times

We started Sizzle Resorts to meet our own needs, and those of other like-minded young vacationers.

Adding More Pages and Objects to Your Site

Session Introduction

So far, you have worked with images and HTML pages. Other types of files are used on Web sites as well. It is common to find different types of files that you can download to your computer, such as zipped files (compressed with programs such as WinZip) or PDF files, which are either read online using Acrobat Reader or downloaded to your computer and read offline. In this session, you add a PDF file to your site. When you test the file, you see how it can be viewed online or offline.

You likely have come across other types of media online as well. In this session, you add motion to your site. You learn how to embed a Flash movie as an example of animated media. Many other types of media exist, and all but animated GIF files require some sort of player to view them. Flash requires a Flash viewer, included with later versions of browsers, so your readers don't have to download any files to view the movie.

You create an imagemap in this session. Specific areas on an image are identified through your HTML code, and they serve as navigation links to pages in the site. After the imagemap is created, you add it to the logo page of your site and then add some dynamic elements using JavaScript. You add a message to the browser window's status bar and add an automatic date to the page.

TOOLS YOU'LL USE
Notepad, Internet Explorer

CD-ROM FILES NEEDED (Image Storage folder)
sizzle stuff.pdf, sizzle.swf

FILES MODIFIED
store.html, logo.html, video.html, 11logo_ismap.html
(reference - in Session11 tutorial files folder)

TIME REQUIRED
90 minutes

Tutorial
» Adding a PDF File to Your Site

Your site contains a page named `store.html`. The file was constructed to test links on the navigation and site map pages. In this tutorial, you attach a PDF file to the page and give your readers the option to view the page online or download it to their computers for use offline. Before you start the tutorial, copy the `sizzle_stuff.pdf` file from the CD to your Sizzle site folder.

```
5  <head>
6  <title>Get your Sizzle goodies!</title>  2
7  <meta http-equiv="Content-Type" content="text/html; charset=utf-8" />
4  8  <link href="sizzle.css" rel="stylesheet" type="text/css" />
9  </head>
10
11  <body>
12  <h1> The Sizzle Store is Now Open! </h1>  5
```

```
13
14  <p> Did you forget to buy a hat and t-shirt at your last visit? </p>
15  <p> It happens. Now you can order them by mail. We have t-shirts
16  and hats available in basic black. One size fits all. </p>
17
18  <h4>Check out the SIZZLE STORE</h4>            6
19
20  <ul>
21  <li>Click the link to open the PDF page in your browser. </li>
22  <li>To download the page to your computer, right-click the link
23  and choose Save Target As from the shortcut menu.</li></ul>
24
```

1. **Open Notepad, choose File→Open, select** `store.html` **from your Sizzle site folder, and click Open.**

2. **Go to line 6, and replace the placeholder title text. Type:** `Get your Sizzle goodies!` **to change the title.**

3. **Go to line 8, and press Enter to add a blank line.**

4. **On line 8, type:** `<link href="sizzle.css" rel="stylesheet" type="text/css" />` The site's style sheet is attached to the page.

5. **On line 12, type:** `<h1> The Sizzle Store is Now Open! </h1>`, **which adds the main heading.**

6. **Add the rest of the text and basic tags to the page as listed in Table 11-1.** You add content and download information to the page. Leave lines 17 and 19 blank.

7. **Choose File→Save to save the modified page.**

Table 11-1: Text and Tags for the `store.html` Page

Line Number	Text
14-16	<p> Did you forget to buy a hat and t-shirt at your last visit? </p>
	<p> It happens. Now you can order them by mail. We have t-shirts
	and hats available in basic black. One size fits all. </p>
18	<h4>Check out the SIZZLE STORE</h4>
20-23	<ul>
	<li>Click the link to open the PDF page in your browser. </li>
	<li>To download the page to your computer, right-click the link
	and choose Save Target As from the shortcut menu.</li></ul>

8. **Open Internet Explorer, and then open the** `store.html` **page.**
   Note the paragraph and heading styles applied to the text. Minimize the browser.

9. **In Notepad, go to line 14. After the opening <p> tag, type:** `<img class="shells" src="Images/shell4.jpg" />`
   You attach one of the site's seashell images to the page. You apply the shells style to the image.

10. **Go to the <h4> tag on line 19, and expand the text to read:**
    `<h4>Check out the <a href="sizzle_stuff.pdf">  SIZZLE STORE</a></h4>`
    You add a link to the "SIZZLE STORE" phrase.

<NOTE>
You add a blank space on the line before the linked text, inserted by using ` `. When the browser reads the characters, a blank space is added to the line.

11. **Go to line 21, and expand the <ul> tag. Type:** `<ul class="square">`
    You attach the site's list style to the list.

12. **Save** `store.html`. **Open Internet Explorer, and then open** `index.html`.
    The frameset for your site opens.

13. **Click Store in the Navigation frame.**
    The Store page loads in the main frame. Note the style and content changes made to the page from Steps 9 through 12.

14. **Right-click the SIZZLE STORE link to see the shortcut menu.**
    From here you can choose different link options, including opening it in a new window or saving it.

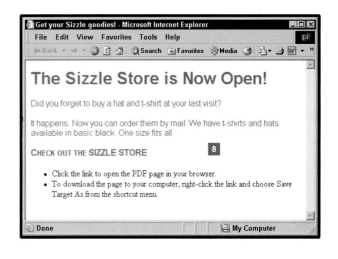

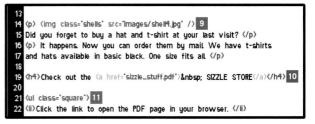

15. **Click the SIZZLE STORE link to load the PDF file.**

<NOTE>

Your computer probably has Acrobat Reader or Adobe Reader already installed. If you cannot open the file, you can download the file to your hard drive, and then download and install Acrobat Reader or Adobe Reader from Adobe's Web site.

16. **Scroll through the page.**

Close Internet Explorer. You completed the page. You added and formatted text and content. You attached a PDF file to the page. Leave Notepad open for the next tutorial.

<NOTE>

The `sizzle_store.pdf` file is a working PDF form. You can fill in the information, order product, and get calculated totals, or you can print the page using the buttons at the bottom of the page.

Tutorial

» Embedding a Flash Movie

You add a movie to your site in this tutorial. Your Sizzle site includes a promo video built in Adobe Premiere and then converted to a Flash file for Web use. Items such as Flash are referred to as objects. The <object> tag provides browsers with information to load and render data types that they could not display otherwise. Also required are parameter tags that specify the run-time settings for the object. To finish the page's design, you add two in-line styles for the background and text colors.

1. **In Notepad, choose File→Open. Choose** `video.html`, **and click Open.**
   You add content to the file.

2. **Go to line 8, and press Enter to add a new line.**
   You attach the style sheet to the page.

3. **On line 8, type:** `<link href="sizzle.css" rel="stylesheet" type="text/css" />`
   The style sheet is attached. Although you use custom colors for the background and text, you use the general style settings for the text supplied by the style sheet.

4. **Expand the <body> tag on line 11. Type:** `<body style="background-color:#333366">`
   You create an in-line style for the background-color using the custom deep blue color.

5. **Add the object information on lines 12 to 17. Type:**
   `<object classid="clsid:D27CDB6E-AE6D-11cf-96B8-444553540000"`
   `codebase="http://download.macromedia.com/pub/shockwave`
   `/cabs/flash/swflash.cab#version=6,0,29,0"`
   `width="160" height="120">`
   `<param name="movie" value="Images/sizzle.swf" />`
   `</object>`
   The information in the <object> and <param> tags is complex; explanations for the content is listed in Table 11-2.

6. **Press Enter to leave a blank line after the <object> tags.**
   Line 18 is blank to separate the content for ease of visibility.

7. **Delete the placeholder text "Sizzle Video". On line 19, type:** `<p style="color: #E1FFFF; font-weight: bold">`
   You start a text paragraph on the page using an in-line style. The styled text uses the pale blue custom color and a bold font.

8. **On line 20, type:** `Right-click the movie to <br /> access the Flash controls.</p>`
   You add the content for the paragraph and close the tag, and you add a line break to display the text over two lines.

```
7  <meta http-equiv="Content-Type" content="text/html; charset=utf-8" />
8  <link href="sizzle.css" rel="stylesheet" type="text/css" /> 3
9  </head>
10
11 <body style="background-color:#333366"> 4
```

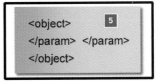

```
<object>         5
</param> </param>
</object>
```

```
12 <object classid="clsid:D27CDB6E-AE6D-11cf-96B8-444553540000"
13 codebase="http://download.macromedia.com/pub/shockwave
14 /cabs/flash/swflash.cab#version=6,0,29,0"
15 width="160" height="120">           5
16 <param name="movie" value="Images/sizzle.swf" />
17 </object>
```

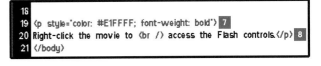

```
18
19 <p style="color: #E1FFFF; font-weight: bold"> 7
20 Right-click the movie to <br /> access the Flash controls.</p> 8
21 </body>
```

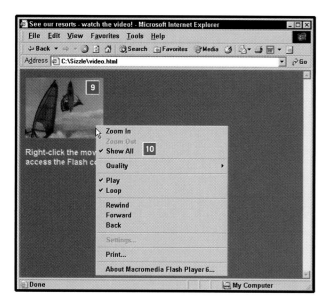

9. **Open Internet Explorer, and then open** `video.html`.

The page opens in the browser, and the movie starts playing.

10. **Right-click the movie to open the Flash control menu.**

Test the controls. Close the browser window.

<NOTE>

Make sure that your sound is turned on because the video includes a sound track.

11. **In Notepad, choose File→Save.**

The `video.html` page is complete with its embedded Flash movie and added text and colors.

Table 11-2: Object Information for Flash Movies

Line Number	Description of the Line's Content
12	This is the opening tag for the <object> element. The `classid` attribute is the ActiveX control number for the movie.
13, 14	This is the `codebase` attribute, the URL where the code for the object is located.
15	These are the `height` and `width` attributes for the movie in pixels; pixels are the only allowed value, so it isn't necessary to include the designation.
16	The <param> element identifies information about the content to be rendered. It is contained in the object element. The `name` attribute is required; the value is the name of the movie file.
17	This is the closing tag for the <object> element.

Discussion
Building Imagemaps

In this session, you create rectangular hotspots on an image used to navigate to pages on your site. The shapes are based on the top left and bottom right x,y coordinates of a rectangle.

Coordinates are always defined in the same way, whether in reference to a page or to an image. Regardless of an image's position on a page, it uses the same coordinates to refer to locations. The upper-left corner has x,y coordinates of 0,0. The bottom right coordinate is based on the size of the image. For example, a location on an image that is 10 pixels from the left of the image and 20 pixels from the top of the image has coordinate values of 10,20.

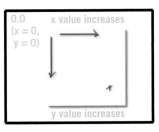

You can create circular shapes. A circle requires only two coordinates. Define the center of the circle as a pair of coordinates and another value for the radius of the circle.

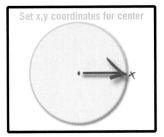

Technically a rectangle is a polygon, but the term is used to refer to a shape with a minimum of three points and any maximum number of points.

Polygons can have any number of sides, and each side of the polygon requires one pair of coordinates. Start at any point and enter the coordinates in sequence.

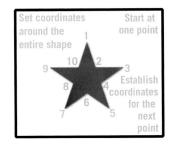

Tutorial

» Determining Page Coordinates for an Imagemap

In the Sizzle site, you use a map of the Caribbean with navigational links from the coordinates on the map to the main pages for each Sizzle resort location. In this tutorial, you add the image to the logo.html page, add map tags, and define page coordinates in a browser. In the next tutorial, based on your testing, you complete the descriptions of the map areas adding tags and information for final use of the imagemap.

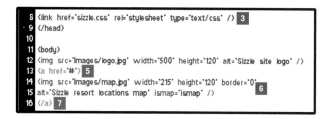

<NOTE>

A copy of the logo.html page complete with the tags used in this testing tutorial is on the CD in the Session 11 folder. The file is named 11logo_ismap.html.

<TIP>

Defining the image as a map allows you to identify locations, a much simpler means of setting coordinates than trial and error or counting pixels.

1. **Open logo.html in Notepad.**
   You add the image to the same page as your site's logo.

2. **Go to line 8, and press Enter.**
   Add a blank line in the <head> tags for the style sheet information.

3. **On line 8, type:** `<link href="sizzle.css" rel="stylesheet" type="text/css" />`
   The style sheet is attached to the page.

4. **Go to line 13, and press Enter.**
   Add a blank line after the logo image's tag.

5. **On line 13, type:** `<a href="#">`
   Add an anchor reference for the image that you insert in the next step.

6. **On lines 14 and 15, type:** `<img src="Images/map.jpg" width="215" height="120" border="0" alt="Sizzle resort locations map" ismap="ismap" />`
   You add the image to the page, and define its size and alternate text. Because the image is a link, remove the border by setting the border attribute as "0". The ismap attribute defines the entire picture as a map.

7. **On line 16, type:** `</a>` **to close the anchor tag.**

8. **Choose File→Save to save the file with the temporary tags.**

9. **Open Internet Explorer, and then open logo.html.**

10. **Move your cursor over the letters on the map. Note the coordinates displayed in the window status bar.**
    Write down coordinates for each letter, including the upper-left, upper-right, lower-right, lower-left coordinates. As you move the cursor over the image, you see that the a:hover style is applied to the image.

11. **Close the browser, and return to Notepad.**
    You used the map.jpg image to experiment with image coordinates by temporarily making it a map. Leave Notepad and the logo.html page open to continue to the next tutorial.

Tutorial
» Using an Imagemap for Navigation

In the previous tutorial, you started work on an imagemap for your site. You defined the entire image as a map and then used your browser to identify coordinate locations. In this tutorial, you modify the tags and complete the imagemap for use on the site.

1. **In Notepad, go to line 13 on** `logo.html`**, which reads** `<a href="#">` **and delete the content.**
   You remove the anchor tag from the page.

2. **Go to line 15, and delete the** `ismap="ismap"` **attribute.**
   You used the attribute to identify image locations; the attribute isn't required for the actual imagemap. The line now reads: `alt="Sizzle resort locations map" />`

3. **On line 15, add a new attribute. Before the closing bracket of the** `<img>` **tag, type:** `usemap="#map"`
   The `usemap` attribute indicates another location on the page named "map" that has the map details.

<NOTE>
The map name's syntax is the same as that used with anchor tags, where a reference within a page is preceded by #.

4. **Go to line 16. Delete the** `</a>` **tag used in the previous tutorial.**

5. **Delete line 13 (a blank line).**
   You don't need the space for visibility purposes, and its content was deleted in Step 1.

6. **On line 15, type:** `<map name="map" id="map">`
   The map element houses information on the hotspots and their reference files. Use both `id` and `name` attributes. Although the `name` attribute is deprecated, older browsers don't recognize the `id` attribute.

7. **Type the information for the first hotspot on lines 16 and 17.**
   Type: `<area shape="rect" coords="100,0,135,40" href="sizzle_east.html" alt="link to Sizzle East resort's page" target="main" />`
   The `<area>` tag lists the shape attribute and the coordinates, as well as the linking reference. Alternate text is required for hotspots. The target frame for the link is the main frame of the frameset.

<TIP>
The area element, nested inside the map element, defines the regions in the imagemap.

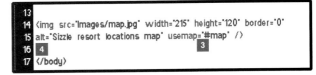

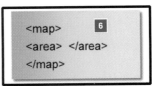

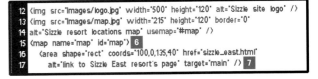

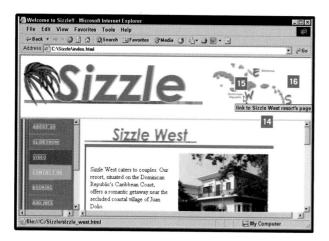

```
18  <area shape="rect" coords="80,60,115,100" href="sizzle_west.html"
19     alt="link to Sizzle West resort's page" target="main" />       9
20  <area shape="rect" coords="185,75,220,115" href="sizzle_south.html"
21     alt="link to Sizzle South resort's page" target="main" />      10
22  </map>  11
```

8. **Copy lines 16 and 17. Paste twice, adding content to lines 18 through 21.**

9. **On lines 18 and 19: change the coordinates on line 18 to** "80,60,115,100"
   change the href **attribute on line 18 to** "sizzle_west.html"
   change the alt **attribute on line 19 to** "link to Sizzle West resort's page"
   The hotspot links to the Sizzle West main page.

10. **On lines 20 and 21: change the coordinates on line 20 to** "185,75,220,115"
    change the href **attribute on line 20 to** "sizzle_south.html"
    change the alt **attribute on line 21 to** "link to Sizzle South resort's page"
    The hotspot links to the Sizzle South main page.

11. **Go to line 22. Type:** </map> **to close the <map> tag.**

12. **In Notepad, choose File→Save to save the** logo.html **page.**

13. **Open Internet Explorer, and then open** index.html.
    You test the imagemap links from within the site's frameset.

14. **Move the cursor over a letter on the map.**
    The alt text for the hotspot displays.

15. **Click a hotspot.**
    The page loads in the main frame of the frameset.

16. **Test the other links.**
    Close the browser. You removed the temporary tags and added a map container, which set coordinates for hotspots to link from the map to the main pages for each Sizzle resort. You targeted the links so the pages load into the main frame of your site. Leave the logo.html file open in Notepad for the next tutorial.

Discussion
Adding Dynamic Content Using JavaScript

JavaScript is a scripting language, which means the code is read, interpreted, and run in real time. JavaScript is not the same thing as Java, a programming language. In the Sizzle site, you use JavaScript for a number of purposes ranging from displaying a status message and date, to controlling windows, to navigation buttons, to validating user input on a form.

You need to answer three basic questions to write JavaScript: When? What? How?

"When?" is the simple question. Some examples are *when* viewers click on a link, or *when* viewers move their cursor over a button. "When" refers to events that can happen at the document level (such as when the page loads or unloads) at the link level (responding to mouse actions) and with form fields.

You must answer "What?" specifically. If you want an image link to change appearance when the cursor is passed over it, then the image and its alternate version answer this second question.

"How?" is probably the most complex question. You must understand how the document object model (DOM) fits into the equation. In other words, what must you define in order to get the item you want to change or work with?

The Document Object Model

JavaScript separates language from objects using a DOM. The DOM describes the syntax that you use for scripting. If you understand the syntax, then you know how to address objects to write your scripts.

There are several major hierarchical objects including the following:

» **window object**—The content area of the browser window where the HTML document appears.

» **document object**—The information that gets loaded into a window becomes a document object.

» **location object**—Information about the URL of the loaded document.

To refer to an object, you write each object above its hierarchy first. To write (the method) to the document (the object) within the window object, write this:

```
window.document.write("Hello World!");
```

All object references are part of the window object because you can have only one document in a window, so the script can be abbreviated to this:

```
document.write("Hello World!");
```

Writing the script in either way displays "Hello World" in a Web browser window.

JavaScript terminology

JavaScript is an object-oriented computer language using a number of terms:

- » **client:** A computer running a Web browser. Web pages are loaded from Web servers and are displayed on Web clients.

- » **event handler:** An attribute that associates an object with an event. For example, a button can be associated with a mouse click using the onClick event handler.

- » **function:** A set of JavaScript statements interpreted all at once by calling the function name. You can reuse functions within the same script or in other documents. You define functions at the beginning of a file (in the head section), and call them later in the document. JavaScript has several built-in functions. You also create your own functions by including the name, values, and statements.

- » **instance:** One copy of an object. A button on a Web page is an object; a button called myButton1 is an instance.

- » **method:** An action that a particular object can perform. Methods are implemented like functions and always associated with a particular object (like a verb).

- » **object:** Any thing, idea, or concept is an object—for example, window, image, document (like a noun).

- » **operators:** Processes used to operate on values; may be arithmetic, or strings of text or letters.

- » **property:** An attribute describing an object. They are one-word attributes, such as name, target, value. An object's properties are written as `objectname.propertyname` and can contain other objects as well. For example, an order form has a check box named blue; the value is written as `document.orderform.blue.value`

- » **variable:** A "container" for storing information.

Tutorial
» Changing the Message on the Browser Status Bar

Links on your site display the address in the status bar at the bottom of the browser window. You have probably seen Web pages that display a custom message in the status bar at the bottom of the window. In this tutorial, you add a message to the `logo.html` page. The process involves writing your first piece of JavaScript. The load function is a built-in JavaScript function. You add the function and its statement to the <head> section of the page and then add the triggering event to the <body> tag of the page. When the page loads, the script loads as part of the <head> content; when the <body> information is loaded into the browser, the script is available for display on the page.

1. **In Notepad, go to line 9 on the `logo.html` page and press Enter.**
   You add script information in the head segment of the page.

2. **On lines 9 and 10, type:**
   ```
   <script type="text/javascript">
   <!-- hide from JavaScript-challenged browsers
   ```
   You add the opening script tag and define the type of script used. You also open a comment tag. If you don't hide the script content, the actual words and characters used to create the script display on the browser's page in older browsers.

3. **On lines 11 through 14, type:**
   ```
   function load()
   {
   window.status = "Sizzle \-\- the hottest
   place to be!!";
   }
   ```
   JavaScript uses specific rules for writing. Each line or statement is ended using a semicolon. The content of each line of the script and what it means is included in Table 11-3.

4. **On lines 15 and 16, type:**
   ```
   // done hiding -->
   </script>
   ```
   You close the comment and the script tags. The </head> tag moves to line 17.

5. **On line 18, press Enter to add a blank line.**
   Separate the <head> from the <body> sections of the page.

6. **On line 19, expand the <body> tag. Type:** `<body onload="load()">`
   The `onload` attribute is new. One of the event attributes, `onload` means that an event is triggered when an action occurs—in this case, when the page loads.

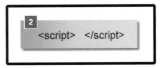

<TIP>
Using comment tags hides the content from older browsers but doesn't affect running the script in JavaScript-enabled browsers.

<NOTE>
In the figures showing JavaScript, script references to some attributes and file locations are shown in italics. This is a function of the program used to display the code captured in the figures; you don't need italics, and can't add them in Notepad.

7. **In Notepad, choose File→Save to save the** logo.html **page.**

8. **Open Internet Explorer, and then open** index.html.
   The frameset for the Sizzle site loads into the browser.

9. **Note the message displayed in the status bar at the bottom of the browser window. Move your cursor over the page.**
   When you move your cursor over other items, such as hotspots on the imagemap or links, you see the content displayed; when the cursor moves off an active area on a page, the scripted message is shown again. Close the browser. You added a script to the page describing a new message for the browser window. Leave the logo.html file open in Notepad to continue with the final tutorial in this session.

<NOTE>
If you have made errors in the code, your script won't run, and you won't see the message. Review the code added in Steps 2 to 4. Pay close attention to punctuation and spacing.

<NOTE>
You identified the function and its statement in the <head> of the page. When the page loads, the head information is loaded before the body information. This means the entire script is loaded before the call is made (when the body loads) to execute the script.

Table 11-3: Writing a JavaScript Function

Content of Line	Means...
function load();	A function is a set of JavaScript statements; some functions, such as the load function, are built in. You define functions at the beginning of a file (in the head section) and call them later in the document. The pair of brackets () signify that the function has no additional arguments.
{	This is the opening bracket for the statement.
window.status = "Sizzle \-\- the hottest place to be!!";	The status bar is a component of the window object, identified as window.status. Content to be displayed is enclosed in quotation marks. A backslash is used before each of the dash characters to identify it as a character and not part of the code
}	An open bracket must have a closing bracket.

Tutorial

» Displaying an Automatic Date

The `logo.html` page now contains the site's logo and an imagemap for linking to the resorts' pages. In the final tutorial for this session, you add an automatic date to the page using JavaScript. The script is added to the <body> tag. You work with variables and an array in the script. A variable is a "container" for storing information—in this case, date information. Arrays hold a collection of similar information, such as names of months. The script that you write displays the date in the format dd "Month" yyyy, as in 01 January 2003.

1. **In Notepad, go to line 20 on the `logo.html` page and press Enter to add a blank line.**
   You insert the new script at this location.

2. **On lines 20 and 21, type:**
   ```
   <script type="text/javascript">
   <!-- hide from JavaScript-challenged browsers
   ```
   You add the opening script tag and start a comment for the script's content. You add the same tags to the body of the page as those added to the head of the page.

3. **On line 22, type:** `var d = new Date();`
   Define (or declare) the new variable with the word "`var`." You add a new variable to the script, variable "d" based on the Date object stored in (). An instance, or copy of the Date object, is identified using the "new" keyword. The Date object is used to work with dates and time.

< N O T E >

Variables are the way JavaScript stores information. For example, if you write "x=5," "x" is a variable that holds the value "5." If you then say "y=x+10," "y" holds the value "15."

4. **On lines 23 and 24, type:**
   ```
   var monthname = new Array ("Jan","Feb",
   "Mar","Apr","May",
   "Jun","Jul","Aug","Sep","Oct","Nov","Dec");
   ```
   Declare a second variable named `monthname`. The names of the months are stored in an array. An array object is used to store a set of values in a single variable name—in this case, `monthname`. You create an instance of the Array object with the `new` keyword.

< N O T E >

The content of the array is split over two lines for visibility in the session's figure.

```
20 <script type= "text/javascript">        2
21 <!-- hide from JavaScript-challenged browsers
```

```
22 var d = new Date();  3
23 var monthname = new Array( "Jan","Feb","Mar","Apr","May",  4
24 "Jun","Jul","Aug","Sep","Oct","Nov","Dec");
25 document.write(d.getDate());
26 document.write(" ");
27 document.write(monthname[d.getMonth()]);  5
28 document.write(" ");
29 document.write(d.getFullYear());
30 // done hiding -->  6
31 </script>
```

5. **On lines 25 through 29, type:**
   ```
   document.write(d.getDate());
   document.write(" ");
   document.write(monthname[d.getMonth()]);
   document.write(" ");
   document.write(d.getFullYear());
   ```
   The JavaScript command for writing output to a page is
   `document.write`. Each statement produces output using
   the `getDate`, `getMonth`, and `getFullYear` objects. The
   variable "d" is used twice to display both the numeric date
   and the numeric year. The variable "monthname" is used to
   display the month, using an element from the array identified
   in the variable.

   < N O T E >
   The two lines `document.write(" ");` each add a blank space
   on the line when the date is written, separating the day, month,
   and year values visually. The blank spaces can be included as part
   of the other statements, but it is simpler to understand when each
   statement is written in full.

6. **On lines 30 and 31, type:**
   ```
   // done hiding -->
   </script>
   ```
   You close the comment and end the script tag.

7. **In Notepad, choose File→Save to save the** `logo.html` **page.**
   You added a script to automatically write the date to the top
   of the page. You configured the date to display the day, the
   month (in words), and the full year.

8. **Open Internet Explorer, and then open** `logo.html`.
   The Sizzle frameset loads in the browser window. You see the
   date added at the upper left of the window. Close the browser.

< T I P >
If you do not see the date displayed, check the code in Steps 2
through 6.

< N O T E >
The date is present, but it distorts the other content in the page.
In the next session, you add styles to place the images in the
`logo.html` page and also style and place the date generated
by the script that you built in this tutorial.

» Session Review

This session covered some of the sophisticated elements that you can add to your Web site for added interest and information. You learned how to work with PDF files and how to insert a Flash movie into a page. The opening image in this session shows the `logo.html` page before you started work in this session.You learned how to create an imagemap, which you added to the logo's page. You tested coordinates on a map image by using special attributes, and then you modified the page to add final coordinates and map attributes to the page. You learned how JavaScript is written and added your first script—a message on the browser window's status bar. Finally, you learned how to write a script using variables and an array to add an automatic date to a Web page. In the next session, you complete the page using styles.

Here are some questions to help you review what you learned in this session. The answer to each question is in the tutorial noted in parentheses.

1. How do you save a PDF file from a Web page? (See Tutorial: Adding a PDF File to Your Site.)

2. What string of characters does a browser read as a blank space? (See Tutorial: Adding a PDF File to Your Site.)

3. When do you use the <object> tag? (See Tutorial: Embedding a Flash Movie.)

4. What are parameters? How are they set? (See Tutorial: Embedding a Flash Movie.)

5. How many shapes or hotspots can be added to a map container? (See Discussion: Building Imagemaps.)

6. Which area of an image has the coordinates 0,0? (See Discussion: Building Imagemaps.)

7. What image attribute makes an entire image work as a map? (See Tutorial: Determining Page Coordinates for an Imagemap.)

8. What does the "usemap" image attribute refer to? (See Tutorial: Using an Imagemap for Navigation.)

9. How do you write the set of coordinates for a rectangular hotspot? (See Tutorial: Using an Imagemap for Navigation.)

10. Is the same type of JavaScript used for client-side and server-side scripting? (See Discussion: Adding Dynamic Content Using JavaScript.)

11. What is the document object model? (See Discussion: Adding Dynamic Content Using JavaScript.)

12. Why should you hide the content of your scripts in the HTML page? (See Tutorial: Changing the Message on the Browser Status Bar.)

13. Why do you organize information into an array? (See Tutorial: Displaying an Automatic Date on the Imagemap.)

14. What is the JavaScript command for writing output to a page? (SeeTutorial: Displaying an Automatic Date on the Imagemap.)

» Other Projects

Use PhotoPlus 5.5 to create the imagemap used in this session. Review the HTML page exported with the image. Compare the HTML page with the session's XHTML page. Notice the differences in content, capitalization, as well as reference points for the hotspots. Modify the HTML for use on an XHTML page. Validate the page with the W3C Validator.

Explore other methods for writing the statements that you used for adding the date to your page. Try incorporating the blank spaces into the `document.write` statements. Research other ways to write the array elements and other ways to configure dates.

Using
JavaScript

Session Introduction

In the previous session, you wrote the first scripts for your Web site. You added a custom message to the browser window and added a date to the logo.html page.

You have some unfinished business to take care of on the logo.html page. The scripted date displays on the page, which is a good thing. When you view the page in a browser, the date sits at the upper left of the page, uses default text, and displaces the other content on the page, which is not a good thing. In this session, you add three styles to your site and attach them to the images and date on the logo.html page. Finally, when the code is added and the content configured, you make a final adjustment to the index.html page to accommodate the changes made on the page.

After the logo.html page is finished, it's on to the slideshow. In this session, you add more styles to the existing slideshow page. Then you work with JavaScript to configure the navigation buttons on the page. Finally, you construct the remainder of the slideshow pages for the site.

TOOLS YOU'LL USE
Notepad, Internet Explorer

CD-ROM FILES NEEDED
ss2a.jpg, ss2b.jpg, ss3a.jpg, ss3b.jpg, ss4a.jpg,
ss4b.jpg, ss5a.jpg, ss5b.jpg, ss6a.jpg, ss6b.jpg

FILES MODIFIED
index.html, logo.html, ss1.html

FILES CREATED
ss2.html, ss3.html, ss4.html, ss5.html, ss6.html

TIME REQUIRED
90 minutes

Tutorial
» Adding the Final Styles to the Logo Page

The `logo.html` page uses a logo image and the imagemap. In this tutorial, you write two positioning styles for the images and apply them to the page. The styles are added to the miscellaneous category on the `sizzle.css` style sheet. The date you previously added uses browser default text and locations. In this tutorial, you write a style for the text and apply it to the page. The script on the `logo.html` page is encased in a <div> tag to allow you to configure the output from the code—the automatic date.

```
151  img.logo {
152  position: absolute;
153  top: 0px;           3
154  }
155
156  img.map {
157  position: absolute;
158  left: 530px;        4
159  top: 0px;
160  }
```

```
32  <img class="logo"  src="images/logo.jpg"  width="500"  height="120"  alt="Sizzle site    7
33  <img class="map"   src="images/map.jpg"   width="215"  height="120"  border="0"  8
```

<NOTE>

The tutorial steps reference line numbers. Your line numbering may differ slightly from that shown in the tutorial figures or listed in the steps. Use the line numbers as references to different areas of a page, but read the content of the line carefully as you follow the steps to ensure you are modifying or adding code to the correct line.

1. **Open Notepad, choose File→Open, and select** `sizzle.css`.

2. **Go to line 151, and press Enter to add a blank line after the closing bracket of the** `img.z` **style.**
   You add another first style in the miscellaneous section of the stylesheet.

3. **On lines 151 to 154, type:**
   ```
   img.logo {
   position: absolute;
   top: 0px;
   }
   ```
   This style sets the logo image's position to the absolute top of the page.

4. **Leave a blank line. On lines 156 to 160, type:**
   ```
   img.map {
   position: absolute;
   left: 530px;
   top: 0px;
   }
   ```
   This positioning style sets the map image at the top of the window and to the right of the logo image, which is 520 pixels wide.

5. **Choose File→Save to save the** `sizzle.css` **style sheet.**
   You added two styles to the site's style sheet.

6. **Choose File→Open, and select the** `logo.html` **page.**

7. **Go to line 32, and add a class attribute to the <img> tag. Type:**
   `class="logo"` **after the opening <img tag.**
   You add the positioning style to the logo image.

8. **Go to line 33, and add a class attribute to the <img> tag. Type:**
   `class="map"` **after the opening <img tag.**
   You add the positioning style to the map image.

9. **In Notepad, choose File→Save to save the** `logo.html` **page.**
   You wrote and applied two styles for placing the logo and map images.

10. **Open Internet Explorer, and open** `logo.html`.

    You see the images are flush with the top of the window, but the date is still at the left margin. Close the browser.

11. **In Notepad, open** `sizzle.css`.

12. **Go to line 162. On lines 162 through 172, type:**
    ```
    div.date {
    color: #FF0033;
    background-color: transparent;
    font-family: Arial,sans-serif;
    font-size:12px;
    font-weight: bolder;
    position: absolute;
    left: 495px;
    top: 95px;
    z-index: 1;
    }
    ```

    This is a custom style for the date. The date is generated dynamically using JavaScript and doesn't have tags such as <p> or <h1> attached; instead it uses the browser's defaults. Enclosing the entire script within <div> tags allows you to control how the text is displayed. The date is configured to overlay the other images on the page. The position of the text is within the borders of the logo.jpg image. In order to be visible, you set the z-index property for the date text to 1.

< N O T E >

Unless a z-index value is specified, the content on a page sits on layer 0; a z-index value of 1 adds content on top of the rest of the page content.

13. **Choose File→Save to save the** `sizzle.css` **page.**

    You added another custom style.

14. **Choose File→Open, and choose** `logo.html`.

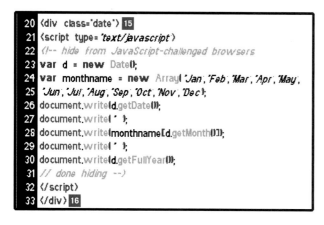

15. Go to line 20. Type: `<div class="date">`
This adds the opening <div> tag, and adds the `class` property and new style.

16. Go to line 33, and press Enter to add a blank line. Type: `</div>`
This adds the </div> tag.

17. In Notepad, choose File→Save.
The `logo.html` page is saved. You wrote styles for placing the images on the page and configuring the automatic date text and applied them to the page's elements. Leave Notepad open for the next tutorial.

18. Open Internet Explorer, and then open `index.html`.
The Sizzle frameset loads in the browser.

19. View the page. Note that the scripted date is styled and placed on the page.
The images are positioned at the top margin; extraneous space appears below the logo and map images. Minimize the browser.

Tutorial
» Adjusting the Sizzle Site's Frameset

In the previous tutorial, you added styles to place the images and automatic date text on the `logo.html` page. You have completed all the work required for this page. In this tutorial, you make some adjustments to the `index.html` page. When the frameset page was constructed, you left additional space in the top frame for testing purposes and also left a border for visibility. Now that the content of the frame, the `logo.html` page, is complete, you fine-tune the frameset.

1. **In Notepad, choose File→Open and choose** `index.html`.
   You finished the page's layout and are ready to make final adjustments to the frameset.

2. **Go to line 10, and change the** `rows` **attribute from** `"165,*"` **to** `"120,*"`
   You used a row size larger than the images when the frameset was initially designed to allow room for placement of objects.

<NOTE>
After you are finished designing the page, remove extraneous space. The `logo.html` frame doesn't need the space, and you can provide more screen display for the content in the second frameset row—the navigation and main frames.

3. **Go to line 17, and change the** `frameborder` **attribute from** `"1"` **to** `"0"`
   This removes the border. Now the placement and design is complete.

4. **Choose File→Save.**
   The `index.html` frameset page is saved. Leave Notepad open for the next tutorial.

5. **Open Internet Explorer, and then open** `index.html`.
   Note that the top frame is now the depth of the images; note also that the frame's border is removed, giving the page a smoother appearance. Close the browser.

Tutorial

» Building Styles for the Slideshow Page

Now it's time for the slideshow. In this tutorial, you add five new styles to the style sheet. The styles are applied to elements on the slideshow page in the next tutorial. Rather than building a style, applying it, and testing the styles one by one, you create the entire set of styles at once, and then apply and test them. The new styles are added to the slideshow style section on the page that starts at line 50. Add the styles to the page in the same order as they are used on the `ss1.html` page. For example, a style used for the text caption on the page is written before a style used for the text links at the bottom of the page.

1. In Notepad, open `sizzle.css`.

2. Go to line 68, and press Enter to add a blank line after the closing bracket of the `tr.textrow` style.
   You add the first new slideshow style.

3. On lines 69 to 80, type:
   ```
   p.textrow {
   text-align: center;
   color: #333366;
   background-color: #D2FFF1;
   font-family: Arial,sans-serif;
   font-size: 11pt;
   line-height: 130%;
   margin: 5px 15px 5px 15px;
   border: solid;
   border-color: #FFFF99;
   border-width: 2px;
   }
   ```
   You write a style for the text caption on the page. The text is similar in layout and format to the style that you wrote earlier for paragraph captions used on other pages of the site.

4. Go to line 87, and press Enter to add a blank line.
   You add tags for the text links at the bottom of the page. On the `sizzle.css` sheet, the link styles are written after the `div.center` style used for the image buttons.

5. **On lines 88 to 93, type:**

```
a.red:visited {
color: #FF0000;
background-color: transparent;
font-family: Arial,sans-serif;
text-decoration: none;
}
```

You add a style for the text tags at the bottom of the page. The text uses the site's custom red color. Set the text-decoration property's value to "none" to remove the default underline from the links.

6. **Press Enter to add a blank line. On lines 95 to 98, type:**

```
a.red:hover {
color: #009966;
background-color:rgb(230,230,179);
}
```

You add a style for the anchor's hover state. The color and background color are the same as that used for the rest of the site.

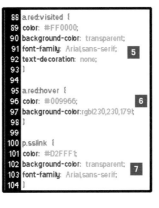

<NOTE>

The style written for the links on the rest of the site use a dark green as the text color; in the slideshow, the dark green is hard to read against the striped background. The new style, a.red:hover, makes the links on the slideshow pages easy to see.

7. **Press Enter to add a blank line. On lines 100 to 104, type:**

```
p.sslink {
color: #D2FFF1;
background-color: transparent;
font-family: Arial,sans-serif;
}
```

You add the last style for the slideshow. The style is used for the vertical bars separating the text links at the bottom of the slideshow page.

8. **Choose File➔Save.**

The sizzle.css style sheet is saved with the five new styles. Leave Notepad open to continue with the next tutorial.

<NOTE>

This would be a good time to test the style sheet using the W3C CSS Validator. You added several complex new styles, and a quick test at this point can save time later.

Tutorial

» Applying Styles and Links to the Slideshow Page

You just built five additional styles for the slideshow page. In this tutorial, you apply the styles. You also add two in-line styles to complete the slideshow page's layout and create links from the text at the bottom of the table. Test the page using the W3C Markup Validator.

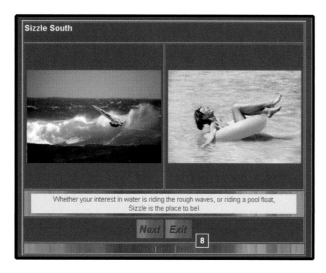

1. **In Notepad, open** `ss1.html`.

2. **Go to line 14 and after** `<td colspan="2">`, **type:** `<h3 style="color:#E1FFFF">`
   You add heading tags and apply an inline style. The line now reads: `<td colspan-"2"><h3style="color:#E1FFFF"> Sizzle South</h3></td>`.

3. **Expand the <p> tag on line 23. After the opening <p tag, type:** `class="textrow"`
   You attach the new paragraph style to the caption text.

4. **Go to line 35 and after the <td> tag, type:** `<div style="text-align: center">`
   You add a <div> tag to serve as a container for aligning the three text links. Create an in-line style for alignment within the <div> tag.

5. **On line 35, expand the <p> tag. Type:** `<p class="sslink">` **and press Enter.**
   You attach another new style. The style is applied only to the three vertical separator bars between the text links. The link text is moved to line 36.

6. **On lines 36 to 38, add link information for each text link. Type:**
   ```
   <a class="red" href="index.html"> BACK </a> |
   <a class="red" href="ss2.html"> NEXT </a> |
   <a class="red" href="index.html"> EXIT
   </a></p></div></td>
   ```
   You attach anchors to each word and use the new anchor styles that you created in the previous tutorial. The BACK and EXIT links both return the user to the Sizzle frameset; the NEXT link takes the reader to the second slideshow page. Each link automatically loads the link into the slideshow's browser window.

7. **Choose File→Save.**
   The `ss1.html` slideshow page is saved. You completed the styles and added them to the page. You also added links to the text at the bottom of the page. Leave `ss1.html` open in Notepad for the next tutorial. You write scripts for the image buttons on the page.

8. **Open Internet Explorer, and open** `ss1.html` **to test the styles and links.**
   Note how the styles are attached to different elements on the page. Click the links at the bottom of the page to test them. Close the browser.

< N O T E >
Make sure that the tags are closed in sequence. The </p> and </td> tags were present in the page; add the </a> tag immediately after the EXIT text; add the </div> tag after the </p> tag. The </td> tag ends the sequence.

< N O T E >
You haven't built the second page yet. When you test the NEXT link, you receive a "Page Not Found" error.

Discussion
More on Writing Variables and Defining Functions

You have written a number of variables so far. In all cases, you write a variable using the prefix `var`. You can write variables without using `var` at the beginning of the statement. However, it is simpler to read and understand what you are writing if you use the term, as in the example:

```
var temperature = degrees
```

The variable name is on the left side of the expression (the equal [=] sign separates the left and right sides of the expression), and the value that you assign to the variable is on the right. Assign a value to the variable such as "75" now the variable "temperature" has the value "75".

You have used some of the built-in JavaScript functions such as `write` and `load` and the `date` functions. You can also write your own functions. Functions are composed of several parts.

» Start with the word "function", just as you started a variable with "var" to identify it in your code.

» Name a value, some sort of descriptive name that helps you understand what you are writing.

» Define the variables that make up the value, often some sort of calculation. Variables used in a function are called "arguments". It isn't necessary to use arguments in all functions as some use absolute values.

» Write the statements. A statement is a way to test a condition. For example, if it rains put on a raincoat, if it is sunny, put on a hat.

Write a function like this:

```
function myfunction (argument1,argument2)
{
statements go here
}
```

» Include parentheses even if you have no arguments in the function:

```
function function1()
{
statements go here
}
```

» Add functions to the head section of the page to make sure that all the code is loaded before the function is called.

Functions that produce a result must use the "return" statement. The statement specifies the value returned. In this example, the function returns the sum of two numbers:

```
function total(a,b)
{
result=a+b
return result
}
```

Here's what the function means:

`function total(a,b)`   The function is identified using the word "function"; the value is named "total", and the value is composed of two arguments with values of "a" and "b".

`{` This open the statements.

`result=a+b`   The first statement is called result, and it is made up of the total of "a" plus "b".

`return result`   The second statement is called return. Its function is to produce the outcome of the result statement.

`}`   This closes the statements.

If you use a function in your code, it is enclosed within the <head> tags. The function is processed, or called, from the <body> of the page. When the function is called, values are sent for the arguments in the statement `result=a+b` such as 2 and 3.

The return result, or the returned value from the function is 5.

Tutorial
» Writing Scripts for Navigation Using Button Images

The slideshow page is visually developed. You added content and wrote styles to configure the appearance of the table, text, and images on the page. You added links from the text at the bottom of the page to other pages on the slideshow and your site. The only incomplete element on the page is the pair of navigation buttons. In this tutorial, you write the script for the navigation buttons. Your script requires four variables in total for the button states. To make it simpler to understand and to decrease error, you write, apply, and test the scripts for one button at a time. You built the navigation buttons in Session 4 and added them to the Images folder at that time.

1. **In Notepad, open** `ss1.html`. **Go to line 9, and press Enter to add a blank line before the closing <head> tag.**

2. **On lines 9 and 10, type:**
   ```
   <script type="text/javascript">
   <!--
   ```
   Add the opening script tag, as well as the opening comment tag to hide the content from older browsers. You don't have to add any text to the comment.

<NOTE>
In the figures showing JavaScript, script references to some attributes and file locations are shown in italics. This is a function of the program used to display the code captured in the figures; you don't need italics, and can't add them in Notepad.

```
 9  <script type="text/javascript">
10  <!--
11  var next_ovr = new Image();
12  var next_out  = new Image();
13  next_ovr.src = "images/nextB.jpg"
14  next_out.src = "images/nextA.jpg"
15  // done hiding -->
16  </script>
17  </head>
```

3. **On lines 11 through 14, type:**
   ```
   var next_ovr = new Image();
   var next_out = new Image();
   next_ovr.src = "Images/nextB.jpg"
   next_out.src = "Images/nextA.jpg"
   ```
   You need a variable for each state of the button that you want to use on the page. You create two new objects of the Image type, one for the state called `next_ovr` and the other for the state called `next_out`. The source (`src`) property of each object is the image's file name. When the page is loaded in a browser, the images are preloaded and display quickly.

4. **Go to line 15. On lines 15 and 16, type:**
   ```
   // -->
   </script>
   ```
   You add the closing comment and ending script tags. The </head> tag is pushed down to line 17.

5. **Go to line 37, and press Enter.**
   Add a blank line below the opening <td> and <div> tags for the button images, which are located on line 36.

<NOTE>
You can use several mouse events, such as onmouseover, onmousedown, onmouseup, and onmouseout. Your page uses two events—onmouseover and onmouseout. The default state shows the button image (blue text on a green background). Moving the mouse over the image invokes the onmouseover state and swaps the image for the second version of the button (yellow text on a blue background). Clicking the button link has no variation attached to it. When you move the mouse away from the button, called onmouseout, the image swaps to the original again.

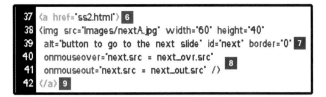

```
37   <a href="ss2.html"> 6
38   <img src="Images/nextA.jpg" width="60" height="40"
39   alt="button to go to the next slide" id="next" border="0" 7
40   onmouseover="next.src = next_ovr.src"
41   onmouseout="next.src = next_out.src" /> 8
42   </a> 9
```

6. **On line 37, type:** $\langle$a href="ss2.html"$\rangle$
   You add a link to the second slideshow page.

7. **Following the** alt **attribute on line 39, type:** id="next"
   border="0"
   You assign a unique name to the button. Because the button
   is used for a link, set the border to "0" to remove it.

8. **On lines 40 and 41, type:**
   onmouseover="next.src = next_ovr.src"
   onmouseout="next.src = next_out.src" />
   Assign an action to the events. When the user moves the cursor over the image, whose id is "next", the script is triggered
   and the source of the image changes to the named variable.
   The JavaScript interpreter understands that the next_ovr.
   src file is the nextB.jpg image based on the variable that
   you wrote in the head of the page and that the next_out.
   src file is the nextA.jpg image. The variables swap in and
   out of the <img /> element's source attribute (src) in
   response to cursor movement.

9. **On line 42, type:** $\langle$/a$\rangle$
   You close the anchor tag.

10. **Choose File➜Save to save the** ss1.html **page.**
    You added the scripts for the first button image and its link.

11. **Open Internet Explorer, and then open** ss1.html.
    You test the link.

12. **Move the cursor over the Next button at the bottom of the page.**
    You see the images swap.

<NOTE>
When you move the cursor over the image, you also see a frame
extending beyond the right and bottom edges of the button. The
frame is actually the a:hover style used on the page.

13. **Click the Next button.**
    An error page loads into the window. Close the browser.
    The error page loads because you haven't created the other
    slideshow pages yet.

14. **In Notepad, go to line 15 and press Enter to add a blank line.**
    You add variables and their values for the second navigation
    button.

15. On line 15 through 18, type:

```
var exit_ovr = new Image();
var exit_out = new Image();
exit_ovr.src = "Images/exitB.jpg"
exit_out.src = "Images/exitA.jpg"
```

You add variables for the Exit button. The two variables are defined and values assigned in much the same way as the Next button's script. The closing comment and </script> tags now follow the script on lines 20 and 21.

```
15  var exit_ovr  = new  Image();
16  var exit_out  = new  Image();
17  exit_ovr.src  =  "Images/exitB.jpg"
18  exit_out.src  =  "Images/exitA.jpg"
19  // -->
20  </script>
```

< T I P >
You can also copy and paste the content from the first pair of variables and their values and then customize for the second button.

16. Go to line 47, and press Enter.

Add a blank line after the </a> tag for the first image on line 46.

17. On line 47, type: `<a href="index.html">`

You add a link to the Sizzle frameset. If the reader clicks the button, the slideshow page is replaced by the site's frameset in the same browser window.

```
47  <a href="index.html">
48  <img src="Images/exitA.jpg" alt="button to exit slideshow"
49  width="60" height="40" id="exit" border="0"
50    onmouseover="exit.src = exit_ovr.src"
51    onmouseout="exit.src = exit_out.src" />
52  </a></div></td>
```

18. Following the `alt` **attribute that ends on line 49, type:**

```
id="exit" border="0"
```

You assign a unique name to the button. Because the button is used for a link, set the border to "0" to remove it.

19. On lines 50 and 51, type:

```
onmouseover="exit.src = exit_ovr.src"
onmouseout="exit.src = exit_out.src" />
```

You assign action to mouse events. Make sure the closing /> for the image tag follows the content on line 51.

20. On line 52, type `</a>` **before the closing <div> and table cell tags.**

You close the anchor tag.

< T I P >
Proper code requires that you open and close each pair of tags in sequence; the first tag opened is the last tag closed.

21. In Notepad, choose File➡Save.

You added navigation scripts to the page and tested the two buttons. The first slideshow page is complete. Leave Notepad and `ss1.html` open for the next tutorial.

22. Open Internet Explorer, and then open `ss1.html`.

The page loads in the browser window.

23. Click the Exit button to test it.

Click the button to load the Sizzle frameset in the window. Close the browser.

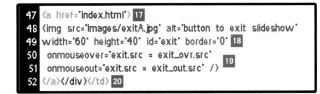

Tutorial
» Constructing the Sizzle Slideshow

The first slideshow page is finished. Early in the development process, you learned that creating a set of similar pages is simpler when one page is complete and tested. You are at that point now with the slideshow. In this tutorial, you create the rest of the slideshow pages and then modify each page. There are eight modifications for each page.

```
5
6  <title>Slideshow 2 </title>
7  <meta http-equiv="Content-Type" content="text/html; charset=utf-8" />
8  <link href="sizzle.css" rel="stylesheet" type="text/css" />
```

```
26    <td colspan="2"><h3 style="color:#E1FFFF">Sizzle East</h3></td>
27    </tr>                                              6
28    <tr class="imagerow">
29  7 <td><img src="Images/ss2a.jpg"  class="sslayout" width="300" height="200"
30    alt="couple standing on a beach with ocean in background"/></td>
31  8 <td><img src="Images/ss2b.jpg" class="sslayout" width="300" height="200"
32    alt="group of people on poolside lounge chairs" /></td>
33    </tr>
34    <tr class="textrow">
35    <td colspan="2"> <p class="textrow">Find that special someone or
36    just get away on your own. <br />                  9
37    Sizzle East is the place to go!</p></td>
```

```
40    <td colspan="2"> <div class ="center">
41 <a href="ss3.html"> 10
```

1. **Transfer the slideshow images to the site's Images folder.**
   The images are located in the Images Storage folder on the CD. You use a set of 12 images for the slideshow.

2. **In Notepad, open** `ss1.html`. **Choose File→Save As. Name the file** `ss2.html`, **and click Save.**
   You save a second copy of the slideshow page.

3. **Repeat Step 2 four more times, and name the pages** `ss3.html` **to** `ss6.html`.
   You have six slideshow pages in total.

4. **Open** `ss2.html`.
   You customize the page.

5. **Go to line 6, and retitle the page:** `Slideshow 2`
   The titles correspond to the name and content of the pages.

6. **Go to line 26, and replace the heading. Type:** `Sizzle East`
   Each slide includes images of the different resorts.

7. **On lines 29 and 30, revise the <img> tag. After the opening <img tag, type:** `src="Images/ss2a.jpg" class="sslayout" width="300" height="200" alt="couple standing on a beach with ocean in background"/>`
   The new image is added. You replaced the alt text for the image.

8. **On lines 31 and 32, revise the <img> tag. Type:** `<img src="Images/ss2b.jpg" class="sslayout" width="300" height="200" alt="group of people on poolside lounge chairs" />`
   You add the second image and revise its attributes.

9. **On lines 35 to 37, modify the page's caption. Type:** `Find that special someone or just get away on your own. <br /> Sizzle East is the place to go!`
   Each caption corresponds with the page's images.

10. **On line 41, add an attribute to the anchor tag. After the opening <a tag, type:** `href="ss3.html"` **followed by the closing >.**
    From the second slideshow page, you want the link to display the third page.

11. **Modify the BACK text anchor tag on line 56. Change the** `href`
    attribute's value to `href="ss1.html"`
    The BACK text links to the first slideshow page.

12. **Modify the NEXT text anchor tag on line 57. Change the** `href`
    attribute's value to `href="ss3.html"`
    The anchor tag is attached to the NEXT text link; clicking the
    link from the page takes the reader to the third slideshow
    page, `ss3.html`.

13. **Choose File→Save.**
    You save the second slideshow page.

14. **Open Internet Explorer, and then open** `ss1.html`.
    You test the links.

15. **Click Next.**
    The `ss2.html` page loads in the browser window.

16. **Click Next on the** `ss2.html` **page.**
    The `ss3.html` page loads in the browser window. Close the
    browser.

17. **Repeat Steps 3 through 13 for** `ss3.html`.
    Make modifications to the page as listed in Table 12-1.

< T I P >

When working with a group of pages, as you are in the tutorial, it's
a good idea to make a list of the changes required on each page.
Systematically go through each page, making the changes. When
testing the pages after construction, follow the same list again to
make sure that your pages are error-free.

18. **Repeat Steps 3 through 13 for** `ss4.html`.
    Make modifications to the page as listed in Table 12-2.

19. **Repeat Steps 3 through 13 for** `ss5.html`.
    Make modifications to the page as listed in Table 12-3.

20. **Repeat Steps 3 through 13 for** `ss6.html`.
    Make modifications to the page as listed in Table 12-4.

21. **Open Internet Explorer, and then open** `ss1.html`.
    Test each page's links. Check the button links as well as the
    text links at the bottom of the page. Check the image sizes
    and the `alt` text for the images. Close the browser.

< T I P >

If any links aren't working, check your code carefully. Make sure
you haven't made any spelling errors or left out closing tags, which
are two common sources of error.

22. **Close Notepad.**
    You created the rest of the slideshow pages. You modified the
    content and tested the pages in your browser.

Table 12-1: Modifications for the Slideshow Page 3 Content (ss3.html)

Line Numbers	Tag or Attribute	Modify Content to Read...
6	page title	Slideshow 3
26	heading	Sizzle West
29-30	image1	<img src="Images/ss3a.jpg" class="sslayout" width="200" height="300" alt="couple at table in private beach cabana" />
31-32	image2	<img src="Images/ss3b.jpg" class="sslayout" width="300" height="300" alt="closeup of breakfast tray showing pancakes and flowers" />
35-37	caption	You can enjoy breakfast in your room or
		by the pool in your private cabana.
		Our room service staff are happy to serve you.
41	href	href="ss4.html"
56	href	href="ss2.html"
57	href	href="ss4.html"

Table 12-2: Modifications for the Slideshow Page 4 Content (ss4.html)

Line Numbers	Tag or Attribute	Modify Content to Read...
6	page title	Slideshow 4
26	heading	Sizzle South (no change)
29-30	image1	<img src="Images/ss4a.jpg" class="sslayout" width="300" height="200" alt="closeup of couple on a sailboat" />
31-32	image2	<img src="Images/ss4b.jpg" class="sslayout" width="300" height="200" alt="man waterskiing" />
35-37	caption	At Sizzle South water sports rule!
		Sailing, surfing, waterskiing -
		we have it all.
41	href	href="ss5.html"
56	href	href="ss3.html"
57	href	href="ss5.html"

Table 12-3: Modifications for the Slideshow Page 5 Content (`ss5.html`)

Line Numbers	Tag or Attribute	Modify Content to Read...
6	page title	Slideshow 5
26	heading	Sizzle East
29-30	image1	<img src="Images/ss5a.jpg" class="sslayout" width="200" height="300" alt="man on a golf course" />
31-32	image2	<img src="Images/ss5b.jpg" class="sslayout" width="240" height="300" alt="seafood baking in a firepit in the sand" />
35-37	caption	Hang out on the beach, by the pool, or play a round of golf. Work up an appetite for one of our regular cookouts on the beach!
41	href	href="ss6.html"
56	href	href="ss4.html"
57	href	href="ss6.html"

Table 12-4: Modifications for the Slideshow Page 6 Content (`ss6.html`)

Line Numbers	Tag or Attribute	Modify Content to Read...
6	Page title	Slideshow 6
26	Heading	Sizzle West
29-30	image1	<img src="Images/ss6a.jpg" class="sslayout" width="200" height="300" alt="young couple embracing on a beach" />
31-31	image2	<img src="Images/ss6b.jpg" class="sslayout" width="200" height="300" alt="couple in the hotel pool" />
35-37	caption	At Sizzle West we offer a quiet, secluded, romantic experience. Spend time on our private beach or at the pool, accessible from every room.
41	href	href="index.html"
56	href	href="ss5.html"
57	href	href="index.html"

» Session Review

The top frame of the frameset showing the site's logo and the imagemap is complete and configured. The opening image in this session shows the `logo.html` page as it looked when you started the session. You created positioning styles for the images, and then wrote a style to place and format the automatic date added to the page using JavaScript. To configure the text generated by the script, you contained the code within <div> tags. The final results are shown in the closing image of this session.

You assembled the slideshow pages. You wrote scripts for the navigation buttons on the first slideshow page. After the page was finished and all styles attached, you made copies for the remaining slideshow pages. You modified each of the additional pages in the slideshow. Aside from another script that you add to the first and last pages in the next session, the slideshow which is now almost complete.

Answer these questions to help you review what you learned in the session. The answer to each question can be found in the tutorial noted in parentheses.

1. Can you define one positioning coordinate in a style, or must you use both x-axis and y-axis coordinates? (See Tutorial: Adding the Final Styles to the Logo Page.)

2. What element allows you to configure text written to a page using JavaScript? (See Tutorial: Adding the Final Styles to the Logo Page.)

3. Should you leave extra room in a frame beyond that required for displaying the contents? Why or why not? (See Tutorial: Adjusting the Sizzle Site's Frameset.)

4. What is one simple way to organize numerous styles used for the same pages in a site? (See Tutorial: Building Styles for the Slideshow Page.)

5. How do you write an inline style? (See Tutorial: Applying Styles and Links to the Slideshow Page.)

6. Can you use a `<div>` element to surround other elements, such as paragraphs? (See Tutorial: Applying Styles and Links to the Slideshow Page.)

7. What is the rule for opening and closing element tags? (See Tutorial: Applying Styles and Links to the Slideshow Page.)

8. Should you use `var` at the beginning of a statement when writing a variable? Why or why not? (See Discussion: More on Writing Variables and Defining Functions.)

9. What do you call a variable used in a function? (See Discussion: More on Writing Variables and Defining Functions.)

10. What are events? How do you write events used with cursor movement on a page? (See Tutorial: Writing Scripts for Navigation Using Button Images.)

11. How do you assign a value to a variable? (See Tutorial: Writing Scripts for Navigation Using Button Images.)

12. How do you trigger an event? (See Tutorial: Writing Scripts for Navigation Using Button Images.)

13. When working with similar pages, is it simpler to construct all pages simultaneously or complete one page and duplicate/modify for the remaining pages? (See Tutorial: Constructing the Sizzle Slideshow.)

14. How should you manage modifying a group of similar pages? (See Tutorial: Constructing the Sizzle Slideshow.)

» Other Projects

Experiment with other events for the slideshow page's buttons such as the `onmousedown` and `onmouseout` events. Write variables and assign values to the variables for the additional events.

Adding a Form to Your Site

We want to hear from you. Complete our Sizzle survey. -...

File   Edit   View   Favorites   Tools   Help

← Back   →   ⊗   🗐   🏠   🔍 Search   ⊛ Favorites   🎬 Media   »

Sizzle Survey

🖹 Done   🖳 My Computer

Session Introduction

You worked with JavaScript in the last two sessions, writing scripts for actions such as button links and displaying dates. In this session, you add more scripts to your site.

The slideshow pages are complete with their content and button links. In this session, you add a scripted message for one button on pages 1 and 6 of the slideshow.

You work with the window object in this session. The site map page opens in a new browser window. You add a script that determines where and how the window displays on the desktop.

As you can see by the session's title, you work with a form in this session as well. Forms are special types of objects, and they have specific elements and scripting requirements. The results of the form that you construct in the session are transmitted via e-mail. You write a script to validate the user's e-mail address on the form.

TOOLS YOU'LL USE
Notepad, Internet Explorer

CD-ROM FILES NEEDED
contact.html, index.html, nav_left.html, ss1.html,
ss6.html

TIME REQUIRED
90 minutes

Tutorial
» Displaying Messages for the Reader

When you tested the set of slideshow pages in the previous session, you noticed that clicking the BACK button on the first slideshow page loads the site's frameset in the window. Likewise, clicking the NEXT button on the last slideshow page also loads the site's frameset. To your user, the links out of the slideshow may appear as errors. In this tutorial, you construct a script that displays a message to the user when these buttons are clicked on slides 1 and 6.

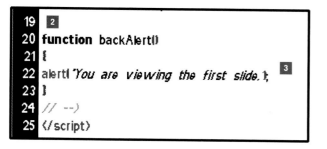

1. **Open Notepad, and then open** `ss1.html`.
   You add another script to the page.

2. **Go to line 19, and press Enter to add a blank line after the final line of the button image scripts, which reads** `exit_out.src = "Images/exitA.jpg"`.
   You add additional script information, so you need to separate the scripts with a blank line.

3. **On lines 20 to 23, type:**
   ```
   function backAlert()
   {
   alert("You are viewing the first slide.");
   }
   ```
   This is a new function named `backAlert`. Alert is a built-in JavaScript function. In the statement, you write the text as it is to appear on the alert message box. Enclose the text in quotation marks and end the statement with a semicolon.

4. **Go to line 61, and revise the `<a>` tag. Type:** `<a class="red" href="#" onclick="backAlert()">BACK</a> |`
   Use the "#" `href` to refer to the current page. The `onclick` event is used to trigger the function. The text remains the same, as does the separator bar at the end of the line.

5. **Choose File→Save.**
   The `ss1.html` page is saved with its alert dialog script.

6. **Open Internet Explorer, and then open** `ss1.html`.
   You test the script.

7. **Click BACK.**
   The alert box displays.

<NOTE>
The status bar at the bottom of the page shows the location on the page as `ss1.html#` or the anchor location that you added in the script in Step 5.

8. **Click OK to close the alert box.**
   Minimize the browser.

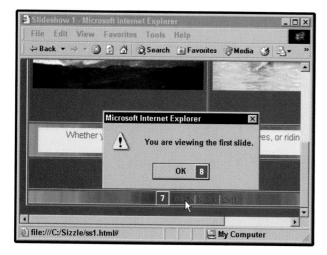

9. **In Notepad, choose File→Open, choose** `ss6.html`, **and click Open.**

   You add an alert box script to the page.

10. **Go to line 19, and press Enter to add a blank line.**

    You add another script, so you need to separate the scripts visually on the page as you did in Step 2.

11. **On lines 20 to 23, type:**

    ```
    function nextAlert()
    {
    alert("You are viewing the last slide.");
    }
    ```

    You add a function similar to that added to the `ss1.html` page. The function is named according to the link that you attach it to in the page.

12. **Go to line 46, and modify the anchor tag to read:** `<a href="#" onclick="nextAlert()">`

    In the last session, you set the NEXT button's link to the `index.html` page temporarily. This replaces the link with an alert. Clicking the NEXT button displays the alert box.

13. **Go to line 62, and revise the anchor tag to read:** `<a class="red" href="#" onclick="nextAlert()">NEXT</a> |`

    In the last session, you set the NEXT text link to the `index.html` page temporarily. This replaces the link with an alert.

14. **In Notepad, choose File→Save to save the** `ss6.html` **page.**

    You added scripts to two pages to control the user's path through the slideshow pages.

15. **Open Internet Explorer, and then open** `ss6.html`.

16. **Click NEXT.**

    The alert dialog box opens.

17. **Click OK to close the alert box.**

    The script works correctly.

18. **Click the NEXT text link.**

    The alert dialog box opens.

19. **Click OK to close the alert box.**

    Close Internet Explorer. Leave Notepad open for the next tutorial.

< N O T E >

The tutorial steps reference line numbers. Your line numbering may differ slightly from that shown in the tutorial figures or listed in the steps. Use the line numbers as references to different areas of a page, but read the content of the line carefully as you follow the steps to ensure you are modifying or adding code to the correct line.

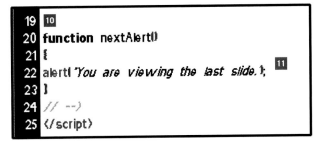

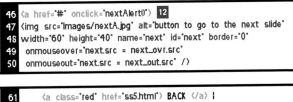

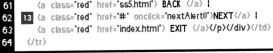

Tutorial
» Managing Open Windows Using JavaScript

Windows are one of the major classes of objects in the document object model, as described in Session 11. The site map page of the Sizzle site opens in a blank window from the frameset. In this tutorial, you write a script to load the `sitemap.html` page into the Sizzle frameset window. You write a new function in the head of the document and then trigger the script using the site map's link on the `nav_left.html` page.

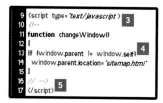

1. **In Notepad, open** `nav_left.html`.
   You write the first script on the navigation frame's page.

2. **Go to line 9, and press Enter to add a line following the** `<link href>` **code attaching the stylesheet to the page.**

3. **On lines 9 and 10, type:**
   ```
   <script type="text/javascript">
   <!--
   ```
   You write the opening script and comment tags.

4. **On lines 11 through 15, type:**
   ```
   function changeWindow()
   {
   if (window.parent != window.self)
    window.parent.location="sitemap.html"
   }
   ```
   The function for the site map page is named `changeWindow`. You write an if-statement based on frame assignments using the `!=` (not equal to) operator. The question, or condition, is this: Is the entire frameset the same as the window loaded? If not, the parent window's location is set to the `sitemap.html` page.

5. **On lines 16 and 17, type:**
   ```
   // -->
   </script>
   ```
   You close the comment and script tags.

< N O T E >

Using the `parent` and `self` frame descriptions is a simple way to define the windows in the argument. `parent` opens the linked document in the parent frameset of the frame in which the link appears, replacing the entire frameset; `self` opens the link in the current frame, replacing the content in that frame. In terms of the Sizzle site, `parent` refers to the `index.html` frameset; `self` refers to `sitemap.html`. If you try to add the `target="self"` attribute to the `sitemap.html` link from the `nav_left.html` frame, the page loads in the navigation frame.

Managing Windows in the Sizzle Site

The site map page opens outside the Sizzle frameset. A user clicks a link on the site map, and another browser window opens; links clicked on the site map page continue to load into the same window. There are three windows open during this process. A better use of screen space and browser windows is for the site map to replace the frameset, for the site map page to be located on a specific location, and for the frameset to reload when the site map is closed.

You can't make the changes without using JavaScript. You write a script to swap windows on the `nav_left.html` page. You write a script on the `sitemap.html` page to control its location and size. When you return to the frameset, it is loaded into the small-sized window. You write one more script for the `index.html` frameset page to control its size as well.

6. **Go to line 71, and modify the link for the** `sitemap.html` **page
   to read:** `<td class="nav2"><a href="sitemap.html"
   onclick="javascript:changeWindow()"> Site
   Map</a></td>`
   You add the `onclick` event attribute and assign the new
   function as the value. The script runs when the link is clicked.

```
70   <tr>
71     <td class="nav2"><a href="sitemap.html" onclick="javascript:changeWindow()">
72       Site Map</a></td>
73   </tr>
```

<NOTE>

The figure shows the content wrapping over lines 71 and 72. The
wrapping was added to display the content in the image; in the
session's file, the text is on line 71 only.

7. **In Notepad, choose File→Save to save the** `nav_left.html`
   page.
   You added a function to load the site map page into the parent
   window.

8. **Open Internet Explorer, and then open** `index.html`.
   You test the first script.

9. **In the navigation frame, click Site Map.**
   The `sitemap.html` page loads into the open browser
   window.

10. **Close the browser.**
   You tested the first script. Now that the `sitemap.html` page
   loads into the single browser window, you need a return link
   from the page back to the frameset. You add that link in the
   next tutorial.

Tutorial

» Controlling Window Sizes Using JavaScript

In the previous tutorial, you wrote a script to open the site map page into the Sizzle frameset browser window. The site map opens at whatever size the frameset was using when you clicked the link from the `nav_left.html` frame. In this tutorial, you write a script to control the size and location of the site map window. The script is triggered when the page loads in the browser. You also add a link to return to the frameset. Finally, you add a script to the frameset to resize it as well.

1. **In Notepad, choose File→Open. Choose** `sitemap.html`, **and click Open.**
   You add a script and a link to the page.

2. **Go to line 9, and press Enter to add a line.**
   You add a script to the page.

3. **On lines 9 and 10, type:**
   ```
   <script type="text/javascript">
   <!--
   ```
   You open the script tag and comment.

4. **On line 11, type:** `function document_onload()`
   You name the function. The function is later called from the <body> tag.

5. **On lines 12 through 14, type:**
   ```
   { self.resizeTo(350,500);
     self.moveTo(0,0);
   }
   ```
   The two statements, surrounded by curly braces, are both applicable to the self object, the `sitemap.html` page. The `resizeTo` property of the `self` object is given values of 350 and 500 pixels (pixels are the default and are understood; you don't have to specify). When the script is run, the page is sized to 350 x 500 pixels. The `moveTo` property of the `self` object is given values of 0 and 0 pixels; when the script is run, the window moves to the top left of the screen. Each statement is ended with a semicolon.

6. **On lines 15 and 16, type:**
   ```
   // -->
   </script>
   ```
   You close the comment and script tags.

7. **On line 18, press Enter to add a blank line.**
   Separate the <head> content from the <body> content.

8. **On line 19, type:** `<body onload="document_onload()">`
   You add the event to the <body> tag. When the body of the page is loaded in the browser, the function is called and the page is resized.

<NOTE>
In the figures showing JavaScript, script references to some attributes and file locations are shown in italics. This is a function of the program used to display the code captured in the figures; you don't need italics, and can't add them in Notepad.

<NOTE>
There are two events associated with the <body> tag. You used the `onload` event that executes when a page loads. You can also use the `onunload` event, which executes when a page unloads.

9. **Go to line 43, and press Enter to add a blank line. On line 44, type:** <a class="red" href="index.html">CLOSE SITE MAP</a>
   You add a blank line for visibility; you add a link to close the site map page and return to the frameset. For added visibility, the link uses the link colors that you set for the slideshow pages.

```
43
44 <a class="red" href="index.html">CLOSE  SITE  MAP</a>  9
45 </body>
46 </html>
```

< N O T E >
If you don't add a return link, your viewers must use the browser's Back button to return to the frameset.

10. **In Notepad, choose File→Save to save the** sitemap.html **page.**
    You added a function to control the size of the window when it displays in a browser.

11. **Open Internet Explorer, and then open** index.html**.**
    You test the pages.

12. **Click Site Map in the navigation frame.**
    The sitemap.html page loads into the same browser window. The page resizes itself and moves to the upper left of the screen.

13. **Scroll down the site map page to the new link. Click CLOSE SITE MAP.**
    The index.html frameset loads into the same window. Close the browser. If the script doesn't run, check the code you added earlier in this tutorial.

< N O T E >
The frameset uses the same size window as the site map page.

14. **Choose File→Open, and then choose** index.html**.**
    You add a sizing function to the frameset.

15. **Go to line 8, and press Enter to add a line.**
    You add a script to the page.

> **281**

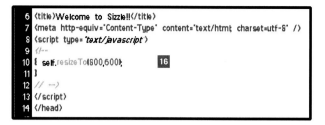

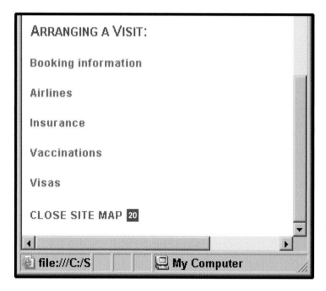

16. On lines 8 through 13, type:
```
<script type="text/javascript">
<!--
{ self.resizeTo(800,600);
}
// -->
</script>
```
The script runs when the page loads into the browser. The window size is reset to a large screen size (using an 800x600-pixel window resolution, the window is full-size) and is already located at the upper left of the window.

< N O T E >
In the figures, numerical values are shown in red.

17. Choose File➔Save and save `index.html`.
You added a function to the `sitemap.html` page to resize the window when the page loads. You added a script to the `index.html` page to resize the window again when the user closes the site map to return to the site.

18. Open Internet Explorer, and then open `index.html`.
The page loads at the large size.

19. Click Site Map in the navigation frame to load `sitemap.html` **in the browser window.**
The page loads at its custom size.

20. Scroll down the site map page. Click CLOSE SITE MAP.
The frameset reloads at the specified larger window size.

21. Close the browser.
You tested the sequence of scripts.

22. In Notepad, choose File➔Save to save the `index.html` **page.**

Writing Window Properties

In the tutorials, you set some size properties for two windows. There are many properties that can be set for a window. You control the appearance and functionality of a new window by specifying different elements, such as toolbar, location, directories, status bar, menu bar, scroll bars, and whether the window is resizable. Control and information structures on the browser window are referred to as "chrome." Write the values in one string of characters separated by commas:

```
function openwindow()
{
```
```
window.open ("URL","window_name","toolbar=yes,
width=400, height=400, status=no, menubar=yes, \
scrollbars=yes, directories=no, resizable=no")
}
```

If you use a long line of characters in JavaScript, you cannot simply wrap the text to another line. You use a backslash \ at the end of the line, which instructs the JavaScript interpreter to continue reading on the next line. If you don't use the backslash, you receive a script error. Don't break the line after `window.open`; a break at that location also produces an error.

Discussion
Adding a Form to a Web Page

In HTML, the <form> element creates a form for user input. A form can contain text fields, check boxes, radio buttons, and more. Forms are used to pass user data to a specified URL. Form markup is quite similar to table markup. Forms, like tables, are block elements and exist mainly as containers for other elements.

Forms need three attributes: name, action, and method. The name attribute is used to refer to the form and is very important when used with scripting.

An action attribute is required for describing the form data. The action may be a URL, Web server, or e-mail program used for managing the form's data.

The method attribute refers to how a form's data is sent to the action URL, a Web server, or e-mail program. The attribute can use either get or post values; get is the default value. If the form values exceed 100 characters or use non-ASCII characters, you must use the post value. You use the post value in your site.

A basic form is written as: <form name="form1" action="address" method="post"> content and controls </form> Content and controls refer to the text, buttons, fields, and other elements you add to the form.

Forms are enclosed in other elements to organize their layout. You can use table, fieldset, and legend elements. A fieldset is similar to a table. It is a block element and can have border, width, height, and other properties defined. It is used to contain other elements. A fieldset has only one cell and is configured through styles.

A legend contains a heading and is nested inside a fieldset, written like: <fieldset> <legend> Question or Choices</legend> </fieldset>. The image shows a form using a fieldset and legend; a fieldset alone; and the form field content alone.

You construct a form for the Sizzle site containing several fieldset elements using different types of data input. The form submits its data by e-mail. You also write a script to make sure that the user has supplied an e-mail address before the form content is submitted.

Tutorial

» Constructing the Basic Form

The Sizzle site contains a page named `contact.html`. You construct and complete the form over three tutorials—first the basic content, then form fields, and then a validation script and some styles. In this tutorial, you add the basic form content to the page, as well as five sets of <fieldset> and <legend> tags. Although the `fieldset` is optional, it helps set the sections of your form apart.

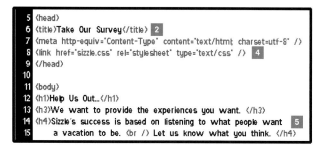

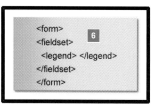

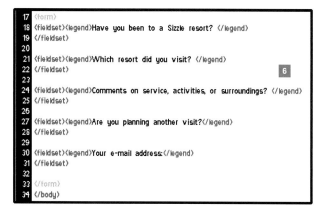

1. **In Notepad, choose File→Open, choose** `contact.html`**, and click Open.**
   You add the form to the page.

2. **Go to line 6, and replace the placeholder title. Type:** Take Our Survey
   This adds a descriptive title to the page.

3. **Go to line 8, and press Enter to add a blank line.**
   You attach the style sheet here.

4. **On line 8, type:** `<link href="sizzle.css" rel="stylesheet" type="text/css" />`
   The site's style sheet is attached to the page.

5. **On lines 12 through 15, type:**
   ```
   <h1>Help Us Out...</h1>
   <h3>We want to provide the experiences you want. </h3>
   <h4>Sizzle's success is based on listening to what people want
   a vacation to be. <br /> Let us know what you think. </h4>
   ```
   You add the headings to the top of the page.

6. **Add the** `fieldset` **elements and their content as described in Table 13-1. Leave blank lines between the tags.**
   In the next tutorial, when you add the form content, it is simpler to find locations on the page if the tags are visually separated. You add the five form segments and their `legend` elements to the page.

<N O T E>
In the figures, the <form> tags and attributes are color-coded orange.

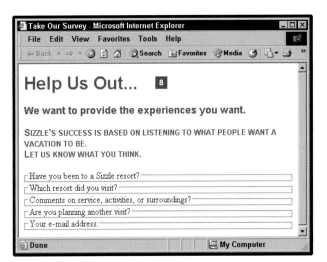

7. **In Notepad, choose File→Save to save the** contact.html **page.**
   You added the basic form information to the page. Leave the
   file open for the next tutorial.

8. **Open Internet Explorer, and then open** contact.html.
   You see the headings at the top of the page using the attached
   sizzle.css styles. The five fieldset elements display on
   the page; the legend elements are inserted into the frames of
   the fieldset elements. Close the browser.

Table 13-1: Basic Content for the Sizzle Site's Form

Line Number	Type:
17	<form>
18	<fieldset><legend>Have you been to a Sizzle resort? </legend>
19	</fieldset>
21	<fieldset><legend>Which resort did you visit? </legend>
22	</fieldset>
24	<fieldset><legend>Comments on service, activities, or surroundings? </legend>
25	</fieldset>
27	<fieldset><legend>Are you planning another visit?</legend>
28	</fieldset>
30	<fieldset><legend>Your e-mail address:</legend>
31	</fieldset>
33	</form>

Tutorial
» Working with Form Attributes

You started writing the form in the previous tutorial. In this tutorial, you add attributes and values for the `fieldset` elements and the form itself, and you also add two buttons at the end of the form. You use a variety of form options on the form, including text areas, radio buttons, and a drop-down list. The `contact.html` page is open in Notepad if you are continuing from the previous tutorial. If you don't have an e-mail program on your computer, you will not be able to test the form data transmission.

```
11 <body>
12 <form method="post" action="mailto:yourname@address.com" name="contactForm"   1
13 enctype="text/plain">
```

```
20 <fieldset><legend>Have you been to a Sizzle resort? </legend>
21   <input type="radio" name="visit_yes" value="yes" /> Yes <br />
22   <input type="radio" name="visit_no" value="no" /> No <br />           3
23     When? <input type="text" name="visit_date" value="month and year" />
24 </fieldset>
25
26 <fieldset><legend>Which resort did you visit? </legend>
27   <select name="resort">    4
28     <option value="East" selected="selected">Sizzle East</option>
29     <option value="South">Sizzle South</option>                  5
30     <option value="West">Sizzle West</option></select>
31 </fieldset>
```

1. **On the** `contact.html` **page, go to line 12. Expand the <form> tag to read:** `<form method="post" action="mailto: yourname@address.com" name="contactForm" enctype="text/plain">`
   The `method`, `action`, and `name` attributes are required. The `"post"` method sends the form contents in the body of the e-mail. The form is named; and an encryption type is specified.

2. **Go to line 21, and press Enter.**
   You add a blank line to add the first form elements' tags after the line containing the opening <fieldset> and <legend> tag.

3. **On lines 21 through 23, type:**
   `<input type="radio" name="visit_yes" value="yes" /> Yes <br />`
   `<input type="radio" name="visit_no" value="no" /> No <br />`
   `  When? <input type="text" name="visit_date" value="month and year" />`
   The first `fieldset` contains three `input` elements. The first two elements are radio buttons. Each item is named and a value assigned. The words "Yes" and "No" appear beside the buttons on the form. The third item is text. The word "When?" appears before the text field, and the text "month and year" is shown in the text box on the form when viewed in the browser. Check that the </fieldset> tag follows the new content you typed on the lines.

<TIP>
To test the form's function later in the tutorial, type your actual e-mail address as the `action` attribute's value rather than yourname@address.com.

<NOTE>
The `enctype` attribute is not required; its value describes a way to encode the form's contents. If you use the attribute, the e-mail content is easily readable.

<TIP>
Input elements are self-closing tags—that is, including / within the right bracket closes the tag.

<NOTE>
You choose only one instance in a set of radio buttons. You can pre-select a button using an attribute-value pair, `checked= "checked"`, or you can leave the set unselected. In the form, the set is unselected.

4. Go to line 27, and press Enter to add a blank line after the
   `<fieldset>` **tags. On line 27, type:** `<select`
   `name="resort">`

   You add an opening <select> tag used to create a drop-down
   list of options. The user clicks an option to choose it.

< N O T E >

The <select> tag is the container for option elements that offer
choices.

5. On lines 28 through 30, type:
   `<option value="East" selected="selected">`
   `Sizzle East</option>`
   `<option value="South">Sizzle South</option>`
   `<option value="West">Sizzle`
   `West</option></select>`

   The select list includes the three Sizzle resort locations listed
   in alphabetical order. The resort's location is used as the value
   for the option. The first option also uses the `selected=`
   `"selected"` attribute; the Sizzle East option is selected by
   default when the form is shown in the browser. Make sure that
   the </fieldset> tag follows the text that you just typed.

6. Go to line 34, and press Enter to add a blank line.
   You add an element to the next <fieldset> tag for the user to
   enter comments.

7. On line 34, type: `<textarea name="comments"`
   `cols="50" rows="*"></textarea>`

   You add a text box element, which is a field for typing text.
   Set the `cols` attribute to a width for the text field in characters (the one you add allows 50 characters). The `rows` attribute is set to any width using `"*"`. When the user types in the
   field, the line wraps to the next line every 50 characters, and
   any number of lines is allowed.

8. Go to line 38, and press Enter to add a blank line.
   This line is for the <fieldset> asking about return visits, which
   uses radio button options.

9. On lines 38 and 39, type:
   `<input type="radio" name="return_yes"`
   `value="yes" /> Yes <br />`
   `<input type="radio" name="return_no"`
   `value="no" /> No`

   You add another pair of radio buttons. To place the buttons on
   separate lines, add a <br /> tag at the end of the first line of
   text. If you don't add the
 tag, the radio buttons sit side
   by side on the page. Make sure that the </fieldset> tag follows
   the text that you type in this step.

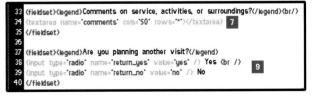

```
42  <fieldset><legend>Your e-mail address:</legend>
43  <input type="text" name="emailAddress" value="" size="50" />  11
44  </fieldset>  12
45
46  <input type="submit" name="submit" id="submit" value="Submit" />  13
47  <input type="reset" name="reset" id="reset" value="Reset" />
```

10. **Go to line 43, and press Enter to add a blank line.**
You add an element for the e-mail address.

11. **On line 43, type:** `<input type="text" name=`
`"emailAddress" value="" size="50" />`
You add another text field. The value is blank, and the field
can hold 50 characters. Make sure that the `input` element
is added to the line before the </fieldset> tag.

< T I P >
Check the spelling of the `name` attribute carefully. The name of the
field is used in the script that you write in the next tutorial.

12. **Press Enter after the </fieldset> tag to add a blank line.**
You add another pair of elements.

13. **On lines 46 and 47, type:**
`<input type="submit" name="submit" id=`
`"submit" value="Submit" />`
`<input type="reset" name="reset" id="reset"`
`value="Reset" />`
You add two action buttons. The buttons are `input` elements:
Submit and Reset. Submit carries out actions indicated by the
form; reset clears all user input and restores the form to its
default state. The value of each button is the text that appears
on the button when you view the page in your browser, which
is why they are capitalized and the others aren't.

14. **Choose File→Save to save the** `contact.html` **page.**
You configured the page's form. Leave the file open in
Notepad to continue to the last tutorial.

15. **Open Internet Explorer, and then open** `contact.html`.
You see that the form is divided into the five `fieldset`
elements, followed by the pair of buttons at the bottom of
the page.

16. **Enter some data in the form:**

» Click an option in the radio button sets

» Type text into the previous visit month and year field

» Type text in the comments block

» Type an e-mail address

17. **Click Reset to test the reset process.**
The data entered in the form is cleared.

18. **Re-enter data in the form. Click Submit.**
An Internet Explorer warning dialog opens regarding address
and content transmission.

<NOTE>
To test Steps 18 through 22 in the tutorial, make sure that you are using your actual e-mail address in the <form> element's action attribute value.

19. **Click OK to accept the warning.**
The dialog box closes.

20. **An Outlook transmission dialog box displays.**
The transmission process is shown on the dialog box.

<NOTE>
If Microsoft Outlook is your e-mail client, you may or may not see the transmission dialog box depending on your system's configuration, such as the presence of firewalls and e-mail program filters. If you are using another e-mail client, you may see different notification dialog boxes.

21. **When the transmission process is complete, click Yes.**
The e-mail message is sent.

22. **Open your e-mail program. When the e-mail arrives, open it.**
Note that the input elements' names and the values entered in the form are listed in the body of the e-mail.

23. **Close Internet Explorer.**
You configured the form for your site. You entered data in the form and tested it. You reviewed the results e-mailed from the form.

Tutorial

» Validating a Field on the Form

One of the most common reasons that a feedback form is added to a Web site is to communicate with site visitors. You need to ensure that the user has added text in the e-mail field on the form before submitting in order for you to respond. In this tutorial, you write a script to validate the e-mail field on the form. `contact.html` is open in Notepad if you are continuing from the previous tutorial.

```
 9  <script type='text/javascript'>
10  <!--
11  function validateEmail(form)
12  {
13  if (form.emailAddress.value == '') {
14    alert ('Please enter your e-mail address.');
15      form.emailAddress.focus();
16  return false;
17  }
18  return true;
19  }
20  //-->
21  </script>
22  </head>
```

```
24  <body>
25  <form method='post' action='mailto:yourname@youraddress.com'
26  name='contactForm' enctype='text/plain' onsubmit='return validateEmail(this);'>
27
```

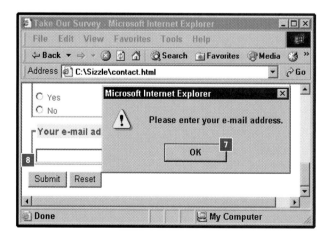

1. **Go to line 9, and press Enter to add a line after the <link> tag for attaching the style sheet.**

2. **On lines 9 through 21, type:**
   ```
   <script type="text/javascript">
   <! --
   function validateEmail(form)
   {
   if (form.emailAddress.value == "") {
     alert ("Please enter your e-mail address.");
   form.emailAddress.focus();
   return false;
   }
   return true;
   }

   //-->
   </script>
   ```
   You write the custom function for the form. With the exclusion of the opening and closing comment and script tags, the script is quite complex and is described in Table 13-2.

3. **Go to line 26 and type:** `onsubmit="return validateEmail (this);"` **before the closing > of the form tag.**
   The function that you wrote requires a return because there is a result from running the script. The script, named `validateEmail`, runs when the Submit button is clicked. Because the function is called from within the form, substitute `(this)` for `(form)` in the `onsubmit` value.

4. **Choose File→Save to save the** `contact.html` **page.**
   You added a script to the page.

5. **Open Internet Explorer, and then open** `contact.html`.
   You test the form again.

6. **Click the Submit button.**
   The alert dialog box displays.

7. **Click OK to dismiss the alert box and return to the form.**
   The cursor is active in the e-mail field.

8. **Enter some text in the e-mail field.**
   You test the second condition by adding text to the e-mail field before clicking Submit.

9. **Click Submit.**

   Internet Explorer displays a warning dialog box for sending the e-mail. The second condition has been met. That is, the form is submitted if the e-mail field contains text.

10. **Click Cancel to dismiss the message. Close Internet Explorer.**

    You tested the custom script. Return to the `contact.html` page to add styles.

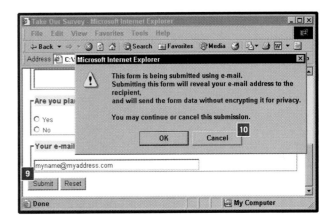

<NOTE>

The script merely tests for any content in the field. It doesn't check for a special configuration, number of characters, or presence of @, required for an e-mail address.

11. **Go to line 22, and press Enter to add a blank line.**

12. **On lines 23 to 33, type:**

```
<style type="text/css">
<!--
fieldset {
color: #333366;
font-family: Arial,sans-serif;
font-size: 12px;
border-top: 3px solid #006666;
border-left: 2px solid #006666;
margin: 10px 5px 10px 5px;
height: 60px;
}
```

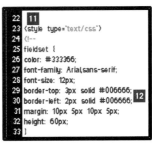

You add a style for the <fieldset> tag. The style can be placed in the head of the page because it is the only place in the Web site where you use the styles. Properties are defined for the height of the `fieldset`, as well as for margins and borders.

<TIP>

If you are using multiple forms on your site, you should add the styles to the site's style sheet.

13. **Leave a blank line to separate the styles on the page. On lines 35 to 42, type:**

```
legend {
font-size: 14px;
line-height: 150%;
font-weight: bold;
background-color: #D2FFF1;
}
-->
</style>
```

You add a style for the <legend> tag. The style gives the text a pale green background. Other style properties, such as the font properties, are inherited from the <fieldset> tag.

14. **Choose File→Save to save the** `contact.html` **file. Close Notepad.**

    You added a script to validate the presence of text in the e-mail field of the form. You tested the form's script and also its e-mail process. You added two styles to configure the appearance of the form.

15. **Open Internet Explorer, and then open** `contact.html`.

    Preview the page. You see the styles applied to both the <fieldset> and <legend> elements. Close the browser.

Table 13-2: Content of the Form Validation Script

Line Number	Code	Means...
11	`function validateEmail(form)`	The function validates the e-mail address, and its name reflects its purpose; the argument (variables in a function are called arguments) names the form.
12	`{`	The opening bracket for the entire script is required.
13	`if (form.emailAddress.` `value == "") {`	The if statement asks if the value of the `emailAddress` field in the form object is blank (the pair of ""). The opening bracket of the action ends the line.
14	`alert ("Please enter your` `e-mail address.");`	If the condition described in line 13 is met, an alert displays asking for the e-mail address.
15	`form.emailAddress.focus();`	When the user closes the alert dialog box, the focus is set on the e-mail field; that is, the cursor is active in the e-mail field.
16	`return false;`	The address is not valid.
17	`}`	The bracket closes the actions that result from testing the if statement and finding the field empty.
18	`return true;`	The address is valid.
19	`}`	The script is closed.

» Session Review

In this session, you added several more scripts to your site as you completed pages and processes. You added alert messages to two of the slideshow pages to identify the first and last pages from button clicks on the pages. You also wrote a set of three scripts to control windows. You wrote one script to open the site map page into the frameset's window, a script to size and position the site map page for ease of use, and a final script to size the frameset page to a constant size. The opening image in the session shows the placeholder contact.html page, which contained nothing but a text title. The final image in the session shows the same page. You built, customized, and stylized the form. You also added a simple validation script and tested the form in this session.

Answer these questions to review what you learned. The answers can be found in the tutorial noted in parentheses.

1. What is the alert function? How is it used? (See Tutorial: Displaying Messages for the Reader.)

2. How do you write text that you want to appear on a message or alert box? (See Tutorial: Displaying Messages for the Reader.)

3. What is the "not equal to" operator? How is it used? (See Tutorial: Managing Open Windows Using JavaScript.)

4. How do you call a JavaScript script from a link in the body of a page? (See Tutorial: Managing Open Windows Using JavaScript.)

5. Do you have to specify units of measurement when adding pixel values in JavaScript statements? (See Tutorial: Controlling Window Sizes Using JavaScript.)

6. What effect does scripting the size of a window have on pages subsequently opened in the same window? (See Tutorial: Controlling Window Sizes Using JavaScript.)

7. How can you break a line when writing a script? (See Tutorial: Controlling Window Sizes Using JavaScript.)

8. What three attributes are required for using a form on a Web page? (See Discussion: Adding a Form to a Web Page.)

9. How are fieldset elements used on a form? When should you use them? (See Tutorial: Constructing the Basic Form.)

10. Why are legend elements used on a form? How does a legend element differ visually from a text string? (See Tutorial: Constructing the Basic Form.)

11. What does the enctype attribute define in a <form> tag? (See Tutorial: Working with Form Attributes.)

12. What different types of data collection elements can you add to a form? (See Tutorial: Working with Form Attributes.)

13. What does "focus" refer to when describing and working with forms? (See Tutorial: Validating a Field on the Form.)

14. How do you call a function from the body of a page when the function returns a result? (See Tutorial: Validating a Field on the Form.)

» Other Projects

Use other window object properties and values to format the sitemap.html page. Try resetting the window using different combinations of "chrome," different sizes, and alternate screen locations.

The contact.html form uses a simple field validation for the e-mail address field. Write additional scripts to validate the other fields on the form. Explore methods to validate the address based on the characters entered in the field.

Help Us Out...

We want to provide the experiences you want.

SIZZLE'S SUCCESS IS BASED ON LISTENING TO WHAT PEOPLE WANT A VACATION TO BE.
LET US KNOW WHAT YOU THINK.

Have you been to a Sizzle resort?
- ○ Yes
- ○ No
- When? `month and year`

Which resort did you visit?
`Sizzle East ▼`

Comments on service, activities, or surroundings?

Are you planning another visit?
- ○ Yes
- ○ No

Your e-mail address:

`Submit` `Reset`

Part VIII

Showing Your Site
to the World

Constructing an Accessible Site

Take Our Survey - Microsoft Internet Explorer

File   Edit   View   Favorites   Tools   Help

Back   Search   Favorites   Media

Address C:\Sizzle\n_contact.html   Go

When? month and year

Which resort did you visit?

Sizzle East

Comments on service, activities, or surroundings?

Are you planning another visit?

○ Yes
○ No

Your e-mail address:

Submit   Reset

Welcome | Booking | Airlines | Travel Info | Contact Us | Back to Frames

Done   My Computer

Session Introduction

At this point, much of your Web site is developed. You have a complete set of pages; you added a form, scripts, a movie, and a variety of links and window assignments to control how the user moves through your site.

In Session 7, you added frames to your site and created an alternate version of the main page to use as a placeholder for the no-frames content for the site. In this session, you return to the `n_main.html` page. Several site pages are renamed to create no-frames versions. You add a navigation structure to each page to allow for simple navigation throughout the site from a single window. You do not combine all the site's content into no-frames pages.

You examine the Sizzle site for accessibility compliance. The Web Accessibility Initiative (WAI) is an arm of the W3C that maintains standards for accessibility just as the organization maintains standards for both XHTML and CSS. As you discover in this session, having created the site to comply with XHTML and CSS standards, you are well on your way to creating an accessible site.

You adjust the content and tags of some elements in the no-frames version of the site to comply with accessibility standards. Although you do not modify the entire site for compliance with strict accessibility standards or use an accessibility validator, you work with and test the no-frames pages from the perspective of users with disabilities using a variety of techniques.

TOOLS YOU'LL USE
Notepad, Internet Explorer, Windows display settings

CD-ROM FILES NEEDED (In Sizzle Site Folder)
booking.html, contact.html, fine_print.html,
n_main.html

For reference, in Storage Folder:
n_nav table.txt

FILES CREATED
n_booking.html, n_contact.html, n_fine_print.html

TIME REQUIRED
90 minutes

Discussion

Accessibility Guidelines and Standards

"The power of the Web is in its universality. Access by everyone regardless of disability is an essential aspect."

Tim Berners-Lee, W3C Director and
Inventor of the World Wide Web

In 1999, the W3C's Web Accessibility Initiative (WAI) released Version 1.0 of the Web Content Accessibility Guidelines (WCAG.) The guidelines consider the needs of people with a range of disabilities and needs, and describe ways to accommodate their needs. The complete guidelines and sets of techniques, checklists, and other materials are available at www.w3.org/WAI.

Some optional accessibility solutions include the following:

» User control of style sheets

» Keyboard equivalents to mouse commands

» Markup of tables and other page elements

» Adding specific tags used by speech synthesizers and Braille displays

One of the most common devices used by people with disabilities is a screen reader. A screen reader literally reads the content of a Web page, or other document, out loud. The screen reader doesn't read like you and I read in that it doesn't process sentence structure, nor does it skim over repetitious material, or assume separation between items on a page that we can see visually. Instead, it reads everything out loud. Imagine how boring it would be to hear the same thing repeated innumerable times as the user worked through a site, or how confusing it would be to read a set of links strung together on one line without any separation.

The guidelines outline lists of methods and techniques to make the Web accessible from the perspectives of different communities, such as Web developers and software and assistive device developers. From the perspective of the Web page developer, there are 14 recommendations, each with numerous descriptions and requirements. The contents of the recommendations are prioritized in three levels according to impact on a user's ability to use a page with a cross-section of assistive devices.

Section 508 is an amendment to the 1973 Rehabilitation Act covering Electronic and Information Technology Accessibility Standards. Section 508 requires access to electronic and information technology; the Access Board developed accessibility standards for the various technologies covered by the law.

The Sizzle site generally complies with the Section 508 requirements. The requirements are not the same as the WAI/WCAG recommendations, which are much more extensive. For example, the page links are valid XHTML, use a valid CSS, and comply with Section 508. However, according to the guidelines, the links should have a text description as well.

Wherever possible, your site should comply with regulations. Where practical, you should also comply with guidelines. When creating content, consider the impact on usability and consider the site's audience. For example, the movie in the Sizzle site works correctly and uses valid XHTML and styles, but it does not completely comply with Section 508. The Act requires that the content have a link to the plug-in source, which it does. However, the movie does not contain captions or have a secondary link to alternate content, so it is not in full compliance.

Tutorial
» Building the No-frames Pages

In Session 7, you created a page for the site's no-frames version when you added the frameset to the site. The page, `n_main.html`, is a renamed copy of the `main.html` page of the site. In this tutorial, you create an additional set of three no-frames pages. You also create a navigation table for the pages.

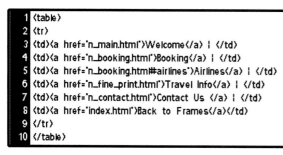

```
1  <table>
2  <tr>
3  <td><a href="n_main.html">Welcome</a> | </td>
4  <td><a href="n_booking.html">Booking</a> | </td>
5  <td><a href="n_booking.html#airlines">Airlines</a> | </td>
6  <td><a href="n_fine_print.html">Travel Info</a> | </td>
7  <td><a href="n_contact.html">Contact Us </a> | </td>
8  <td><a href="index.html">Back to Frames</a></td>
9  </tr>
10 </table>
```

1. **Open Notepad. Choose File→Open, choose** `booking.html`, **and click Open.**
   You reuse this page.

2. **Choose File→Save As, and save the file as** `n_booking.html`.
   You create a file to use for the no-frames version of the site.

3. **Repeat Steps 1 and 2. Create alternate versions of the following pages, and save the files with "n_" prefix.**

   » `fine_print.html`

   » `contact.html`

   You now have a set of four pages using the "n_" prefix denoting that the pages are used for the no-frames version of the site.

4. **In Notepad, choose File→New.**
   You create the navigation structure for the pages.

5. **On lines 1 through 10, add the content for the table as listed in Table 14-1.**
   The code and comments are in Table 14-1. You add text links for the pages and one anchor in the no-frames site.

< N O T E >
All links except the final link are followed by a vertical separator bar. The bar is named by a screen reader for users working with a screen reader, and the content is separated verbally as well as visually. You can use vertical separators or encase the links in square brackets.

< N O T E >
The named anchors on the `n_fine_print.html` page are not included in the list. The anchors are removed later in the tutorial. Speech synthesizers or screen readers read links aloud individually, so you should strive to minimize the overall number of links.

6. **Choose File→Save, name the file** n_nav table.txt, **and click Save.**
   You save the content for the navigation table.

<**N O T E**>
The n_nav table.txt file is available on the CD in the Sizzle site's Storage folder.

7. **Choose Edit→Select All to select the content in the text file.**
   Copy the content.

8. **Choose File→Open, select** n_main.html, **and click Open.**
   You add the table to this page.

9. **Go to line 41, and press Enter.**
   You add a blank line after the closing tag of the page's original table.

10. **On line 42, type:** ⟨br /⟩
    You add a new table with its own styles; add a break to separate the tables visually on the Web page.

11. **Paste the copied text starting on line 43, and continuing to line 52.**
    The table is copied to the page, starting after the inserted <br /> tag, and ending before the closing </body> tag.

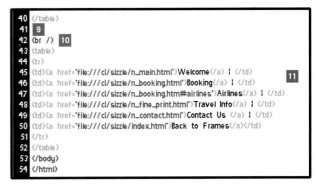

```
40 </table>
41 9
42 <br />  10
43 <table>
44 <tr>
45 <td><a href="file:///c/sizzle/n_main.html">Welcome</a> | </td>      11
46 <td><a href="file:///c/sizzle/n_booking.html">Booking</a> | </td>
47 <td><a href="file:///c/sizzle/n_booking.html#airlines">Airlines</a> | </td>
48 <td><a href="file:///c/sizzle/n_fine_print.html">Travel Info</a> | </td>
49 <td><a href="file:///c/sizzle/n_contact.html">Contact Us </a> | </td>
50 <td><a href="file:///c/sizzle/index.html">Back to Frames</a></td>
51 </tr>
52 </table>
53 </body>
54 </html>
```

Table 14-1: Content for No-frames Navigation Table

Line Number	Type	Note
1	<table>	Open the table tag.
2	<tr>	Insert a table row.
3	<td><a href="n_main.html"> Welcome</a>	</td>	Insert a cell. Text is linked to no-frames main page, followed by vertical separator bar.
4	<td><a href="n_booking.html"> Booking</a>	</td>	Text is linked to booking info.
5	<td><a href="n_booking.html#airlines"> Airlines</a>	</td>	Text is linked to airlines anchor.
6	<td><a href="n_fine_print.html"> Travel Info</a>	</td>	Text is linked to fine print page.
7	<td><a href="n_contact.html"> Contact Us </a>	</td>	Text is linked to survey page.
8	<td><a href="index.html"> Back to Frames</a></td>	Text is linked to return to frameset.
9	</tr>	Close the row tag.
10	</table>	Close the table tag.

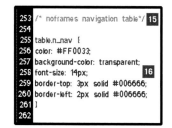

12. **Choose File→Save to save the** n_main.html **page.**
    You added the navigation table.

13. **Open Internet Explorer, and then open** n_main.html.
    You see the table added to the bottom of the page. The links
    use the site's default link styles. Minimize the browser.

14. **Choose File→Open, select** sizzle.css, **and click Open.**
    You add a style for this table.

15. **Go to the end of the** sizzle.css **page, and add a blank line for
    separation. On line 253, type:** /* noframes navigation
    table */
    Add a comment to identify the new style's application.

16. **Leave a blank line for spacing. On lines 255 through 261, type:**
    ```
    table.n_nav {
    color: #FF0033;
    background-color: transparent;
    font-size: 14px;
    border-top: 3px solid #006666;
    border-left: 2px solid #006666;
    }
    ```
    The style is similar to that used on the contact.html page's
    fieldsets. The color and font size are applied to the vertical
    separator bars in the table's cells.

17. **Choose File→Save.**
    You save the sizzle.css file with the new table style.

18. **Choose File→Open, choose** n_main.html, **and click Open.**
    You apply the style.

19. **Go to line 43, and expand the table tag to read:** <table
    class="n_nav">
    You attach the table style.

20. **In Notepad, choose File→Save to save the** n_main.html **page.**
    You assembled the basic no-frames pages for the site. You cre-
    ated navigation table content. You applied the navigation table
    and a style to the first no-frames page. Leave Notepad open
    for the next tutorial.

21. **Open Internet Explorer, and then open** n_main.html.
    View the table at the bottom of the page. You see the style
    applied. Test the links. Close the browser.

Tutorial
» Adding Navigation Tables to the No-frames Pages

In the previous tutorial, you built a file containing links for a text link table to use on the no-frames pages. You applied it to the n_main.html page, added and applied a style to the new table, and tested the page. In this tutorial, you apply the table and style to the remaining no-frames pages. The WAI/WCAG guidelines suggest that tables be used for data rather than styling unless the tables "degrade gracefully," meaning that the table content is legible and readable regardless of whether the content is set in a table. The tables in your site are very graceful.

1. In Notepad, open n_nav table.txt.
   You apply the content to the other pages.

2. Choose Edit→Select All to select the text.

3. Choose File→Open, select n_booking.html, and click Open.
   You apply the table to the page.

4. Go to line 60, and press Enter after the </table> tag to add a blank line after the closing tag of the page's final table. On line 62, type:
   Add a break to visually separate the content on the page when viewed in the browser.

5. On lines 63 to 72, paste the text from the clipboard.
   You add the navigation table content.

6. On line 63, expand the opening <table> tag to read: <table class="n_nav">
   You apply the style.

7. Choose File→Save to save the n_booking.html page.
   You added the navigation table and its style to the page.

8. Choose File→Open, select the n_fine_print.html page, and click Open.

9. Go to line 42, which reads <a name="vaccinations" id="vaccinations"></a>, and select the anchor information. Delete the line.
   You don't use the anchor in the text links.

10. Go to line 50, which reads <a name="visas" id="visas"></a>, and select the anchor information. Delete the line.
    You remove the other unnecessary anchor.

11. Go to line 55, and press Enter to add a blank line.
    You insert the copied text after this blank line.

12. On lines 56 through 65, paste the copied table code.
    You add the table to the page.

13. Expand the <table> tag on line 56 to read: <table class="n_nav">
    You attach the table style.

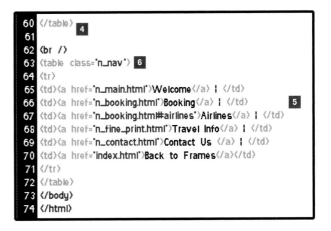

```
60 </table>       4
61
62 <br />
63 <table class="n_nav">  6
64 <tr>
65 <td><a href="n_main.html">Welcome</a> | </td>
66 <td><a href="n_booking.html">Booking</a> | </td>       5
67 <td><a href="n_booking.htm#airlines">Airlines</a> | </td>
68 <td><a href="n_fine_print.html">Travel Info</a> | </td>
69 <td><a href="n_contact.html">Contact Us </a> | </td>
70 <td><a href="index.html">Back to Frames</a></td>
71 </tr>
72 </table>
73 </body>
74 </html>
```

```
53 on your arrival. Be careful when filling out the cards. They are controlled
54 documents and you have to pay an additional fee for a new one.</p>
55       11
56 <table class="n_nav">   13
57 <tr>
58 <td><a href="file:///c/sizzle/n_main.html">Welcome</a> | </td>
59 <td><a href="file:///c/sizzle/n_booking.html">Booking</a> | </td>       12
60 <td><a href="file:///c/sizzle/n_booking.htm#airlines">Airlines</a> | </td>
61 <td><a href="file:///c/sizzle/n_fine_print.html">Travel Info</a> | </td>
62 <td><a href="file:///c/sizzle/n_contact.html">Contact Us </a> | </td>
63 <td><a href="file:///c/sizzle/index.html">Back to Frames</a></td>
64 </tr>
65 </table>
66 </body>
67 </html>
```

< N O T E >

It isn't necessary to use the <br /> tag before the table on the page. The table is added following a paragraph, which already includes spacing after the text.

```
80  </form>
81  16
82  <table class="n_nav">  18
83  <tr>
84  <td><a href="n_main.html">Welcome</a> ¦ </td>
85  <td><a href="n_booking.html">Booking</a> ¦ </td>
86  <td><a href="n_booking.htm#airlines">Airlines</a> ¦ </td>
87  <td><a href="n_fine_print.html">Travel Info</a> ¦ </td>   17
88  <td><a href="n_contact.html">Contact Us </a> ¦ </td>
89  <td><a href="index.html">Back to Frames</a></td>
90  </tr>
91  </table>
92  </body>
```

14. **Choose File→Save to save the** n_fine_print.html **page.**
    You removed extra anchors and added the navigation table and its style to the page.

15. **Choose File→Open, select the** n_contact.html **page, and click Open.**
    You add the table to the page.

16. **Go to line 81, and press Enter to add a blank line.**
    You add the table to the page.

17. **On lines 82 through 91, paste the copied table code.**
    You add the table to the page.

< N O T E >
You don't need the <br /> tag inserted before the table. The form's fieldsets include space following the frame.

18. **Expand the <table> tag on line 82 to read:** <table class="n_nav">
    You attach the style to the page.

19. **In Notepad, choose File→Save to save the** n_contact.html **page.**
    You modified the remaining pages for the no-frames set. You removed extra anchors and added spacing where required between previous page content and the new table. You tested the links. Leave Notepad open for the next tutorial.

Your e-mail address:

[Submit] [Reset]   20

|Welcome | Booking | Airlines | Travel Info | Contact Us | Back to Frames

My Computer

---

20. **Open Internet Explorer. Open** n_contact.html, **and scroll down the page.**
    Note the spacing between the final fieldset and the table. Test the links. Close the browser.

Discussion
Using an Entire Page as an Object

One of the W3C techniques suggested for frames-free sites is to use an object on the site's pages. The object references another page, containing a set of links for the site, and is written on the page as:

```
<object data="n_nav1.html" name="n_links"> </object>
```

where the object is named, and the data attribute has the value of the page's URL.

The process is very convenient because only one page of links is required. However, issues arise regarding using the <object> tag in this manner. In the image on the left, the Web page containing the object is shown in Netscape 7.0. You can see the small menu bar at the bottom of the page. The image on the right shows the same page in Internet Explorer, but the object (the inserted Web page) isn't visible.

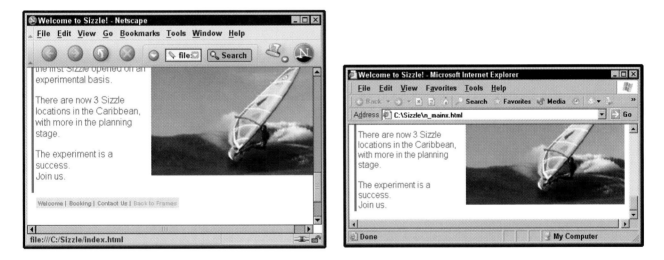

The no-frames version of the Sizzle site does not use the inserted object method; instead, the navigation links are added in a table at the bottom of each no-frames page. Although the method is more time-consuming when updating pages, it is visible regardless of the browser used.

Tutorial

» Tweaking the Main No-frames Pages for Accessibility

Your no-frames site has four pages. In this tutorial, you add some new information to the pages. You also see how a commercial accessibility checker scores the pages and how the content can be modified. The accessibility test result samples shown in the tutorial use the UsableNet Section 508 Accessibility Tests v. 2.0 and the UsableNet WAI/WCAG Accessibility Tests v. 2.0 programs; two commercially available tools used for testing sites.

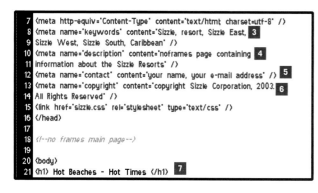

1. **In Notepad, open** n_main.html.
   You modify the page for the no-frames version of the site.

2. **Go to line 8, and press Enter to add a blank line.**
   You expand the heading tags for the page.

3. **On line 8, wrapping to line 9, type:** `<meta name="keywords" content="Sizzle, resort, Sizzle East, Sizzle West, Sizzle South, Caribbean" />`
   This defines keywords for search engines.

4. **On line 10, wrapping to line 11, type:** `<meta name="description" content="noframes page containing information about the Sizzle Resorts" />`
   You define a description of the Web page.

5. **On line 12, type:** `<meta name="contact" content="your name, your e-mail address" />`
   You add contact information for users of your site.

6. **On line 13, wrapping to line 14, type:** `<meta name="copyright" content="copyright Sizzle Corporation, 2003. All Rights Reserved" />`
   You add copyright information to the page.

7. **Go to line 21, and delete the attributes from the <h1> tag. The line now reads** `<h1> Hot Beaches - Hot Times</h1>`.
   You remove the deprecated tags.

8. **Choose File→Save.**
   You modified the page's content to make it more accessible. Leave Notepad and the n_main.html page open to continue with the next tutorial.

9. **Open Internet Explorer, and then open** n_main.html.
   Check the main heading on the page. It uses the site's style for the `<h1>` heading, which is very similar to the style you originally defined using the color, font face, and font weight attributes deleted in Step 7.

How the n_main.html Page Scored

The main page for the no-frames site complies with Section 508. However, it fails at the WCAG Priority 2 level on two points, as you can see in the figure.

There are deprecated tags in the page (although the page is valid XHTML), and the page is missing <meta> tag information. You removed deprecated tags and added <meta> tag information in the tutorial.

The test results described in the tutorials were generated by commercial software. When your site is posted to a Web server (in the Bonus Session on the CD-ROM) you can test pages individually online for free, using a service named Bobby available at www. cast.org/bobby. Bobby is a service developed and supported by Watchfire, a company providing Web site management solutions.

File	Line	Description
✕ n_main.html	14	Avoid deprecated features of W3C technologies [WCAG 11.2 P.2] -- FAILED --
? n_main.html	45	Clearly identify the target of each link [WCAG 13.1 P.2] -- MANUAL -- The TITLE attribute is missing in link text element.
? n_main.html	46	Clearly identify the target of each link [WCAG 13.1 P.2] -- MANUAL -- The TITLE attribute is missing in link text element.
? n_main.html	47	Clearly identify the target of each link [WCAG 13.1 P.2] -- MANUAL -- The TITLE attribute is missing in link text element.
? n_main.html	48	Clearly identify the target of each link [WCAG 13.1 P.2] -- MANUAL -- The TITLE attribute is missing in link text element.
? n_main.html	49	Clearly identify the target of each link [WCAG 13.1 P.2] -- MANUAL -- The TITLE attribute is missing in link text element.
? n_main.html	50	Clearly identify the target of each link [WCAG 13.1 P.2] -- MANUAL -- The TITLE attribute is missing in link text element.
✕ n_main.html	3	Provide metadata to pages and sites [WCAG 13.2 P.2] -- FAILED --

Complete.

Tutorial

» Completing Content in the No-frames Pages

You added and changed the content in the first of the no-frames pages to comply with some accessibility issues. In this tutorial, you modify the content in the n_fine_print.html and n_booking.html pages. Start by copying the <meta> tag information for reuse.

```
 8 <meta name="keywords" content="Sizzle, resort, Sizzle East, 3
 9 Sizzle West, Sizzle South, Caribbean" />
10 <meta name="description" content="noframes page containing
11 information about booking vacations and airline flights" />   4
12 <meta name="contact" content="your name, your e-mail address" />
13 <meta name="copyright" content="copyright Sizzle Corporation, 2003.
14 All Rights Reserved" />
15 <link href="sizzle.css" rel="stylesheet" type="text/css" />
16 </head>
17
18 <body class="bookingbkgd">
19 <h1> Staying at Sizzle</h1>
20
21 <p class="caption"> Visit Sizzle when YOU want to visit. <br />
22 For a long weekend, for a month -- the choice is yours!</p>
23 <img src="Images/shell1.jpg" class="shells" 5
24 alt="brown and white spotted seashell image"/>
```

1. **In Notepad, scroll to the top of the** n_main.html **page and select the content in lines 8 through 14.**
   You copy the <meta> tag information to the clipboard.

2. **Choose File→Open, select** n_booking.html, **and click Open.**
   You open the next no-frames page.

3. **Go to line 8, and press Enter to add a blank line. Paste the content from the clipboard to the page.**
   This adds the <meta> tag information to the page.

4. **Go to lines 10 and 11. Change the text for the content attribute to read:** content="noframes page containing information about booking vacations and airline flights" />
   This changes the page's description to match the content of the page.

<NOTE>

The tutorial steps reference line numbers. Your line numbering may differ slightly from that shown in the tutorial figures or listed in the steps. Use the line numbers as references to different areas of a page, but read the content of the line carefully as you follow the steps to ensure you are modifying or adding code to the correct line.

5. **Go to line 23, and change the** alt **attribute for the seashell image. Type:** alt="brown and white spotted seashell image"/>
   The alt attribute is now in compliance with Section 508 guidelines. In the figure, the <image> tag is shown wrapped over two lines for demonstration; the tag is on line 23 only in the session's sample page.

<NOTE>

The original alt attribute read alt="seashell image" which is not in compliance with Section 508 because it isn't descriptive. The original attribute alt="seashell image" was defined as a placeholder only, the new attribute added in Step 5 is much more descriptive of the image's content.

6. **Go to line 36. Select the original** alt **attribute for the seashell image** alt="seashell image" **and type:** alt=" dark yellow starfish image"/>

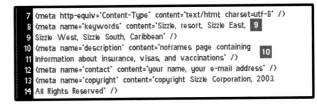

```
36  <p><img src="Images/shell4.jpg" class="shells"
37  alt="image of dark yellow starfish"/>
38  Spring Break is another story. Since Sizzle is built around the idea of Spring
```

`< N O T E >`

In the figure, the starfish image tag is shown wrapped over two lines for demonstration; the tag is on one line in the session's sample page on the CD. In the sample page, line 37 reads: `<p><img src="Images/shell4.jpg" class="shells" alt="image of dark yellow starfish"/>`

7. **Choose File→Save.**
   You modified the `n_booking.html` page to comply with accessibility standards.

8. **Choose File→Open, choose** n_fine_print.html, **and click Open.**
   You amend the page's content.

9. **Go to line 8, and press Enter to add a blank line. Paste the content from the clipboard to the page.**
   This adds the <meta> tag information to the page after the `<meta http-equiv="Content-Type" content="text/html; charset=utf-8" />` code in line 7.

```
7   <meta http-equiv="Content-Type" content="text/html; charset=utf-8" />
8   <meta name="keywords" content="Sizzle, resort, Sizzle East,     9
9   Sizzle West, Sizzle South, Caribbean" />
10  <meta name="description" content="noframes page containing     10
11  information about insurance, visas, and vaccinations" />
12  <meta name="contact" content="your name, your e-mail address" />
13  <meta name="copyright" content="copyright Sizzle Corporation, 2003.
14  All Rights Reserved" />
```

10. **Go to lines 10 and 11, and modify the content attribute to read:**
    content="noframes page containing information about insurance, visas, and vaccinations" />
    You modify the tag's value to describe the page's content.

11. **Go to line 29. Select the original** alt **attribute for the seashell image that reads** alt="seashell image" **and type:**
    alt="spiny white and brown seashell image" />
    to expand the attribute.
    The alt attribute's content is modified to comply with standards.

```
29  <p><img src="Images/shell2.jpg" class="shells"
30  alt="spiny white and brown seashell image" />     11
31  You never know when something happens that forces you to return
```

12. **Go to line 51, and select the original** alt **attribute for the seashell image that reads** alt="seashell image" **and change the** alt **attribute. Type:** alt="beige and pink spiral seashell image" />
    The alt attribute's content is modified to comply with standards.

```
51  <p><img src="Images/shell3.jpg"
52  class="shells" alt="beige and pink spiral seashell image" />     12
53  You don't need vaccinations to visit our resorts. If you are the
```

`< N O T E >`

In the figures, the spiral and spiny seashells image tags are shown wrapped over two lines for demonstration; the tags are each on one line in the session's sample page.

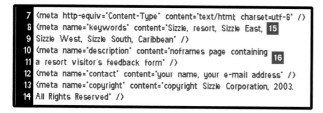

```
 7 <meta http-equiv="Content-Type" content="text/html; charset=utf-8" />
 8 <meta name="keywords" content="Sizzle, resort, Sizzle East,
 9 Sizzle West, Sizzle South, Caribbean" />
10 <meta name="description" content="noframes page containing
11 a resort visitor's feedback form" />
12 <meta name="contact" content="your name, your e-mail address" />
13 <meta name="copyright" content="copyright Sizzle Corporation, 2003.
14 All Rights Reserved" />
```

13. **Choose File➜Save, and save the** n_fine_print.html **page.**
    You modified the Fine Print page to make it more accessible.

14. **Choose File➜Open, choose** n_contact.hmtl, **and click Open.**
    You add more content to the page.

15. **Go to line 8, and press Enter to add a blank line. Paste the content from the clipboard to the page.**
    This adds the additional <meta> tag information to the page.

16. **Go to lines 10 and 11, and modify the content attribute to read:**
    content="noframes page containing a resort visitor's feedback form" />
    Modify the tag's value to describe the page's content.

17. **Choose File➜Save to save the** n_contact.html **page.**
    You modified three content pages for the no-frames version of the site, adding identification information and expanding image descriptions. Close Notepad.

How the Remaining No-frames Pages Scored

The main page for the no-frames site complies with Section 508. However, it fails at the WCAG Priority 2 level on two points, as you can see in the figure.

There are deprecated tags in the n_main.html page (although the page is valid XHTML), and the page is missing <meta> tag information. Both these items are corrected in the tutorial.

The n_contact.html page fared better. No compliance issues were discovered at either the Section 508 or WAI/ WCAG Priority 1 levels. At the Priority 2 level, the page failed because it requires that labels for each of the form's fields be attached to the form content. That way, a visitor using a device such as a screen reader hears the name of the choices along with the actual content of each option.

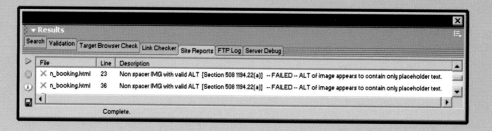

Tutorial
» Reviewing the Sizzle Site's Pages

A preliminary review is used to identify the scope of potential issues on a Web site. The review doesn't test every aspect of a site or include a full range of testing for different users' disabilities. Instead, a preliminary review uses some specific browser settings. You can also test a site using text-only or voice-based browsers. To simulate a text-only browser, place a piece of paper on the computer screen so that you can see a page's content only one line at a time. What you read across the page is the same as what a text or voice-based reader generates.

1. **Open Internet Explorer, and choose Tools→Internet Options.**
   The Internet Options dialog box opens.

2. **Click Advanced to open the tab. Scroll down to the Multimedia section.**

3. **Deselect the Show Pictures options, which is selected by default.**

4. **Click OK to close the dialog box and return to the browser window.**

5. **Click Refresh in your browser window.**
   The option change takes effect.

6. **Open the** n_main.html **page.**
   Scroll through the page, and you see that the pictures are hidden.

<NOTE>
Your site's images have width and height defined, which means that the image blocks remain at the defined size even when the pictures are hidden. If the sizes are undefined, the image block appears as a small square.

7. **Click Booking at the bottom of the** n_main.html **page to load the** n_booking.html **no-frames page.**
   The page loads into the browser window. Scroll through the page, and check the image locations.

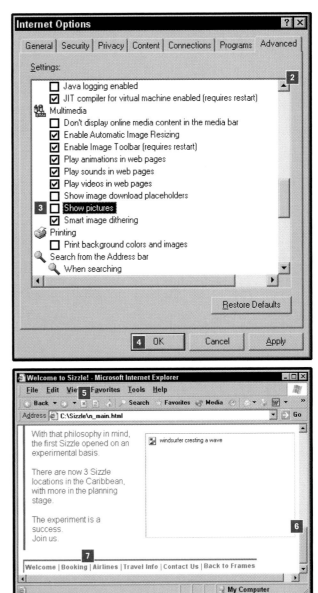

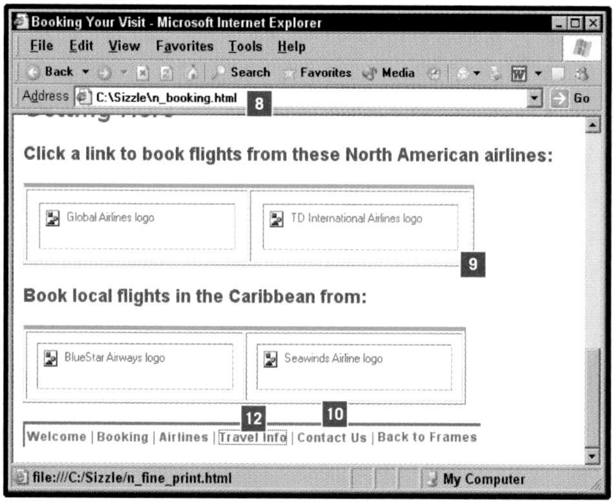

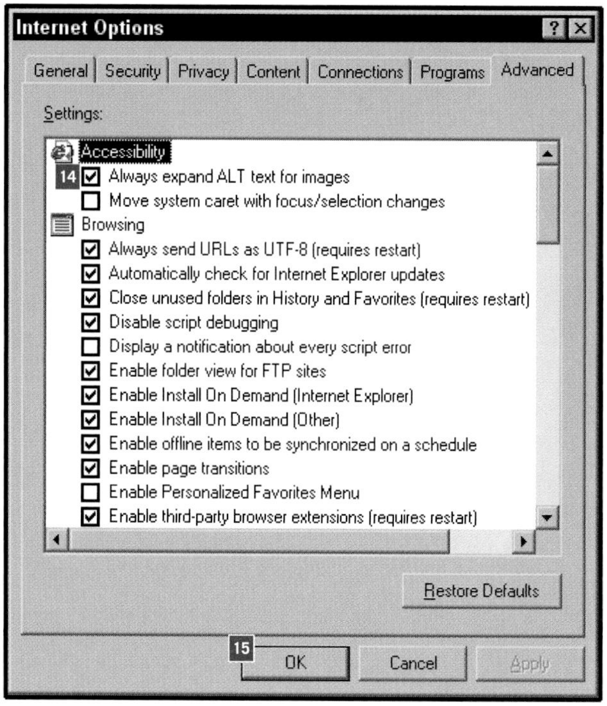

8. **Press the Tab key.**

The focus, which is the active element on the page, jumps to the page's address on the address bar. The address is highlighted.

9. **Continue to press Tab through the set of airline image links.**

You can see the focus at each link display as a thin, hatched frame around the link, both text and image links. Check the link against the description in the status bar at the bottom of the window.

<NOTE>

In the figure, the focus is shown on the Travel Info link.

10. **Click Contact Us in the text links at the bottom of the page.**

The n_contact.html page loads in the browser window.

11. **Press Tab repeatedly, and watch the focus shift through the form.**

The focus jumps from selection to selection through the form, and then from link to link across the bottom text links.

12. **Click Travel Info.**

The n_fine_print.html page loads in the browser window.

13. **Choose Tools→Internet Options→Advanced.**

The Internet Options dialog box opens.

14. **Click Always expand ALT text for Images.**

The option is selected.

15. **Click OK to close the dialog box.**

You return to the browser window.

16. Click Refresh in your browser window.

The page reloads.

17. Scroll down the page to the seashell image.

You see that the image frame displays the entire alt text that you added to the tag.

18. Choose Tools→Internet Options→Advanced.

The Internet Options dialog box opens.

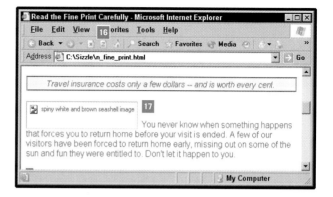

19. Click Restore Defaults.

The custom settings revert to the program's default settings.

20. Click OK to close the dialog box.

You return to the browser window.

21. Click Refresh to reset the browser's settings.

You tested your no-frames pages for several common accessibility features. You tested the tab order and tab function, and viewed the pages without images and with expanded alt text. Leave Internet Explorer open for the next tutorial.

Tutorial
» Modifying the Page Display for Page Testing

In the final tutorial, you continue testing your no-frames site. You tested general functionality and visibility in the previous tutorial, and also evaluated the pages for tabbing order. In this tutorial, you make several tests using browser controls for font and color scheme, as well as with changes to the system's display settings.

1. **In Internet Explorer, choose Tools→Internet Options.**
   The Internet Options dialog box opens.

2. **Click Accessibility.**
   The Accessibility dialog box opens.

3. **Select all three formatting options.**
   Your page's font colors, sizes, and styles are turned off.

4. **Click OK to close the Accessibility dialog box. Click OK again to close the Internet Options dialog box.**

5. **Scroll through the page in the Explorer window.**
   You see that the text on the page remains legible.

6. **Click Contact Us.**
   The survey form page loads in the browser window.

7. **Choose View→Text Size→Largest.**
   The font size changes.

8. **Scroll through the survey form.**
   Note that the content and structure of the form remains legible and usable because of the tags that you used.

9. **Choose View→Text Size→Medium.**
   The font size returns to the browser's default size.

10. **Repeat Steps 1 and 2. In the Accessibility dialog box, deselect the formatting options. Click OK to close the Internet Options dialog box.**
    The page's color, fonts, and styles are restored.

11. **Minimize the browser. Right-click the desktop to open a shortcut menu, and choose Properties from the shortcut menu.**
    The Display Properties dialog box opens.

12. **In the Display Properties dialog box, click the Appearance tab.**

< N O T E >

If you are working with an earlier operating system version, omit Step 13.

13. **Click the Windows and buttons drop-down arrow, and choose Windows Classic style.**
    You can set Windows XP's appearance to that of earlier operating system versions.

14. **Click the Color Scheme drop-down arrow, and choose one of four High Contrast options from the list.**

15. **Click OK.**
    The dialog box closes, and the alternate color scheme is applied to the display.

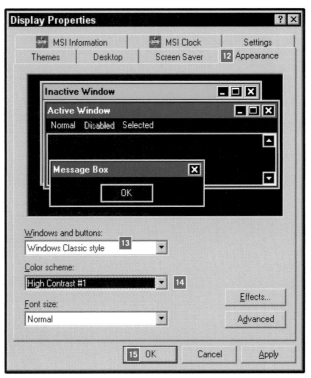

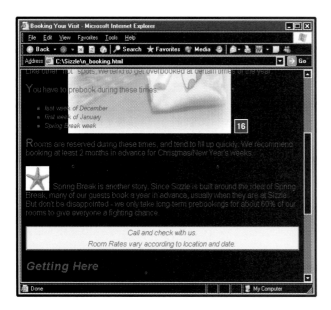

16. Maximize the browser window.

Test the pages for contrast. Close the browser.

<NOTE>

The page shown in the figure is the n_booking.html page. With a high-contrast color scheme, the content is difficult to read due both to the text color and the background image.

17. Repeat Steps 11 through 13.

Reset the window style to the style in use before you started the tutorial.

18. Repeat Step 14, choosing your previous color scheme.

Click OK to close the dialog box and reapply your color scheme. You tested your site using a variety of visual settings and color schemes.

Logical Compromise Is Key

You have experimented with your site's pages using a range of different browser configurations and display settings. Some of the pages look fine in the modified versions; others don't. You have two choices if you anticipate that your site visitors may use devices such as screen readers, text browsers, or magnifiers.

You can reset all your site's styles to appear more visible in a high contrast color scheme and remove the background images, or you can add a note to the page providing instructions for assistive device users. The figure shows the same location on the n_booking.html page as shown in the tutorial.

The content is more legible. The Accessibility format options available in the Internet Options menu in Internet Explorer are all selected, which bypass the page's styles. Add a note to your pages explaining to your users how to achieve the same page clarity. You can use the styles for visual design and provide assistance for optimal accessible use of the site.

» Session Review

This session covers the creation and testing of the no-frames version of your Sizzle site. You created one page in Session 7. In this session, you add three more no-frames pages. You built a navigation table to use for the pages and applied a style to the table. The opening image in the session shows the survey form complete with its navigation links.

You learned what accessibility standards are and the different types of standards in existence. You modified the pages to comply with Web usability standards, and then tested the content of the no-frames pages using a variety of browser-based accessibility options including the use of a high contrast color scheme similar to that shown in the final image in this session.

Use these questions to help you review the information in this session. The answer to each question can be found in the tutorial noted in parentheses.

1. Who are the accessibility guidelines from the WAG/WAIC designed for? (See Discussion: Introducing Accessibility Guidelines.)

2. What is Section 508? (See Discussion: Introducing Accessibility Guidelines.)

3. Why is it important to physically separate text content on a page with a vertical separator or other similar character? (See Tutorial: Building the No-frames Pages.)

4. How do screen readers and similar devices handle links on a page? (See Tutorial: Building the No-frames Pages.)

5. What does it mean for a table to "degrade gracefully"? (See Tutorial: Adding Navigation Tables to the No-frames Pages.)

6. Is it always necessary to insert a `<br />` tag before adding a table to a page? When is it necessary? (See Tutorial: Adding Navigation Tables to the No-frames Pages.)

7. How do you insert a page into another page? Is the method reliable? (See Discussion: Using an Entire Page as an Object.)

8. What types of information can you add to the `<meta>` tag in the `<head>` of a page? (See Tutorial: Tweaking the Main No-frames Pages for Accessibility.)

9. Is all `alt` text for an image considered in compliance with Section 508 standards? (See Tutorial: Completing the Content in the No-frames Pages.)

10. Can deprecated tags be used on a page containing valid XHTML? (See Tutorial: Completing the Content in the No-frames Pages.)

11. Are the placeholders for images the same whether or not you define dimensions in the page's code? (See Tutorial: Reviewing the Sizzle Site's Pages.)

12. How do you test tab order and functionality on a page? (See Tutorial: Reviewing the Sizzle Site's Pages.)

13. How do you disable font style, size, and color in Internet Explorer? (See Tutorial: Modifying the Page Display for Testing.)

14. Why is it valuable to test your site using high contrast color schemes? (See Tutorial: Modifying the Page Display for Testing.)

» Other Projects

Continue to create additional no-frames pages to duplicate content in both the frames and no-frames versions of the site.

Explore the WAI/WACG guidelines. Evaluate the content of your site's pages for compliance with the standards. Can you find instances where the site does not comply fully with the guidelines? (Here is an example: Not all pages use the headings in a consistent order.)

The scripted links in the site are triggered with mouse actions. Explore using equivalent keyboard commands such as `onkeyup` in addition to `onmouseup`, and so on.

SIZZLE'S SUCCESS IS BASED ON LISTENING TO WHAT PEOPLE WANT A VACATION TO BE. LET US KNOW WHAT YOU THINK.

⌐Have you been to a Sizzle resort?─

○ Yes
○ No
When? │month and year│

⌐Which resort did you visit?─

│Sizzle East ▾│

⌐Comments on service, activities, or surroundin

│   ▴▾│

Evaluating and Testing Your Site

Take Our Survey - Microsoft Internet Explorer

File   Edit   View   Favorites   Tools   Help

Back

Search   Favorites   Media

Have you been to a Sizzle resort?
- ○ Yes
- ○ No

When? month and year

Which resort did you visit?

Sizzle East ▼

Comments on service, activities, or surroundings?

Are you planning another visit?
- ○ Yes
- ○ No

Your e-mail address:

Submit   Reset

Done   My Computer

Session Introduction

Before you finish constructing your site, there are still a few things to finish. The site's pages must be checked for content, errors, style use, and active links. You test the site using different screen resolutions and make some final changes to the pages.

TOOLS YOU'LL USE
Notepad, Internet Explorer

CD-ROM FILES NEEDED (In Image Sources Folder)
flower.jpg

FILES MODIFIED
contact.html, main.html, n_contact.html, n_main.html, sizzle.css, sizzle_east.html, sizzle_south.html, sizzle_west.html

TIME REQUIRED
90 minutes

Discussion

Understanding Screen Resolution

The Sizzle site uses an 800 x 600-pixel display, which is the optimal size for developing a Web site. A pixel is a distinct dot on the screen. At 800 x 600 pixels the screen can display 800 distinct dots on each of 600 lines, or 480,000 pixels. Actually, some of the pixel space is taken up by the edges of the monitor, giving you only 760 x 420 pixels of visible area.

Changing resolution changes the number of pixels seen on the screen. The content of the pixel doesn't change; only the size of the pixel changes. In the figure, the same content is shown at a low-resolution, and a high resolution. You see the images use different amounts of screen space to display the same content. The resolution of the screen is not the same as the size of the monitor. A 14-inch monitor may be capable of using the same resolution as a 19-inch monitor.

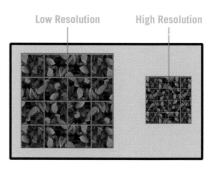

If your screen is configured to use an 800 x 600-pixel resolution, the Sizzle site displayed at full window size fills the entire screen, as shown in the left figure. However, if the screen is set to 1600 x 1200, the same image fills only a portion of the screen, shown in the right figure below.

Using the 800 x 600-pixel resolution, you know that your viewers can see the content at 800 x 600 pixels as well as any higher-resolution settings they may be using. If you design a page using a high resolution, such as 1600 x 1200, viewers using a lower-resolution page may not be able to see all your content correctly.

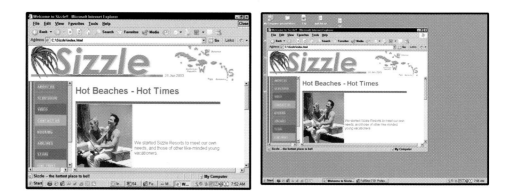

Tutorial
» Testing Your Site on Different Screens

Your project has come a long way! It is nearly complete. You constructed a suite of pages and validated the HTML and CSS content. You created a frames version and a representative no-frames version, and you conducted some accessibility testing as well. Your site may look and behave quite well on your own computer, but that doesn't mean that it will look good on other computers. A common design error is building pages that don't display well when viewers use different screen resolutions. Your site is built for a screen using a resolution of 800 x 600 pixels, a low resolution. In this tutorial, you test the page with both a higher resolution and a lower resolution screen size.

1. **Open Internet Explorer, and then open** index.html.
   You test the site's interface using different resolutions. Leave the browser and page open as you continue with the next steps.

2. **Right-click the desktop, and click Properties from the shortcut menu.**
   The Display Properties dialog box opens.

3. **Click the Settings tab.**
   You make adjustments to the screen's resolution here.

4. **Drag the Screen resolution slider.**
   Stop when the values below the slider read "1024 by 768 pixels."

5. **Click Apply.**
   The screen blacks out and then resets itself. A Monitor Settings message displays.

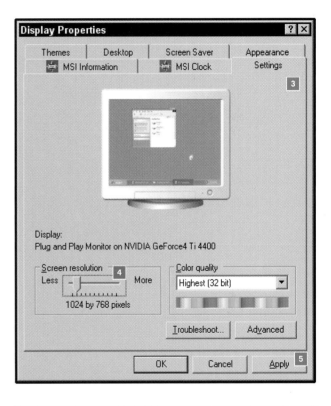

6. **Click Yes to resize the screen.**
   The message box closes, and the screen is resized. Leave the Display Properties dialog box open.

<NOTE>
If you don't select Yes or No in the dialog box, the screen automatically reverts to the last-used resolution after a specified number of seconds. You see a countdown display on the message.

7. **Click the Internet Explorer window to make it the active window.**

8. Drag the resize handle at the bottom right of the window.
You can resize the window to display the entire navigation table without scroll bars. The text on the page is sufficiently large to read clearly at the higher resolution.

<NOTE>
If you are working with Windows XP, you can't do Steps 9 through 14 as Windows XP doesn't allow a screen resolution of 640 x 480 pixels. Please continue at Step 15. Steps 9 through 14 are shown using Windows 2000 Professional.

9. Click the Display Properties dialog box to make it the active window again.

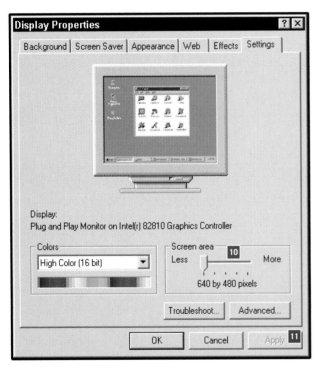

10. If you are using Windows 2000 or an older version of Windows, drag the slider to the left to set the screen resolution to 640 x 480 pixels.
You reset the screen resolution to a low resolution.

11. Click Apply.
The screen blacks out and then resets itself. The Monitor Settings message displays.

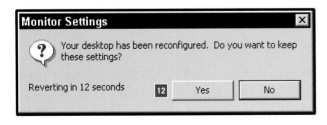

12. Click Yes to resize the screen.
The screen is resized, and the message box closes. Leave the Display Properties dialog box open.

13. Click the Internet Explorer window to make it the active window.

14. Maximize the window.

A large portion of the navigation table requires scroll bars for display. Portions of the imagemap are beyond the limits of the window.

15. Click the Display Properties dialog box to make it the active window.

You restore the screen resolution settings.

16. Drag the resolution slider to 800 x 600 pixels.

The value is shown below the screen slider.

17. Click Apply.

The screen blacks out and is restored; the Monitor Settings message displays.

18. In Windows XP, click Yes to reset the window; in Windows 2000 or an older version, click OK to reset the window.

You tested the Web site's interface with both high and low resolution screen sizes. The site's content is designed for a display using 800 x 600 pixel resolution, and it displays well at higher resolutions. Leave Internet Explorer open and the frameset loaded to continue with the next tutorial.

Tutorial
» Starting a Final Check of the Sizzle Web Site

In this tutorial, you follow a path to check your site one last time to make sure that everything is in order before you show it to the world. In both this tutorial and the one following, you work through the site using a systematic method for testing and evaluating the content. You evaluate the site for appearance, layout, errors in content and spelling, and functionality. As you evaluate different pages, make note of changes that should be made. You can either make changes individually, or check the entire site and then modify pages as required. In the tutorials, you evaluate the site first, and then make changes.

1. **Open Internet Explorer, and then open** `index.html`.
   If you are continuing from the previous tutorial, the program and file are already open.

2. **Check the logo frame of the page:**
   - » Do the items fit on the screen horizontally and vertically?
   - » Is the scripted date correct? Placed correctly? Using the correct style?

3. **Click the imagemap link to Sizzle East.**
   The page loads in the main frame of the frameset.

4. **Click the Sizzle West and Sizzle South links on the imagemap.**
   The respective pages load in the frameset.

5. **Click ABOUT US on the navigation frame to reload the** `main.html` **page in the main frame.**
   You tested the imagemap links and evaluated the logo frame's layout.

<TIP>
Finish evaluating the site before making changes and retesting to keep track of what has been tested and what remains to be tested. Make a list of items to repair or change as you review the pages.

<TIP>
If any of your pages are not loading correctly, check its code. Check the anchor tags for spelling mistakes, and check the target frame attribute.

6. **Scroll down the** `main.html` **page in the main frame.**
   Check the content for error, and check that the styles are applied.

7. **Note the irregular layout of the title and links at the bottom of the** `main.html` **page.**
   The layout requires some modification.

8. **Click the Sizzle East link to load the page.**
   The Sizzle East page loads in the main frame.

9. **Click Back on the browser to return to the** `main.html` **page.**
   Test the other two text links.

10. **Click the SIZZLE EAST text link to load the page.**
    You review the first resort page.

11. **Scroll down the page, and evaluate the content.**
    Check for accuracy and application of styles.

12. **Click the SLIDESHOW link to load the slideshow in a separate browser window.**
    Close the slideshow window.

13. **Click the BOOKING link.**
    The `booking.html` page loads in the browser. The booking link uses "book HERE" as the text for the link. In Session 14, you learned about accessible features to consider when planning and building a Web site. One of the simplest features is explanatory links. The link text should be more descriptive.

<NOTE>
Changing the booking link's text is an item to be modified; Table 15-1 at the end of the next tutorial shows a list of corrections to be made according to the review you are doing in this tutorial and the following tutorial.

14. **Click ABOUT US on the navigation frame to reload the `main.html` page in the main frame of the page.**
    You test the two other resort pages.

15. **Scroll down the `main.html` page to the text links. Repeat Steps 11 through 14 with the Sizzle West and Sizzle South pages.**
    Test the pages for content, and test their links. Because the pages were designed at the same time, they should work similarly; they also require changes to the text link content.

16. **Click the SLIDESHOW link on the navigation frame.**
    The slideshow opens in a separate browser window.

17. **Evaluate the set of slides. Check for the following:**

    » Content accuracy

    » Spelling and grammar

    » Application of styles

    » Valid links

18. **Close the slideshow browser window.**
    You return to the frameset. The slideshow pages are tested.

<TIP>
If you find errors in the content or layout of the slides, note the errors. Open the slideshow page containing the error, and read the code. Check for spelling errors in links and styles.

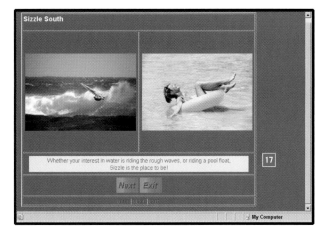

19. **Click VIDEO in the navigation frame.**
    The movie loads in the main frame.

20. **Right-click the movie, and test the controls.**
    The movie works and runs correctly.

21. **Click CONTACT US on the navigation frame.**
    The survey form loads in the main frame.

22. **Scroll through the page.**
    Evaluate the content for accuracy and appearance. The form's content is correct, but its appearance is less decorative than the rest of the site. The page needs an image.

23. **Test the form. Enter some data, and click Submit.**
    You can test the e-mail function or dismiss the dialog box. You evaluated several pages of your site for content, layout, and correct function. The next tutorial completes the testing process; leave Internet Explorer open and the index.html frameset loaded.

Tutorial
» Completing the Review of the Site

In the previous tutorial, you started evaluating the site one last time prior to posting. You are checking for accuracy of content, spelling and grammatical errors, styles, layouts, links, and scripts. The final changes are contained in a table at the end of this tutorial. You continue from the previous tutorial, with the `index.html` frameset open in your browser.

1. **On the navigation frame of the `index.html` frameset, click the BOOKING link.**
   The `booking.html` page loads in the main frame.

2. **Click the AIRLINES link.**
   The `booking.html` page jumps to the airline anchor.

3. **Test the image links to the airlines.**
   Each link opens in a new browser window. You see the Page Not Found message because the links are fictitious. Close the extra browser window.

4. **Click the STORE link in the navigation frame.**
   The `store.html` page loads in the main frame.

5. **Click the SIZZLE STORE link.**
   The page opens in the main frame using Acrobat Reader 5.x or Adobe Reader 6.0.

`<NOTE>`
The products use different names depending on version; any version up to the newest is called Acrobat Reader; the latest version is named Adobe Reader. Both products display content the same way.

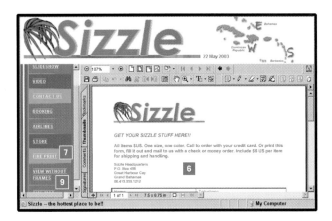

6. **Scroll through the form.**
   Test the form fields.

7. **Click FINE PRINT on the navigation frame.**
   The `fine_print.html` page loads in the main frame.

8. **Scroll through the `fine_print.html` page.**
   Check the content.

9. **Click VIEW WITHOUT FRAMES in the navigation frame.**
   The first no-frames page loads in a blank browser window.

10. **Scroll through the page.**
    Note that the first paragraph doesn't use the site's blue color and should be corrected.The text is missing <p> tags.

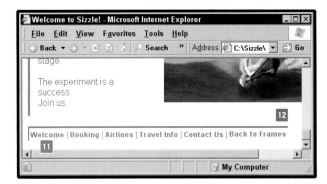

11. **Test the links at the bottom of the page.**
    As each page loads, scroll to the bottom and click Welcome to return to the Booking page.

12. **Test and evaluate the content of the remaining no-frames pages, and then click Back to Frames**.
    You return to the site's frameset.

    <NOTE>
    The `n_contact.html  page` should have an image.

13. **Click SITE MAP on the navigation frame.**
    The site map page loads and resizes the window at its custom size.

14. Check that the script for positioning the page is correct.

The page opens at the upper left of the window at the custom size.

<TIP>

If you have any window resizing errors, check your JavaScript pages for punctuation and spelling errors.

15. Scroll through the page testing the links.

The links are valid.

<TIP>

If you discover any invalid links, check for spelling errors in the links in the page's code.

16. Click CLOSE SITE MAP.

The site map page closes, and the frameset reloads at a screen size of 800 x 600 pixels.

17. **Close Internet Explorer.**

You have tested and reviewed the content in your site. After some final touchups, the site will be ready for the world. The corrections noted during this tutorial and the previous one are listed in Table 15-1. You make the final corrections in the next tutorial.

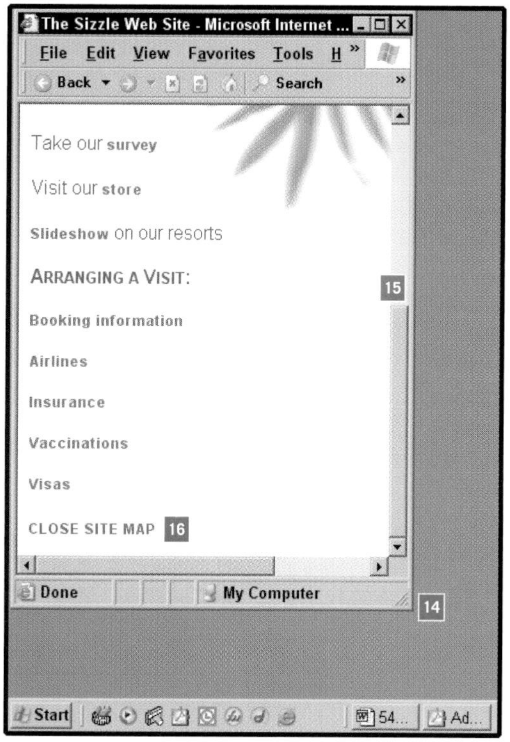

<NOTE>

You may want to make changes to other elements of the site as well. Use your own sense of style to customize content, styles, and so on, to your liking.

Table 15-1: Final Changes Required for the Sizzle Site

Page	Correction to Be Made
main.html	Align the title and text links at the bottom of the page.
sizzle_east.html	Add descriptive alt text for the Click Here link to the booking page.
sizzle_west.html	Add descriptive alt text for the Click Here link to the booking page.
sizzle_south.html	Add descriptive alt text for the Click Here link to the booking page.
contact.html	Add a background image to keep the page from being bland.
n_main.html	Correct the color on the first block of text.
n_contact.html	Add a background image to keep the page from being bland.

Tutorial

» Making Final Content and Layout Corrections

In the previous two tutorials, you evaluated the site looking for errors, reviewing layout and style issues, and checking scripts and processes. Changes that need to be made are listed in Table 15-1 at the end of the previous tutorial. In this tutorial, you make the corrections to the site's pages. You need one final image for your site. It is located in the Image Sources folder on the CD and is named `flower.jpg`. Copy or move the file into the Sizzle site's Image folder.

```
40  <table class="booking" border="0" cellpadding="12">
41    <tr>
42  2    <td><p>Read about our Resorts:</p></td>
43      <td><a href="sizzle_east.html" target="main"> SIZZLE EAST</a></td>
```

```
36  <p>Watch our Sizzle <a href="ss1.html" target="blank"> slideshow </a></p>
37  <hr />
38  <p>Ready to visit? <a href="booking.html" target="main">
39    Click for booking information.</a></p>  4
40  </body>
```

1. **Open Notepad, and then open** `main.html`.
   You modify the text at the bottom of this page.

2. **Go to line 42, and change the tags from <h4> to <p> tags. The line now reads** `<td><p>Read about our Resorts: </p></td>`
   The text and links were misaligned due to the heading style. Changing the <h4> tags to <p> corrects this.

3. **Choose File→Save. Choose File→Open, and select the** `sizzle_east.html` **page.**
   The `main.html` page closes. You made a heading correction in the `main.html` page and now open the next page for correcting because the link to the booking page isn't descriptive.

4. **Go to line 39, and replace the link text on line 39. Lines 38 and 39 now read.** `<p>Ready to visit? <a href="booking.html" target="main">Click for booking information. </a></p>`
   The tag's information is expanded and more useful for a visitor using a screen reader. Move the closing period (.) to appear before the </a> tag.

<NOTE>
The text is wrapped over lines 38 and 39 in the figure for display. The session file contains the tag on line 38 only.

5. **Choose File→Save. Open** `sizzle_west.html`.
   You modified the text link on the first resort page and opened the second page for modification.

<NOTE>
The text displays on different lines based on the page's descriptive content. Look for the final <p> tag before the </body> tag.

6. **Repeat Step 4. Replace the link text. The lines read** `Ready to`
   `visit? <a href="booking.html"`
   `target="main">Click for booking informa-`
   `tion.</a>`
   Depending on your page's layout, the final `<p>` tag is on line
   37.

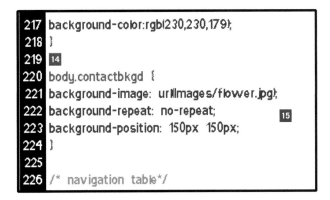

7. **Choose File→Save. Open** `sizzle_south.html`.
   You modified the tag on the second resort page and opened
   the final page for modification.

8. **Repeat Step 4.**
   Depending on your page's layout, the final `<p>` tag is on line
   39.

9. **Choose File→Save. Open** `n_main.html`.
   This page is missing a tag, and it must be added.

10. **Go to line 31, and insert a `<p>` tag after the `<tr>` tag.**
    The text needs `<p>` tags to use the site's basic paragraph
    style.

11. **Go to line 33, and insert a `</p>` tag before the `</tr>` tag.**
    The paragraph needs a closing tag.

12. **Choose File→Save.**
    The missing tag is added to the no-frames main page.

13. **Choose File→Open, and select** `sizzle.css`.
    You need one more style for the site's style sheet. The `con-`
    `tact.html` page contains the survey form. Unlike the other
    pages on the site, the form's page has no images and is quite
    bland in comparison to the rest of the site. The image is
    added to the page using a style.

14. **Go to line 219, and press Enter to add a blank line following the
    closing bracket of the `a:hover` style.**
    You add the final style to the miscellaneous category on the
    style sheet.

15. **On lines 220 through 224, type:**
    ```
    body.contactbkgd {
    background-image: url(Images/flower.jpg);
    background-repeat: no-repeat;
    background-position: 150px 150px;
    }
    ```
    The style is similar to the style that you created for the book-
    ing page's background. The position sets the image at 150
    pixels from the top and 150 pixels from the left side.

16. **Choose File→Save.**
    You save the style sheet.

17. **Choose File→Open, and select** `contact.html`.
    You attach the new style to the page.

```
45  <body class="contactbkgd"> 18
46  <form method="post" action="mailto:yourname@youraddress.com"
47  name="contactForm" enctype="text/plain" onsubmit="return validateEmail(this)">
48
```

18. **Go to the <body> tag on line 45, and expand it. Type:** <body class="contactbkgd">
    The style that you just created is attached to the page.

19. **Choose File→Save.**
    You save the completed contact.html page.

20. **Choose File→Open, and select** n_contact.html.
    You attach the style to the no-frames version of the survey.

21. **Repeat Steps 18 and 19.**
    The <body> tag on the n_contact.html page is located further down the page on line 52 because the no-frames version of the page has attached <meta> attributes. The style is attached to the page. Close Notepad.

22. **Open Internet Explorer, and then open** index.html.
    You test the page corrections and alterations.

23. **Click CONTACT US in the navigation frame.**
    The survey form loads in the main frame.

24. **Scroll down to see the newly placed image.**
    The flower image is placed behind the survey items.

25. **Check the other changes made in the tutorial. Close the browser.**
    You finished modifications to your Web site. If you have an Internet Service Provider (ISP) and would like to test the Sizzle site live, continue to the Bonus Session located on the CD-ROM.

» Session Review

In this session, you completed the final evaluation and tweaking of the site. You tested the site using different screen resolutions. You methodically evaluated and tested the site for content, appearance, and functionality. You made some last-minute changes to the pages, modifying some tags and adding an image to the site. The opening image in this session shows the survey page as it appears in the no-frames version of the site. The final image shows the same page, but with the addition of an image placed using a style.

Here are some questions to help you review the information in this session. You'll find the answer to each question in the tutorial noted in parentheses.

1. Is it better to design a page for a high-resolution or low-resolution screen size? Why? (See Tutorial: Testing Your Site on Different Screens.)

2. How does a high-resolution display differ from a low-resolution display? (See Tutorial: Testing Your Site on Different Screens.)

3. Is it better to complete a site evaluation and then make corrections or to make corrections as you discover them? Why? (See Tutorial: Starting a Final Check of the Sizzle Web Site.)

4. What types of errors are you looking for when performing a final test of site? (See Tutorial: Completing the Review of the Site.)

5. How should links be worded when considering page use by screen readers? (See Tutorial: Making Final Content and Layout Corrections.)

6. Is all text content on your site automatically formatted using styles? (See Tutorial: Making Final Content and Layout Corrections.)

7. How do you define a location for a background image in a style? (See Tutorial: Making Final Content and Layout Corrections.)

» Other Projects

See the Bonus Session on the CD-ROM when you are ready to upload the site for online use.

Experiment with other display devices such as television. Download the MSN Web TV viewer. Test your site's pages. How would you modify your site's structure and page layouts for television display?

Build your own site!

File   Edit   View   Favorites   Tools   Help

Back ▼ | Search | Favorites | Media | »

┌─ **Have you been to a Sizzle resort?** ─────────────┐
│ ○ Yes
│ ○ No
│ When? | month and year |
└──┘

┌─ **Which resort did you visit?** ──────────────────┐
│
│ | Sizzle East ▼ |
└──┘

┌─ **Comments on service, activities, or surroundings?** ─┐
│ | ▲ |
│ | ▼ |
└──┘

┌─ **Are you planning another visit?** ─────────────┐
│
│ ○ Yes
│ ○ No
└──┘

┌─ **Your e-mail address:** ─────────────────────┐
│ | |
└──┘

| Submit | | Reset |

Bonus Session

Posting Your Site

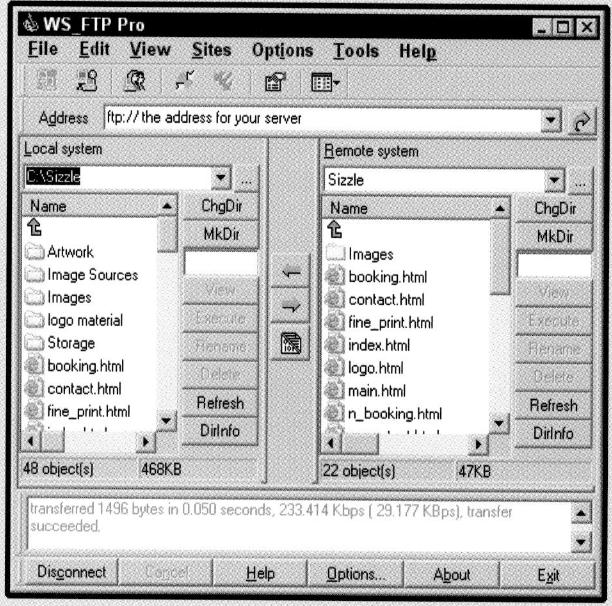

Session Introduction

Throughout the book you learned how to build a Web site, how to validate its content, and how to add interactivity through JavaScript. Before your site can be shared with the world, you have to post it to a Web server. On the CD, you will find a Bonus Session named Posting Your Site. This short session teaches you about FTP, and then shows you how to post a Web site to a Web server using WS FTP software, which is also included on the CD.

Appendix

What's on the CD-ROM?

This appendix provides you with information on the contents of the CD-ROM that accompanies this book. For the latest and greatest information, please refer to the ReadMe file located at the root of the CD-ROM. Here is what you find:

>> System Requirements

>> Using the CD-ROM

>> What's on the CD-ROM

>> Troubleshooting

System Requirements

There are virtually no system requirements to complete the book's project! However, you must meet minimum requirements to use Web browser software and the book's CD.

Recommended System Configuration for Windows 2000, Windows NT, Windows Me, or Windows XP

» Intel® Pentium® III

» Windows Millennium Edition, Windows 2000 with Service Pack 2, Windows XP

» 128MB of RAM

» Super VGA (800 x 600) or higher-resolution monitor with 256 colors

» CD-ROM drive

» Modem or Internet connection

Minimum Requirements

» Computer with a 486/66-MHz processor or higher (Pentium processor recommended)

» Windows 98, Windows 98 Second Edition, Windows Millennium Edition (Windows Me), Windows NT(r) 4.0 SP 6a and higher, Windows 2000, or Windows XP

» 16 MB to 32 MB RAM (depending on Operating System)

» Super VGA (800 x 600) or higher-resolution monitor with 256 colors

» CD-ROM drive

» Modem or Internet connection

Using the CD-ROM

To install the items from the CD-ROM to your hard drive, follow these steps:

1. Insert the CD-ROM into the CD-ROM drive.

2. The interface launches. If you have autorun disabled, click Start→Run. In the dialog box that appears, type D:\setup.exe. Replace *D* with the proper letter if the CD-ROM drive uses a different letter. (If you don't know the letter, see how the CD-ROM drive is listed under My Computer.) Click OK. A license agreement appears.

3. Read through the license agreement, and then click the Accept button if you want to use the CD. (After you click Accept, the License Agreement window never bothers you again.) The CD interface Welcome screen appears.

4. The interface coordinates installing the programs and running the demos. The interface basically enables you to click a button or two to make things happen.

5. Click anywhere on the Welcome screen to enter the interface. This next screen lists categories for the software on the CD.

6. For more information about a program, click the program's name. Be sure to read the information that appears. Sometimes a program has its own system requirements or requires you to do a few tricks on your computer before you can install or run the program. This screen tells you what you may need to do.

7. If you don't want to install the program, click the Back button to return to the previous screen. You can always return to the previous screen by clicking the Back button. Using this feature, you can browse the different categories and products, and then decide what you want to install.

8. To install a program, click the appropriate Install button. The CD interface drops to the background while the CD installs the program you chose.

9. To install other items, repeat Step 8 for each program.

10. When you finish installing programs, click the Quit button to close the interface. You can eject the CD now. Carefully place it back in the plastic jacket of the book for safekeeping.

<CAUTION>
Use the interface to install the project files on your hard drive rather than installing them directly from the CD. If you install them directly and are using any version of Windows except Windows XP, you have to change the read-only status of the copied tutorial files. Otherwise, you won't be able to write over the files as you work through the tutorials. To change the status, select all the files in a folder that you copied to your computer. Right-click one of the files and choose Properties. In the Properties dialog box, click Read-only to deselect it.

I suggest that you instruct Windows to display the filename extensions of the copied tutorial files, if it isn't already set up to show them, so that you can see the file formats (e.g., .html, .gif, .jpeg, and so on). Find your Folder Options dialog box. It's located in a slightly different place in different versions of Windows: in Windows XP, it's in the Appearance and Themes Control Panel; in Windows 2000 and ME, it's in the My Computer→Tools folder; in Windows 98, it's in the My Computer→View folder. Click the View tab. Click Hide File Extensions for Known File Types to deselect it.

Do not work on the project using the files directly from the CD. Copy files from the CD to your hard drive. Open and rename project page files as you require them. Graphics files can be copied directly into your project's Images folder. Each session has its own folder containing the project complete to that point.

What's on the CD-ROM

The following sections provide a summary of the software and other materials you find on the CD.

Author-created materials

All author-created material from the book, including project files, source material, and samples, are on the CD in the folder named Tutorial Files. This folder contains many files in several subfolders.

Sizzle — This folder contains the HTML, style sheet, and PDF files for the complete site, and has one subfolder:

Images — This folder contains the images and Flash files used in the finished site.

session01 through session15 — A collection of 15 folders each containing a set of the HTML files for the project complete to the named session's point in development.

Storage — This folder contains several text and HTML files used as source material for page content.

Artwork — This folder contains the component parts that are used to construct the graphics for the Sizzle logos, buttons, and backgrounds.

Image Sources — This folder contains the source files and raw images used in the Sizzle site.

Images — This folder contains the finished images and graphics used in the Sizzle site.

Confidence Builder — This folder contains one subfolder:

> **MY SITE** — This folder contains the complete HTML, image, and graphic files for the Confidence Builder project. There are 3 HTML pages, and 5 images in the folder.

Applications

The following applications are on the CD:

Adobe Reader 6.0 from Adobe Systems, Inc.

Freeware version—for Windows. This is the reader required to view PDF files. For more information, check out www.adobe.com/products/acrobat/readermain.html.

FTP Commander from InternetSoft Corporation

This is a freeware FTP client with a simple and easy to use interface. The program displays local and remote server panels. Set up a connection and use a set of buttons to move your files. For more information, go to www.internet-soft.com/ftpcomm.htm.

HandyTools for Web Designers power pack from SilverAge Software

This set of tools are, as the name states, handy for working with Web pages. Included in the set are File Find & Replace, Handy Image Mapper, GIF Color Mapper, ColourSpy and Gradientex tools. Check out their website for more information at www.silveragesoftware.com/handytools.html.

HandyHTML Studio from SilverAge Software

This is a trial version of HandyHTML Studio. The program is designed to enhance the hand coding process. You can use syntax highlighting to keep track of your tags, work with templates, and manage your Web site. The studio also includes built-in FTP upload tools. Find out more at www.silveragesoftware.com/hhs.html.

IrfanView from Irfanview

This program is used for converting file formats. It originally began as a simple graphics convertor and has become a very powerful tool. In addition to the basic conversions, you can also download and install a number of extensions for specialized file formats. Read about the program and its uses at www.irfanview.com.

Photo Plus from Serif Software Inc.

You use PhotoPlus to prepare the graphics in the book. PhotoPlus has an expansive set of tools and features, including the ability to use and configure layers and text. This is only one of the products available from Serif Software. See more information on the freeware version of PhotoPlus at www.freeserifsoftware.com/serif/ph/ph5/index.asp and other Serif products at www.serif.com.

WS FTP Pro Version 7.6 from Ipswitch, Inc.

30-day Evaluation version of WS FTP client for Windows. This is the FTP client used in the Bonus Session to transfer the completed project to a Web server for online viewing. For more information, go to www.ipswitch.com/Products/WS_FTP/index.html.

Troubleshooting

If you have difficulty installing or using anything on the companion CD-ROM, try the following solutions:

» **Turn off any antivirus software that you may have running.** Installers sometimes mimic virus activity and can make your computer incorrectly believe that it is being infected by a virus. (Be sure to turn the antivirus software back on later.)

» **Close all running programs.** The more programs you're running, the less memory is available to other programs. Installers also typically update files and programs; if you keep other programs running, the installation may not work properly.

» **Reference the ReadMe:** Please refer to the ReadMe file located at the root of the CD-ROM for the latest product information at the time of publication.

If you still have trouble with the CD-ROM, please call the Wiley Publishing Customer Care phone number: (800) 762-2974. Outside the United States, call 1(317)572-3994. You can also contact Wiley Publishing Customer Service by e-mail at techsupdum@wiley.com. Wiley Publishing will provide technical support only for installation and other general quality control items; for technical support on the applications themselves, consult the program's vendor or author.

Wiley Publishing, Inc.
End-User License Agreement

READ THIS. You should carefully read these terms and conditions before opening the software packet(s) included with this book "Book". This is a license agreement "Agreement" between you and Wiley Publishing, Inc. "WPI". By opening the accompanying software packet(s), you acknowledge that you have read and accept the following terms and conditions. If you do not agree and do not want to be bound by such terms and conditions, promptly return the Book and the unopened software packet(s) to the place you obtained them for a full refund.

1. **License Grant.** WPI grants to you (either an individual or entity) a nonexclusive license to use one copy of the enclosed software program(s) (collectively, the "Software," solely for your own personal or business purposes on a single computer (whether a standard computer or a workstation component of a multi-user network). The Software is in use on a computer when it is loaded into temporary memory (RAM) or installed into permanent memory (hard disk, CD-ROM, or other storage device). WPI reserves all rights not expressly granted herein.

2. **Ownership.** WPI is the owner of all right, title, and interest, including copyright, in and to the compilation of the Software recorded on the disk(s) or CD-ROM "Software Media". Copyright to the individual programs recorded on the Software Media is owned by the author or other authorized copyright owner of each program. Ownership of the Software and all proprietary rights relating thereto remain with WPI and its licensers.

3. **Restrictions On Use and Transfer.**

   (a) You may only (i) make one copy of the Software for backup or archival purposes, or (ii) transfer the Software to a single hard disk, provided that you keep the original for backup or archival purposes. You may not (i) rent or lease the Software, (ii) copy or reproduce the Software through a LAN or other network system or through any computer subscriber system or bulletin-board system, or (iii) modify, adapt, or create derivative works based on the Software.

   (b) You may not reverse engineer, decompile, or disassemble the Software. You may transfer the Software and user documentation on a permanent basis, provided that the transferee agrees to accept the terms and conditions of this Agreement and you retain no copies. If the Software is an update or has been updated, any transfer must include the most recent update and all prior versions.

4. **Restrictions on Use of Individual Programs.** You must follow the individual requirements and restrictions detailed for each individual program in the What's on the CD-ROM? appendix of this Book. These limitations are also contained in the individual license agreements recorded on the Software Media. These limitations may include a requirement that after using the program for a specified period of time, the user must pay a registration fee or discontinue use. By opening the Software packet(s), you will be agreeing to abide by the licenses and restrictions for these individual programs that are detailed in the What's on the CD-ROM? appendix and on the Software Media. None of the material on this Software Media or listed in this Book may ever be redistributed, in original or modified form, for commercial purposes.

5. **Limited Warranty.**

   (a) WPI warrants that the Software and Software Media are free from defects in materials and workmanship under normal use for a period of sixty (60) days from the date of purchase of this Book. If WPI receives notification within the warranty period of defects in materials or workmanship, WPI will replace the defective Software Media.

   (b) WPI AND THE AUTHOR(S) OF THE BOOK DISCLAIM ALL OTHER WARRANTIES, EXPRESS OR IMPLIED, INCLUDING WITHOUT LIMITATION IMPLIED WARRANTIES OF MERCHANTABILITY AND FITNESS FOR A PARTICULAR PURPOSE, WITH RESPECT TO THE SOFTWARE, THE PROGRAMS, THE SOURCE CODE CONTAINED THEREIN, AND/OR THE TECHNIQUES DESCRIBED IN THIS BOOK. WPI DOES NOT WARRANT THAT THE FUNCTIONS CONTAINED IN THE SOFTWARE WILL MEET YOUR REQUIREMENTS OR THAT THE OPERATION OF THE SOFTWARE WILL BE ERROR FREE.

   (c) This limited warranty gives you specific legal rights, and you may have other rights that vary from jurisdiction to jurisdiction.

6. Remedies.

(a) WPI's entire liability and your exclusive remedy for defects in materials and workmanship shall be limited to replacement of the Software Media, which may be returned to WPI with a copy of your receipt at the following address: Software Media Fulfillment Department, Attn.: *HTML Complete Course*, Wiley Publishing, Inc., 10475 Crosspoint Blvd., Indianapolis, IN 46256, or call 1-800-762-2974. Please allow four to six weeks for delivery. This Limited Warranty is void if failure of the Software Media has resulted from accident, abuse, or misapplication. Any replacement Software Media will be warranted for the remainder of the original warranty period or thirty (30) days, whichever is longer.

(b) In no event shall WPI or the author be liable for any damages whatsoever (including without limitation damages for loss of business profits, business interruption, loss of business information, or any other pecuniary loss) arising from the use of or inability to use the Book or the Software, even if WPI has been advised of the possibility of such damages.

(c) Because some jurisdictions do not allow the exclusion or limitation of liability for consequential or incidental damages, the above limitation or exclusion may not apply to you.

7. U.S. Government Restricted Rights.
Use, duplication, or disclosure of the Software for or on behalf of the United States of America, its agencies and/or instrumentalities "U.S. Government" is subject to restrictions as stated in paragraph (c)(1)(ii) of the Rights in Technical Data and Computer Software clause of DFARS 252.227-7013, or subparagraphs (c) (1) and (2) of the Commercial Computer Software - Restricted Rights clause at FAR 52.227-19, and in similar clauses in the NASA FAR supplement, as applicable.

8. General.
This Agreement constitutes the entire understanding of the parties and revokes and supersedes all prior agreements, oral or written, between them and may not be modified or amended except in a writing signed by both parties hereto that specifically refers to this Agreement. This Agreement shall take precedence over any other documents that may be in conflict herewith. If any one or more provisions contained in this Agreement are held by any court or tribunal to be invalid, illegal, or otherwise unenforceable, each and every other provision shall remain in full force and effect.

Index

About Seybold Seminars and Publications

Seybold Seminars and Publications is your complete guide

to the publishing industry. For more than 30 years it

has been the most trusted source for technology events,

news, and insider intelligence.

Workflow
Media Te
Creation [
Manageme
Digital As
Fonts an
Digital M
Content
Manageme
Workflow
Media Te
Creation [
Manageme
Digital As
Fonts an
Digital M
Content
Manageme
Workflow
Media Te
Creation [
Manageme

SEYBOLD
CONSULTING / PUBLICATIONS

SEYBOLD
SEMINARS

Produced by

K3M Key3 Media Group

SEYBOLD
CONSULTING PUBLICATIONS℠

PUBLICATIONS

Today, Seybold Publications and Consulting continues to guide publishing professionals around the world in their purchasing decisions and business strategies through newsletters, online resources, consulting, and custom corporate services.

- ○ **The Seybold Report: Analyzing Publishing Technologies**
  The Seybold Report analyzes the cross-media tools, technologies, and trends shaping professional publishing today. Each in-depth newsletter delves into the topics changing the marketplace. *The Seybold Report* covers critical analyses of the business issues and market conditions that determine the success of new products, technologies, and companies. Read about the latest developments in mission-critical topic areas, including content and asset management, color management and proofing, industry standards, and cross-media workflows. A subscription to *The Seybold Report* (24 issues per year) includes our weekly email news service, *The Bulletin,* and full access to the seyboldreports.com archives.

- ○ **The Bulletin: Seybold News & Views on Electronic Publishing**
  The Bulletin: Seybold News & Views on Electronic Publishing is Seybold Publications' weekly email news service covering all aspects of electronic publishing. Every week *The Bulletin* brings you all the important news in a concise, easy-to-read format.

For more information on **NEWSLETTER SUBSCRIPTIONS,**
please visit **seyboldreports.com**.

CUSTOM SERVICES

In addition to newsletters and online information resources, Seybold
Publications and Consulting offers a variety of custom corporate services
designed to meet your organization's specific needs.

○ **Strategic Technology Advisory Research Service (STARS)**
The STARS program includes a group license to *The Seybold Report* and
The Bulletin, phone access to our analysts, access to online archives at
seyboldreports.com, an on-site visit by one of our analysts, and much more.

○ **Personalized Seminars**
Our team of skilled consultants and subject experts work with you to create a
custom presentation that gets your employees up to speed on topics spanning
the full spectrum of prepress and publishing technologies covered in our publications. Full-day and half-day seminars are available.

○ **Site Licenses**
Our electronic licensing program keeps everyone in your organization, sales
force, or marketing department up to date at a fraction of the cost of buying
individual subscriptions. One hard copy of *The Seybold Report* is included with
each electronic license.

For more information on **CUSTOM CORPORATE SERVICES,**
please visit **seyboldreports.com**.

SEYBOLD SEMINARS

EVENTS

Seybold Seminars facilitates exchange and discussion within the high-tech publishing community several times a year. A hard-hitting lineup of conferences, an opportunity to meet leading media technology vendors, and special events bring innovators and leaders together to share ideas and experiences.

Conferences

Our diverse educational programs are designed to tackle the full range of the latest developments in publishing technology. Topics include:

- Print publishing
- Web publishing
- Design
- Creative tools and standards
- Best practices

- Multimedia
- Content management
- Technology standards
- Security
- Digital rights management

In addition to the conferences, you'll have the opportunity to meet representatives from companies that bring you the newest products and technologies in the publishing marketplace. Test tools, evaluate products, and take free classes from the experts.

For more information on **SEYBOLD SEMINARS EVENTS,** please visit **seyboldseminars.com**.